Alaska in Maps

A Thematic Atlas

Edited by
Roger W. Pearson and Marjorie Hermans

GIS Map Production
John Stroud and Bo Wilmer

Cartography
Jason Geck, David Pray, Keith Ziolkowski

Atlas design
Elizabeth Knecht

University of Alaska Fairbanks   Alaska Department of Education   Alaska Geographic Alliance

The Alaska Geographic Alliance textbook and publications activities were established by a grant from the Alaska Legislature. This Atlas was produced through the cooperation of the Alaska Department of Education; the University of Alaska Fairbanks, Department of Geography; the Alaska Pacific University GIS laboratory; and the Alaska Geographic Alliance, a statewide organization of educators and others supportive of geography education. The Institute of the North at Alaska Pacific University in Anchorage is home to the Alaska Geographic Alliance.

First edition, 1998   Printed in Hong Kong
Second priting with corrections, 2000   Printed in Hong Kong
Third printing, 2001   Printed in Hong Kong

Grateful acknowledgment is made to the individuals, agencies, and institutions who granted permission for the use or adaptation of materials produced or controlled by them. Complete credits are listed under References to Sources at the back of the atlas.

GIS maps in the atlas were produced in ARC/INFO and ARCVIEW software, products of Environmental Systems Research Institute Inc. Diagrammatic maps, graphs, and other graphics by Elizabeth Knecht unless otherwise indicated. Pre-press and print coordination by Exact Imaging.

Any views expressed or implied in this publication should not be interpreted as official positions of the University of Alaska, the Alaska Department of Education, the Alaska Geographic Alliance, the Institute of the North, or Alaska Pacific University.

Alaska State Library Cataloging-In-Publication Data

Alaska in maps : a thematic atlas / edited by Roger W. Pearson and Marjorie Hermans ; GIS map production, John Stroud and Bo Wilmer ; cartography, Jason Geck, David Pray, Keith Ziolkowski ; atlas design, Elizabeth Knecht.

1st ed.
100 p. : ill., maps ; cm.
Produced by: University of Alaska Fairbanks ; Alaska Department of Education ; Alaska Geographic Alliance.
Includes bibliographical references.
ISBN 1-887419-02-0

1. Alaska – Maps. I. Pearson, Roger W. II. Hermans, Marjorie. III. University of Alaska, Fairbanks. IV. Alaska Dept. of Education. V. Alaska Geographic Alliance.
G1530.A45 1998
912/.798

Alaska Geographic Alliance
935 W. Third Avenue
Anchorage, AK 99501
http://www.AK-Geo-
Alliance.org

Institute of the North
Alaska Pacific University
P.O. Box 101700
Anchorage, AK 99510-1700
http://www.institutenorth.org

Acknowledgments

This atlas reflects the ongoing work of hundreds of agencies, organizations, and individuals throughout the state of Alaska. People in schools, university departments, state and federal offices, and private organizations were unfailingly generous and willing to contribute their knowledge and expertise when they knew this was a work to benefit Alaska students. We would like to thank everyone who contributed, while resting responsibility for any errors, omissions, or misinterpretations solely on the shoulders of the editors, who revised and adapted much of what they were told or given.

Deepest thanks go to members of the Alaska Geographic Alliance Textbook Advisory Committee, who guided this project from its inception. Former Representative Terry Martin of Anchorage provided leadership in the Alaska State Legislature to win support for funding the atlas and its companion publication for elementary schools, *Alaska, A Land in Motion*. All committee members helped with crucial decisions about content and manner of presentation, and they reviewed many maps and narratives as they were in process. The committee's contribution reflects extensive expertise and the members' dedication to promoting geography education in Alaska.

For reviewing all or large portions of the maps and narratives we would like to thank Tom Bundtzen, Tom Eley, Donna and Megan Emerson, K. L. Kirk, Don Lynch, and Patricia Partnow.

The editors would specifically like to acknowledge the work of John Stroud and Bo Wilmer, who spent long hours helping to develop and bring to life the information and ideas contained in the GIS maps reproduced here. Jason Geck, David Pray, and Keith Ziolkowski contributed many ideas and hours of work during production of the maps.

George Plumley provided much-needed assistance in creating an in-house web site as a virtual work center so members of the atlas team could review maps from their workplaces in four Alaska communities and in Montana. Thanks to Super Software, Inc. of Homer for use of the web page for editing the maps.

The Anchorage office of Environmental Systems Research Inc. (ESRI) kindly provided meeting space and computer equipment at several crucial points during production. We thank them and Charles Barnwell, manager of the Anchorage office of ESRI, for their support and encouragement.

Alaska Geographic Alliance Textbook Advisory Committee

Roger W. Pearson, Fairbanks
co-coordinator

Marjorie Menzi, Juneau
co-coordinator

Phyllis Bowie, Anchorage

Harvey Brandt, Sitka

Brenda Campen, Sitka

Bob Henning, Angoon and Edmonds, Washington

Bobbie Lowden, Juneau

Jody Marcello, Sitka

Representative Terry Martin, Anchorage

Dorothy Moore, Valdez

Marlene Pearson, Kenai

Julie Wiley, Thorne Bay

Louie Yannotti, Juneau

We wish to thank the National Geographic Society for its long-term support of the Alaska Geographic Alliance, which over a period of 10 years has built a network of trained and dedicated educators with the expertise to undertake a project such as this.

Any atlas of Alaska rests on the foundation of two pioneering works completed in the 1970s: the *Environmental Atlas of Alaska* by Charles W. Hartman and Philip R. Johnson, and the extensive six-volume *Alaska Regional Profiles* produced by the State of Alaska and edited over a period of years by Lidia L. Selkregg. We are grateful for the encouragement and support of Charles Hartman and Lidia Selkregg in preparation of this atlas, and for the information, background, and perspective their works provided to ours. Any errors or misinterpretations, of course, are our own.

We are grateful to the Alaska Division of Tourism, the U.S. Geological Survey, and the other agencies and individuals who provided photos.

Sincere thanks also to the following people, who helped with information, referrals, reviews, and countless acts of support during development of the atlas. They represent many others whose names are not mentioned but to whom we are also indebted: Tammy Alexander, Jo Antonson, Scott Banks, Ken Barrick, Emily F. Binnian, Sue Ann Bowling, Tim Brabets, Gordon Brower, John Byler, Terri Campbell, Richard Carstensen, Greg Chaney, Ron Cleveland, Debbie Corbett, Peggy Cowan, Ron Cowan, Tim Deasis, Bucky Dennerlein, Ken DeRoux, Jo Donner, Kathy Doogan, Gregory Emmanuel, Michael D. Fleming, Harry Gamble, Roger Graves, Martin Gutoski, Jim Haga, Jonathon Hall, John Hebard, Lexi Hill, Jim Ingraham, Kurt Jacobsen, Susan Joling, Jim Kari, John Kelley, Kerry Kirkpatrick, Michael Krauss, Carol Lewis, Chuck Logsden, John Manley, Carl Markon, Bill Marshall, Charles Mattioli, Gary Matthews, John Meyer, Mike Mills, Todd O'Sullivan, Karl Ohls, David Oliver, Tom Osborn, Elise Sereni Patkotak, Donna Parker, Tom Paul, Steve Peterson, Richard Pierce, Sharon Planchon, Dwight D. Pollard, Laura Lee Potrikus, Gordon Preecs, John Quinley, Kathryn Reid, Penny Rennick, Harry Reynolds, Joni Robinson, Susan Rogers, Lou and Richard Rountree, Herman Savikko, Paula Savikko, Ann Lillian Schell, John Schoen, Mike Sfraga, Mark Shasby, Perry and Linda Shipman, Carl Siebe, Ron Somerville, David Stone, Dick Swainbank, Wanda Thaggard, Mary Ann Ward, Marty White, Tim Wilson, Greg Williams, Bob Wolfe, Kes Woodward.

Alaska Division of Tourism

Table of Contents

4 Environment and Society   61

Seasonality

Natural Hazards
   Volcanoes • Earthquakes • Floods • Wildfires
Land Ownership and Specially Managed Places

Wild Harvests

Major Resource Industries
   Oil, Gas, and Coal • Commercial Fisheries •
   The Visitor Industry • Forest Products • Minerals •
   Agriculture and Grazing

5 Uses of Geography   87

Exploring Your School
   Forest, stream, and wetland studies at Dzantik'i Heeni
   Middle School *by Richard Carstensen*
Oil Spill Mapping Along Alaska's Southcentral Coast
   by Greg Chaney
Aleut Settlements in the Western Aleutians
Sharing the Excitement of Discovery
   30 years of *Alaska Geographic*
Technology and Tradition in the North Slope Borough

New Tools for Land Management
   Welcome to the NPR-A web site
Athabaskan Place Names for Rivers in Alaska

References to Sources   97

Chitina River near the Edgerton Highway in Southcentral Alaska

Alaska Division of Tourism

Introduction

The first peoples to enter Alaska from Eurasia launched an "Age of Discovery" of a new world. Most of what they learned and observed was recorded in oral traditions that were passed on over many generations. We have an inkling of this vast knowledge from Alaska Native names and stories associated with places and geographic features.

The spatial understandings people keep in their memories are known today as "mental maps." On one level, we all use this type of spatial knowledge to find our way to school, to go to hunting or recreation areas, and to better understand the world around us. In addition to our mental maps, we also use maps, globes, and atlases.

During the 15th and 16th centuries of the European Age of Discovery, rulers and merchants needed geographic knowledge about newly found areas of the world more than ever before. Explorers and scholars made maps, sketches, and reports to create atlases of newly discovered places. Today we are still producing atlases of the world and of specific places. For each of us as individuals the process of geographic discovery goes on. We want and need to know about places, and modern maps and atlases provide this kind of information.

This atlas is a collection of thematic maps—more than 50 of them, all focused on the geographic characteristics of Alaska. Each map displays information about a single topic, such as transportation, climate, or where Alaska is located in relation to other nations in the North Pacific. Together the maps form a picture of Alaska and the physical and human qualities that characterize the most northwesterly peninsula of North America.

This atlas does not attempt to name all the communities in Alaska, though they are located by type of local governmental organization on **Map 28 Communities.** On many maps in the following pages five cities, one in each region of Alaska, are located and named as a guide to orienting topical features. To locate other communities or specific geographic features, users are encouraged to consult atlases, maps, and gazetteers that provide local geographic information.

The maps and their accompanying narratives are organized according to five categories of geographic knowledge. Maps in the first section deal with **Perspectives,** or spatial dimensions of Alaska. They show where the state is located within the world, its dimensions, and how it might be divided into regions.

Maps in the second section portray the **Physical Geography** of the state. They show the shape of the land, the age and tectonic structure of Alaska, water features, and two major elements characteristic of Alaska as a northern location, glaciation and permafrost.

Maps in the third section depict the **Human Geography** of Alaska. They deal with population, transportation, cities, communication, and services.

Like people everywhere, Alaskans are constantly interacting with their environment. These relationships are shown in the fourth section of the atlas, which focuses on **Environment and Society.** The maps gathered in this section deal with natural hazards such as earthquakes (an important way the environment affects people) and with various ways Alaskans use the environment, such as for subsistence hunting or commercial fishing.

In the final section of the atlas, maps and narratives show the **Uses of Geography,** emphasizing the fact that geography and mapping are important in a wide variety of activities and occupations pursued by Alaskans all across the state.

The word *geography* means literally "description of the earth." A description implies a visual orientation. Geography is a very visually oriented field of study. Therefore, this atlas includes other visual elements besides maps. Graphs and diagrams within each narrative show such concepts as how geography and time are related. For example, the population of Alaska is graphed over a period of 100 years, and the cyclic nature of gold mining is shown on a time chart. From another point of view, a north-south transect of Alaska gives a much different sense of spatial relationships than Map 1 and Map 11, which show land elevations above sea level in different colors over the entire state.

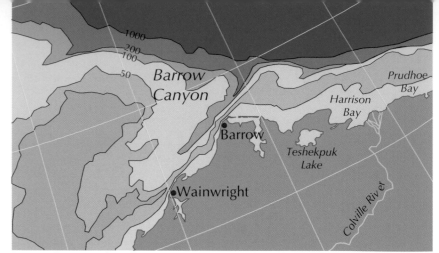
Barrow Canyon – See Figure 10

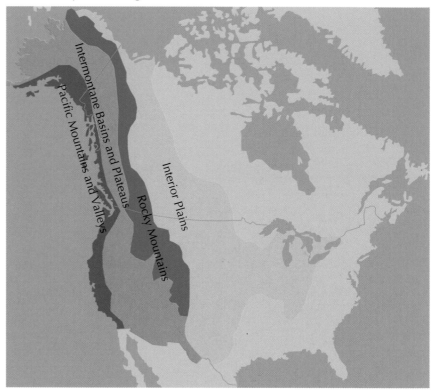
Physiographic Regions of Western North American – See Figure 3

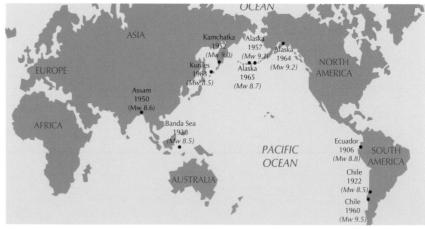
Top Ten Earthquakes in the World – See Figure 22

The atlas also includes photos—yet one more type of visual description. A map can show the spatial distribution of Alaska's coastal forest lands. A photo can expand upon what the map shows by visually recreating the actual shapes and colors of a coastal forest.

Only a globe, which reflects the spherical shape of the earth, can show proper area, shape, distance, *and* direction. Any projection onto a flat map emphasizes one or two of these traits and compromises on the others. Most of the maps in this atlas use the Albers Equal Area Conic Projection, which reflects the actual area of Alaska. This means that the area of Kodiak Island can be visually compared to the area of Prince of Wales Island, for example.

Most of the maps in this atlas are drawn to scale. That means a certain measure anywhere on the map—say, one inch—always represents the same distance on the earth's surface. Distances on the maps can be measured using the bar scale, which translates inches or centimeters on the map to miles or kilometers on the earth's surface. These measurements are accurate for general purposes; however, there is always a certain amount of distortion when curved surfaces are projected onto a flat surface.

Cartographers must generalize when they create maps. Scale is one way of generalizing, as shown in the figures reproduced opposite this page. Large-scale maps can show small areas in considerable detail. The Barrow Canyon, a

Sea stars near Hooper Bay

trench lying beneath the Arctic Ocean, is clearly shown in the large scale map in Figure 10, which appears in Section 2–Physical Geography. Small-scale maps can show larger areas, but they cannot show much local detail. The highly generalized physiographic regions of western North America are shown on a small scale map in Figure 3, which also appears in Section 2. Locations at which the world's 10 largest earthquakes have been recorded are shown on an even smaller scale map, Figure 22 in Section 4.

Most maps in this atlas are on a scale of 1:10,000,000. That is a relatively small scale. Many details had to be eliminated, but the whole state of Alaska can be displayed on a single page. On the map of mineral distribution only large deposits of minerals are located, but the map shows how deposits are distributed across the entire state. The map of permafrost shows only general patterns of permafrost distribution, approximate occurrences of permafrost one could expect to find in various regions and locations within the state.

In developing the base map for maps in the atlas, cartographers had to make a difficult decision about how to portray the state. Alaska is not Kansas or Colorado. It does not fit neatly into the rectangular shape of a book. When the entire state is shown on a single page, individual features have to be very small. When map features are shown at a larger scale so they can be read easily, then something has to be cut off. The obvious cartographic solution is to cut off the Aleutian Islands and place them below Southcentral Alaska. On most maps in the atlas, the solution works well because Alaska can be shown at a slightly larger scale, and map features are large enough for readers to see. In some cases, however, as in depicting ocean currents, it is important to show the actual physical layout of all of Alaska. On those maps, the state is displayed whole, at a smaller scale without any geographic scissoring.

Words, maps, graphs, and photos give us many views of Alaska, but they do not necessarily provide composite views. For example, how are climate and the distribution of forests related? Is there a spatial relationship between climate and population distribution? The individual maps in this atlas do not show these relationships, but much can be learned by comparing various maps with one another, and the Teacher's Guide that accompanies the atlas suggests how such complex geographic relationships can be explored.

All geographers know that no atlas can give a complete description of a place. There is always something else that could have been mapped or something that is difficult or impossible to show on a map. Alaska is often called "The Last Frontier," but what exactly is a "frontier?" Can the individual characteristics of a frontier be mapped, and if so, at what scale?

These maps are a starting point, a staging area for continued geographic explorations of Alaska. The editors invite readers to enjoy the maps, learn from them, and ask questions about them. May they spark exciting personal discoveries within the vast and changing landscape of Alaska geography.

Map 1– Alaska

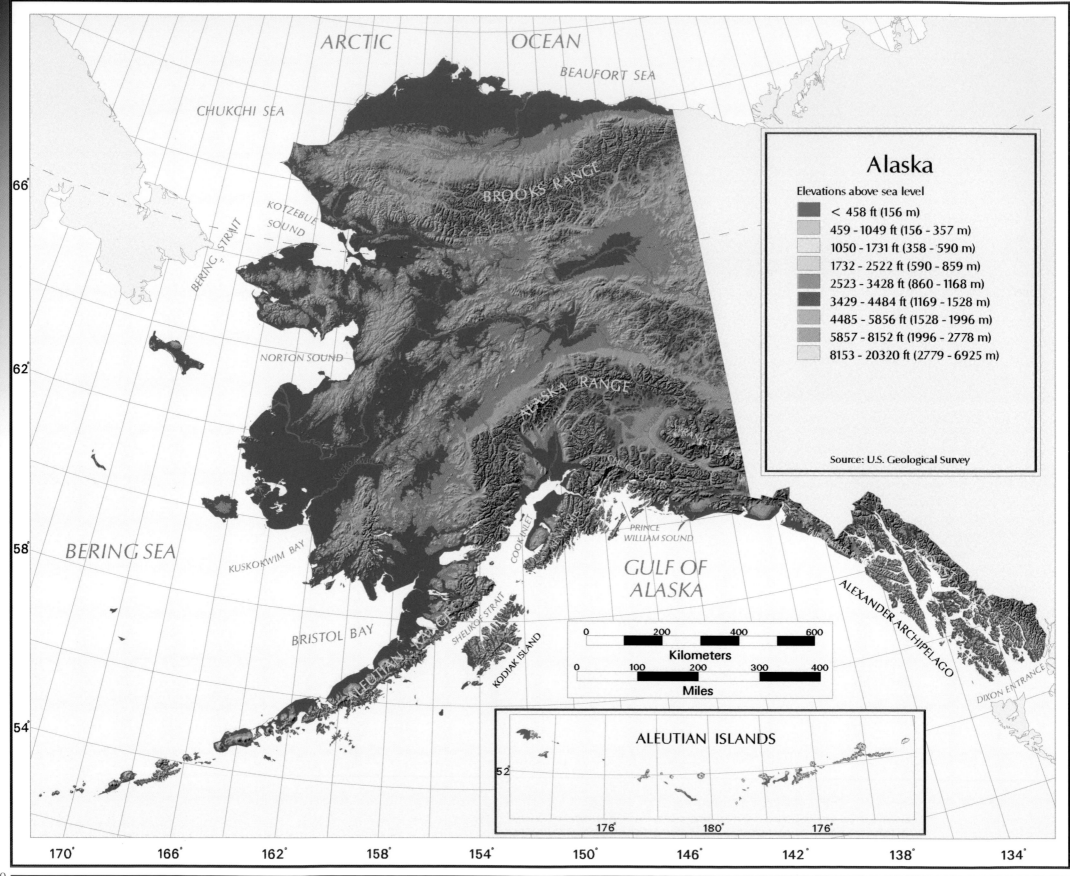

ARCTIC OCEAN

BEAUFORT SEA

CHUKCHI SEA

BROOKS RANGE

KOTZEBUE SOUND

66°

BERING STRAIT

62°

NORTON SOUND

ALASKA RANGE

58°

BERING SEA

KUSKOKWIM BAY

PRINCE WILLIAM SOUND

COOK INLET

GULF OF ALASKA

ALEXANDER ARCHIPELAGO

BRISTOL BAY

SHELIKOF STRAIT

KODIAK ISLAND

DIXON ENTRANCE

54°

Alaska

Elevations above sea level

- < 458 ft (156 m)
- 459 - 1049 ft (156 - 357 m)
- 1050 - 1731 ft (358 - 590 m)
- 1732 - 2522 ft (590 - 859 m)
- 2523 - 3428 ft (860 - 1168 m)
- 3429 - 4484 ft (1169 - 1528 m)
- 4485 - 5856 ft (1528 - 1996 m)
- 5857 - 8152 ft (1996 - 2778 m)
- 8153 - 20320 ft (2779 - 6925 m)

Source: U.S. Geological Survey

```
0        200      400      600
Kilometers
0    100      200      300      400
Miles
```

ALEUTIAN ISLANDS

52°

176°   180°   176°

170°   166°   162°   158°   154°   150°   146°   142°   138°   134°

How people view any part of the world depends on where they are from and what knowledge they have about it. These views are what geographers refer to as perspectives.

Perspectives—The Ways We Look at Things

The Chinese saw their country as the Middle Kingdom—in effect, the center of the world. In contrast, later European maps identified China as part of the Far East. The Russians named a group of the Aleutian Islands the Near Islands because they were close to Russia. The western Aleuts saw these same islands as their center point and a rich homeland. Most Alaskans today think of the Near Islands as remote and climatically inhospitable.

Alaskans living in the age of satellites and space travel enjoy a perspective on their homeland that generations before them hardly dreamed of. Every day satellites orbit hundreds, or even thousands, of miles above the earth. They transmit more images and information about Alaska than people can yet process.

Map 2 Alaska is a composite satellite view of Alaska. It was composed from several satellite images of portions of the state. The images were taken at different times so that clouds would not obscure the landscape. They were then pieced together by computer into a mosaic to show the entire state. Next, colors were added to create a picture that is easier for the eye to interpret. Since the

colors are not "real" this kind of map is called a "false-color" image.

The assigned colors illuminate features of the landscape that otherwise might not be easily seen. Lakes stand out as distinctly dark blue, especially on the Alaska Peninsula and in the Tikchik Lakes region north of Dillingham. The intertwining red and blue lines linking Prudhoe Bay and Valdez show the road system (red) and the TransAlaska Pipeline (blue). The state's extensive glaciers appear white and show up as particularly significant in Southcentral and Southeast Alaska.

The satellite image emphasizes the enormous size of the state, 591,004 square miles (1,530,700 square kilometers) as well as its expansive configuration. Alaska is what geographers describe as a "fragmented" and "prorupt" state. It has thousands of islands, many of them quite large, so the state's land mass is broken up, or fragmented. It also has two long extensions, the Southeast Panhandle, and the Alaska Peninsula and Aleutian Islands, so in geographic terms it is stretched out, or "prorupt."

The satellite image also highlights the tenuous geographic connection between Southeast Alaska and the rest of the state. The link between Southeast and Southcentral Alaska, extending southeastward from the 141st meridian, is ruggedly mountainous and glaciated, and at its narrowest extent is a mere 18 miles (29 kilometers) wide.

Map 3 Alaska as Part of the North is a satellite mosaic

showing Alaska from a polar perspective. One of the most striking observations from this view is how small Alaska is in comparison to the rest of "the North," those areas in the northern hemisphere described as arctic (dominated by tundra) or boreal (dominated by northern coniferous forest). This perspective differs a great deal from the enormous appearance of the state in **Map 2**.

Alaska's geography is in many ways dominated by its northern location. Alaska's north coast faces the Arctic Ocean, and much of the state lies directly east of the Bering Sea and Bering Strait. Like its northern neighbors Russia, Canada, Greenland, and Scandinavia, Alaska is distinguished from places at lower latitudes by relatively cold temperatures and dramatic

seasonal shifts in daylight hours. It has large areas underlain by permafrost ground that has been frozen for centuries. It has species of plants and animals specifically adapted to life in northern environments.

As recently as 11,000 to 12,000 years ago, during the Pleistocene Epoch, Alaska and northeastern Russia were connected by the Bering Land Bridge. The first people who came to North America probably made their way across that land bridge. Today descendants of these groups are reclaiming their ancient heritage in international organizations such as the Inuit Circumpolar Conference, which held its first meeting in Barrow, Alaska in 1977.

Scientists and traditional Native experts throughout the North conduct joint expeditions

Perspectives On Alaska

Walker Lake in Gates of the Arctic National Park

Alaska Division of Tourism

and exchange information about the unique characteristics of northern polar areas. The Eskimo Whaling Commission and the Conference on Protection of the Arctic Environment are only two among a variety of organizations through which people from northern nations join in managing common resources and environmental hazards. Russian and American research on the Arctic Ocean is being brought together, and medical findings on effects of seasonal sunlight deprivation are being

The Alaska Highway, Alaska's main overland connection with the rest of North America

Alaska Division of Tourism

shared, as polar nations search for a better understanding of northern environments and how they affect the people who live in them.

Map 4 Alaska and the North Pacific focuses on Alaska as a place bordering on the North Pacific Ocean. This perspective shows that Alaska is connected to or close to Canada, Russia, Japan, China, and Korea. All these countries are important trading nations with access to the North Pacific.

Associations between these nations and Alaska are familiar history. For centuries early Native people traveled and traded between Alaska and northeastern Russia. From the 1740s to 1867 Russia claimed Alaska and extracted a fortune in furs, which were sent to Russia and China.

Alaska's most important trading partners today are Pacific neighbors: Japan, South Korea, Taiwan, and Canada. Great Circle Routes (the shortest distances because of the earth's spherical shape) bring ships and planes close to Alaska, as can be seen in the air routes linking San Francisco and Seattle with Tokyo. Since 1990 Anchorage has grown dramatically as a refueling and distribution center for cargo carried by air, particularly to and from Japan, South Korea, and Taiwan.

Alaska's North Pacific location has also been of military importance. During World War II, Japan briefly achieved its only occupation of U.S. soil by invading the Aleutian Islands of Attu and Kiska, little more than 2,000 miles (3,200 kilometers) from Tokyo. Beginning in the 1950s, an elaborate defense system was established in

Alaska to provide a defense and warning system against what was then the Soviet Union. Modern defense systems, including several military bases, are still important in Alaska today.

Environmentally, Alaska shares with its North Pacific neighbors ocean currents and wind patterns that influence climate, weather, and the ocean's abundant fish and sea mammals. Northern people share concern over pollution of arctic air (industrial wastes and radioactive fallout carried on arctic wind currents) and the threat of global warming. The entire region shares the tectonic instability of the "Pacific Rim of Fire" and the associated hazards of earthquakes, volcanic eruptions, and tsunamis.

Map 5 shows **Alaska as Part of North America**. From a continental perspective Alaska, like Hawaii, is separated from the "contiguous" United States. The Alaska Highway, built cooperatively by Canada and the United States during World War II, is the sole land link between Alaska and what Alaskans traditionally call "the Lower 48" states.

This map is also a reminder that the physical environment of Alaska is closely tied to the rest of North America. Alaska's landforms, as shown in Section 2 in both **Figure 3– Physiographic Regions of Western North America** and the inset to **Map 11 Topography,** are essentially continuations of larger systems that extend through Canada and the continental United States.

Many species of plants and animals, such as spruce trees and caribou, for example, are found

throughout the northern part of the continent. Connections among aboriginal people are illustrated by the distribution of Athabaskan languages, which extend from Alaska as far east as Hudson Bay, Canada, and as far south as Arizona.

During the 1800s the British sought to link parts of Alaska with Canada to the east, mainly through trading posts at Wrangell and Fort Yukon. It was only in 1867, when the United States purchased Alaska from Russia, that Alaska's political linkage to a North American country became official. Today airlines, several highways, ferries, barges, and advanced communication systems link Alaska to the continental United States and neighboring parts of Canada, the province of British Columbia, and the Yukon Territory.

Distances in Alaska

From all these perspectives, we can see that Alaska covers a large land area. At one-fifth the size of the United States it is larger than many countries. Because of its shape—a central land mass with the long arm of the Aleutians stretching west and the "Panhandle" stretching southeast—it also extends far geographically. In fact, Alaska extends as many miles from west to east as the Lower 48 states do from coast to coast. It stretches as far from north to south as the Lower 48 states do from Canada to Mexico.

As **Figure 1–Alaska Time Zones** shows, Alaska once spanned four time zones, just as the continental United States does today. They ranged from the

Pacific Zone (the zone that includes Washington, Oregon, and California) in Southeast Alaska, to the Bering Zone, which stretched across the Aleutians to the International Date Line. With the shift to Daylight Savings Time on October 30, 1983, that changed dramatically.

Most of Alaska was moved into what had been the "Yukon" time zone and which had previously included only Yakutat. Settlements from Ketchikan to Nome, which range over 34 degrees in longitude, were brought into the new "Alaska" time zone, one hour later than Pacific Time. Only the Aleutian Islands were placed in the former Alaska time zone, now called the "Hawaii-Aleutian" Zone.

If time is used as the scale, Alaska has been shrunk to half its former size. And that was the idea of the change—to bring Alaskans closer together in time.

What does it mean to live in a state that stretches 1,420 miles (2,285 kilometers) from its northernmost point (71°23'N at Point Barrow) to its southernmost (51°13'N at Amatignak Island in the Aleutian Islands)? Does it matter that Alaska extends 2,400 miles (3,862 kilometers) from east to west?

Such great distances matter because a single state government must create laws and provide services appropriate for Alaskans living under extremely different conditions of climate, terrain, and accessibility. They matter because state and federal agencies in Juneau, Anchorage, or Washington, D.C., must manage forests, wetlands, or wildlife populations that are both vastly different from each other and far from the seats of administration. They matter because for many reasons people want and need to travel from one part of Alaska to another.

The impact of great distances is magnified by rugged landscape—towering mountains, glaciers, winding rivers, and expanses of tundra. It is intensified by fierce winds, snowfall, fog, and extremely cold temperatures.

Map 6 Distances Within Alaska shows air miles between major settlements within Alaska and to Seattle, Washington. The distances are not only large, but are magnified by indirect air routes. Bethel and Fairbanks are 503 miles (809 kilometers) apart, but air routes linking them only go through Anchorage, making the trip 652 miles (1,049 kilometers) and an extra stop.

Figure 2–Distance and Cost of Air Travel from Anchorage shows how costs of travel in Alaska are not always related to actual distances between points. Cost differences can be attributed to many factors, including weather and "economy of scale." When more people travel, as between Anchorage and Seattle, costs can be reduced. When fewer people travel, as between Anchorage and Dutch Harbor, the port for Unalaska, costs are generally higher. Whatever their cause, cost differences like these have considerable impact on both Alaskans and visitors. If we think of dollars as our scale rather than miles or kilometers, then the strange circumstance arises that Hong Kong is almost the same dollar distance from Anchorage as Dutch Harbor.

Regional Perspectives

Geographers use the concept of regions as a tool for distinguishing smaller areas within larger ones. Because Alaska is so large, viewing the state from a regional perspective can be very useful. Regions are usually delineated on the basis of similarities and differences. One region might include places that have climates more similar than the climates of other places surrounding them. Or regions might be designated on the basis

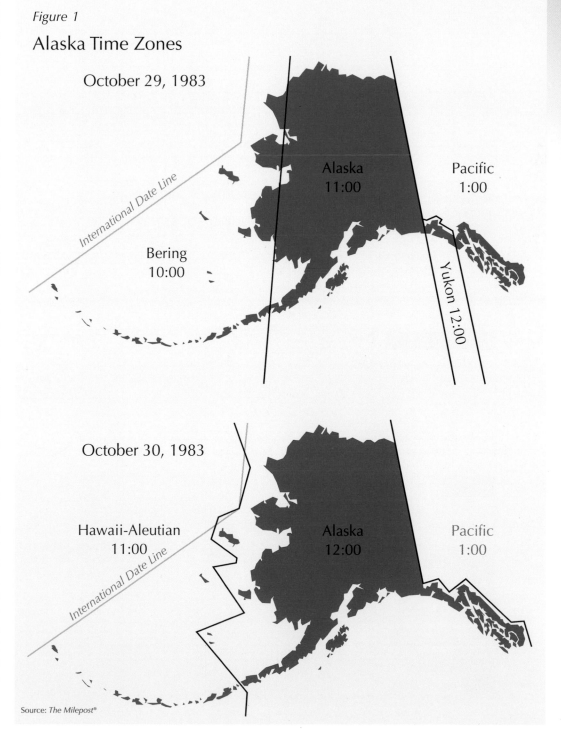

Figure 1

Alaska Time Zones

October 29, 1983

International Date Line

Alaska 11:00

Pacific 1:00

Bering 10:00

Yukon 12:00

October 30, 1983

Hawaii-Aleutian 11:00

International Date Line

Alaska 12:00

Pacific 1:00

Source: *The Milepost*®

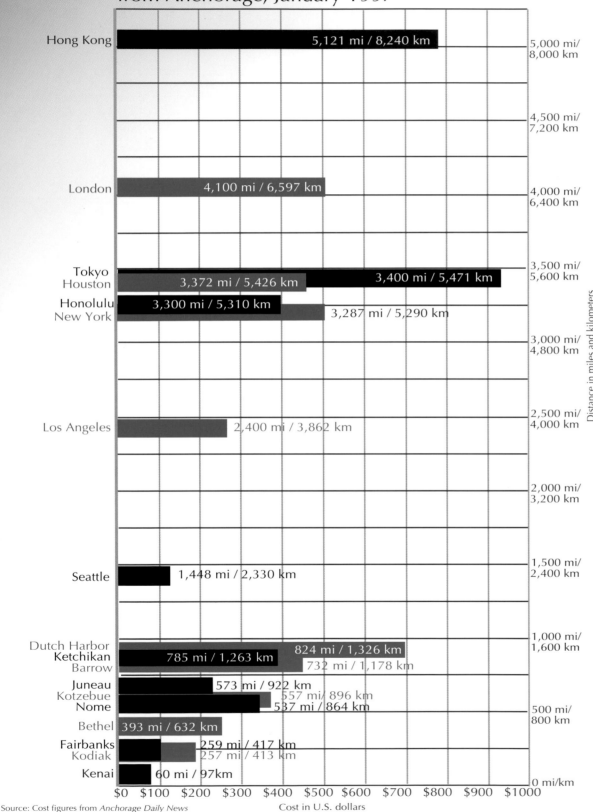

Figure 2

Distance and Cost of Air Travel from Anchorage, January 1997

City	Distance
Hong Kong	5,121 mi / 8,240 km
London	4,100 mi / 6,597 km
Tokyo	3,372 mi / 5,426 km
Houston	3,400 mi / 5,471 km
Honolulu	3,300 mi / 5,310 km
New York	3,287 mi / 5,290 km
Los Angeles	2,400 mi / 3,862 km
Seattle	1,448 mi / 2,330 km
Dutch Harbor	824 mi / 1,326 km
Ketchikan	785 mi / 1,263 km
Barrow	732 mi / 1,178 km
Juneau	573 mi / 922 km
Kotzebue	557 mi / 896 km
Nome	537 mi / 864 km
Bethel	393 mi / 632 km
Fairbanks	259 mi / 417 km
Kodiak	257 mi / 413 km
Kenai	60 mi / 97km

Distance in miles and kilometers

Cost in U.S. dollars

$0 $100 $200 $300 $400 $500 $600 $700 $800 $900 $1000

5,000 mi/8,000 km
4,500 mi/7,200 km
4,000 mi/6,400 km
3,500 mi/5,600 km
3,000 mi/4,800 km
2,500 mi/4,000 km
2,000 mi/3,200 km
1,500 mi/2,400 km
1,000 mi/1,600 km
500 mi/800 km
0 mi/km

Source: Cost figures from *Anchorage Daily News*

of topography, vegetation, or ethnic populations.

Sometimes geographers use "perceptual" regions as seen in **Map 7 Alaska as Five Regions** and **Map 8 Alaska as Six Regions**. Neither map is right or wrong. The two of them show different ways people may think about Alaska. Notice how the Kodiak area appears in Western Alaska in **Map 7**, but in Southcentral Alaska in **Map 8**. Kodiak is environmentally similar to southwestern Alaska, as is its commercial fishing economy. Relationships among Kodiak's Native populations have historically been stronger with southwestern Alaska as well.

Yet eastern Kodiak is also environmentally similar to Southcentral Alaska. Like Kodiak, Seward and other coastal communities in Southcentral Alaska have strong commercial fishing economies. Kodiak's transportation and communication links with Anchorage strengthen the case for considering it part of Southcentral Alaska.

Designating regions for political or administrative purposes is often very controversial because resources and political power may be allocated according to regional identity. The equity or fairness of regional designations can change as population, economics, and government policies change. **Map 9 Election Districts, 1960** and **Map 10 Election Districts, 1994** show how election districts in Alaska have changed over time.

In 1960, two years after Statehood, the first state election districts reflected the broad regions of Alaska with little concern for factors such as

population size. However, a series of U.S. Supreme Court decisions in the 1960s (*Baker v. Carr, 1962; Reynolds v. Sims, 1964;* and *Wesberry v. Sanders, 1964*) required states to make their election districts as equal as possible in population size. Those decisions, plus substantial population growth in urban areas such as Anchorage, led to a dramatic change in the number and shape of the state's election districts for 1994.

The Alaska Constitution mandates that election districts be restructured every 10 years, so election districts change periodically, and reapportionment is a political issue that is highly charged and extremely important to the balance of political power within the state.

Many maps in Sections 3 and 4 of this altas show the use of regions for other purposes, such as gathering population statistics (**Map 25 Alaska Population by Boroughs and Census Areas**), providing government services (**Map 29 Regional Governments**), or managing wildlife and other natural resources (**Map 44 Sportfishing, Map 45 Hunting and Trapping,** and **Map 47 Commercial Fisheries**).

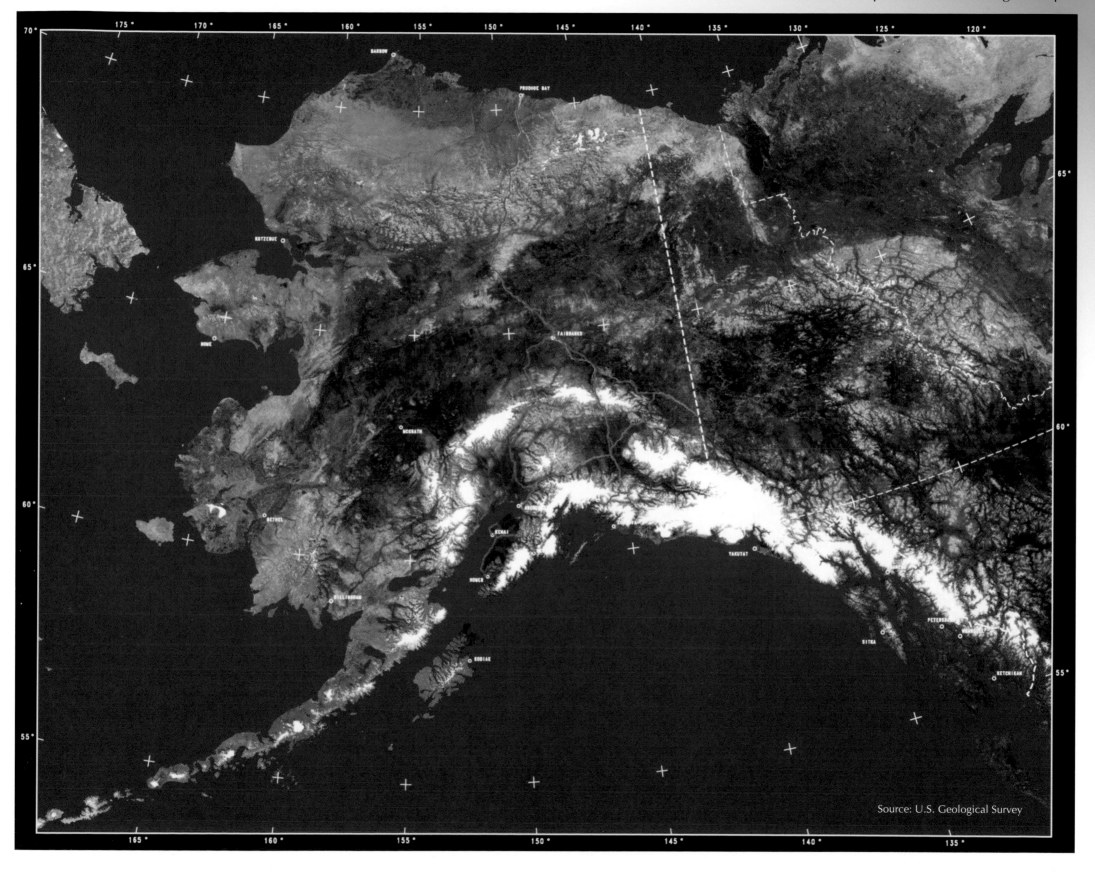

Source: U.S. Geological Survey

Map 3–Alaska as Part of the North

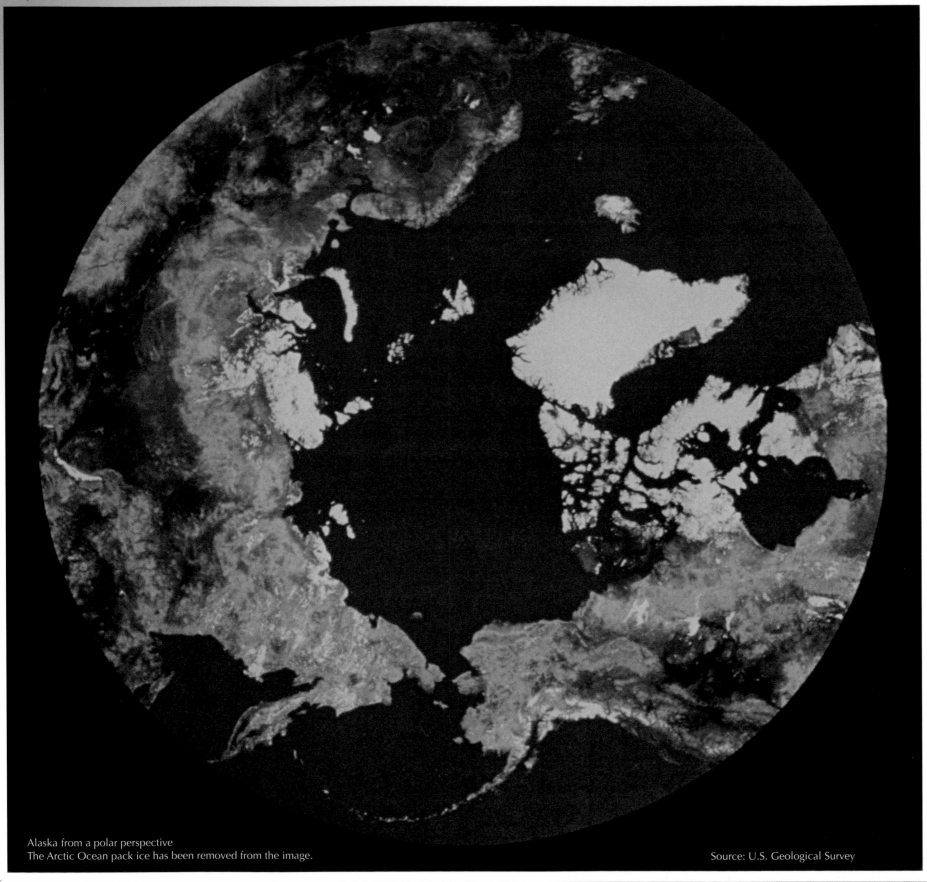

Alaska from a polar perspective
The Arctic Ocean pack ice has been removed from the image.

Source: U.S. Geological Survey

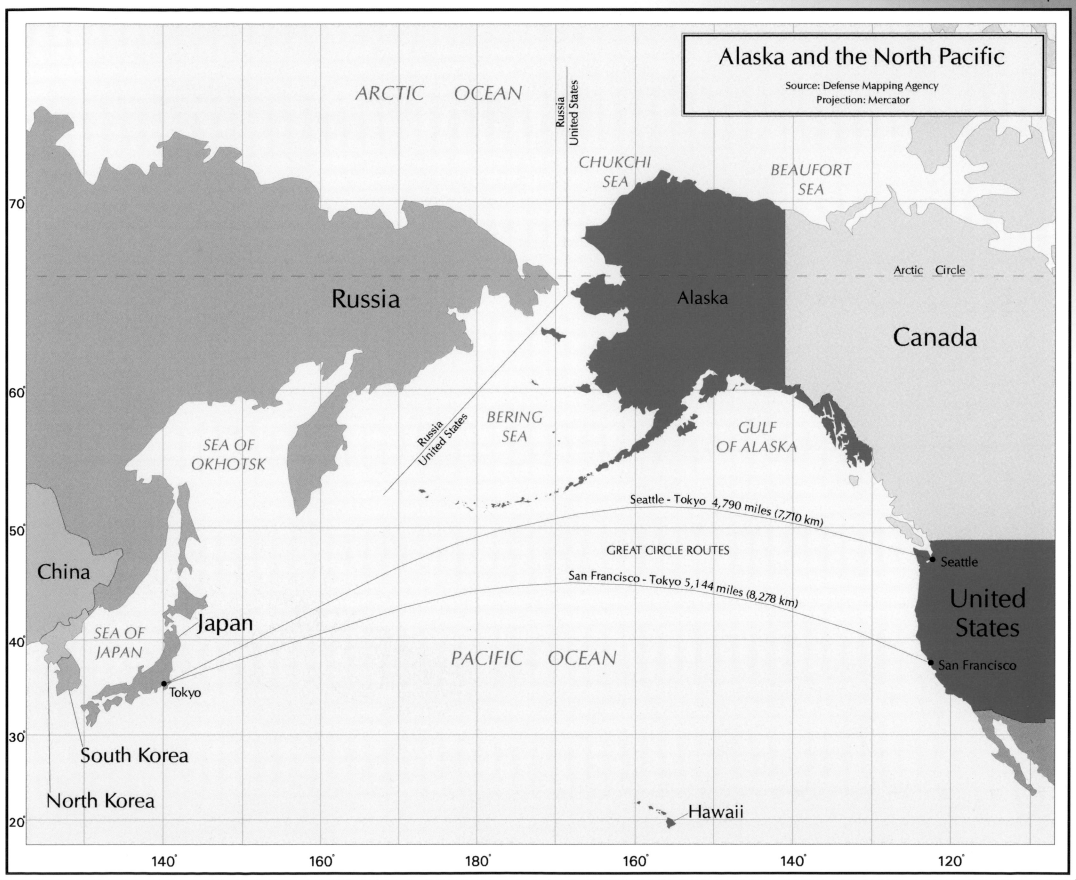

Alaska and the North Pacific

Source: Defense Mapping Agency
Projection: Mercator

ARCTIC   OCEAN

Russia
United States

CHUKCHI
SEA

BEAUFORT
SEA

70°

Arctic   Circle

Russia

Alaska

Canada

60°

Russia
United States

BERING
SEA

GULF
OF ALASKA

SEA OF
OKHOTSK

Seattle - Tokyo 4,790 miles (7,710 km)

50°

GREAT CIRCLE ROUTES

China

San Francisco - Tokyo 5,144 miles (8,278 km)

Seattle

United
States

Japan

SEA OF
JAPAN

40°

PACIFIC   OCEAN

San Francisco

Tokyo

30°

South Korea

North Korea

20°

Hawaii

140°   160°   180°   160°   140°   120°

Map 5—Alaska as Part of North America

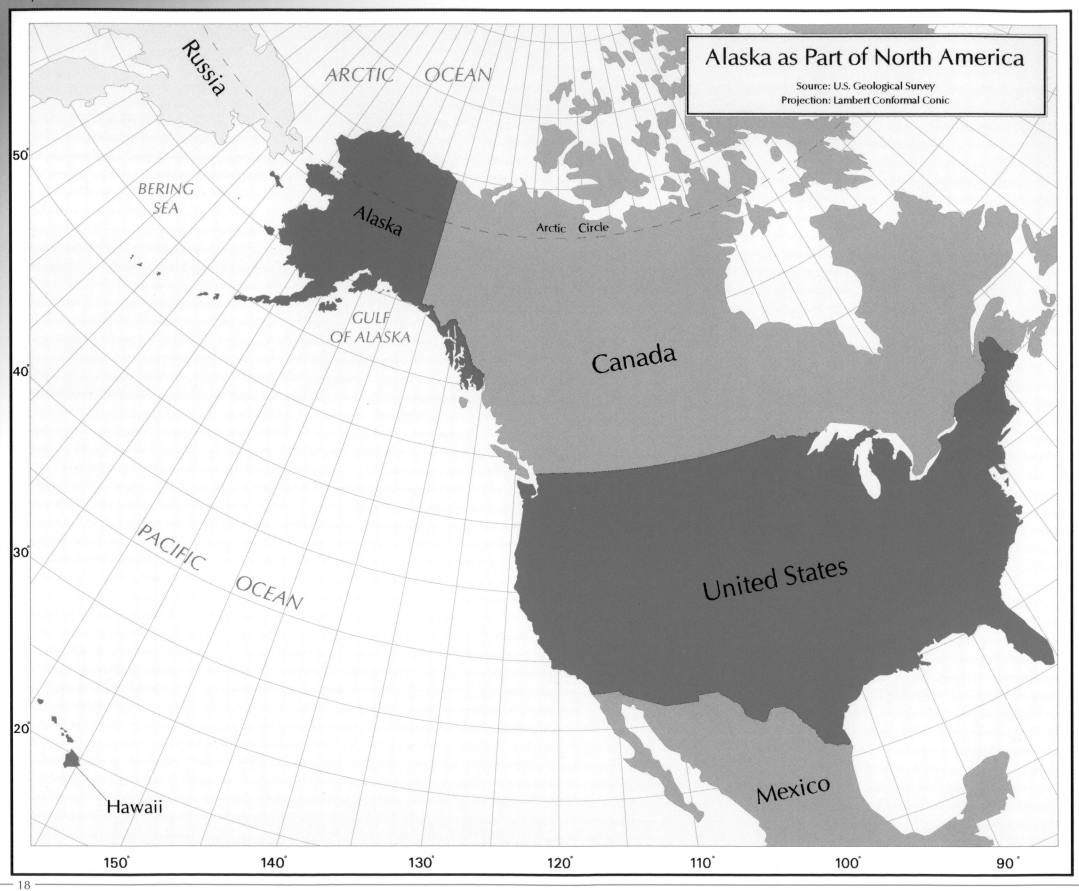

Alaska as Part of North America

Source: U.S. Geological Survey
Projection: Lambert Conformal Conic

Russia

ARCTIC   OCEAN

BERING
SEA

Alaska

Arctic   Circle

GULF
OF ALASKA

Canada

PACIFIC

OCEAN

United States

Mexico

Hawaii

50°

40°

30°

20°

150°   140°   130°   120°   110°   100°   90°

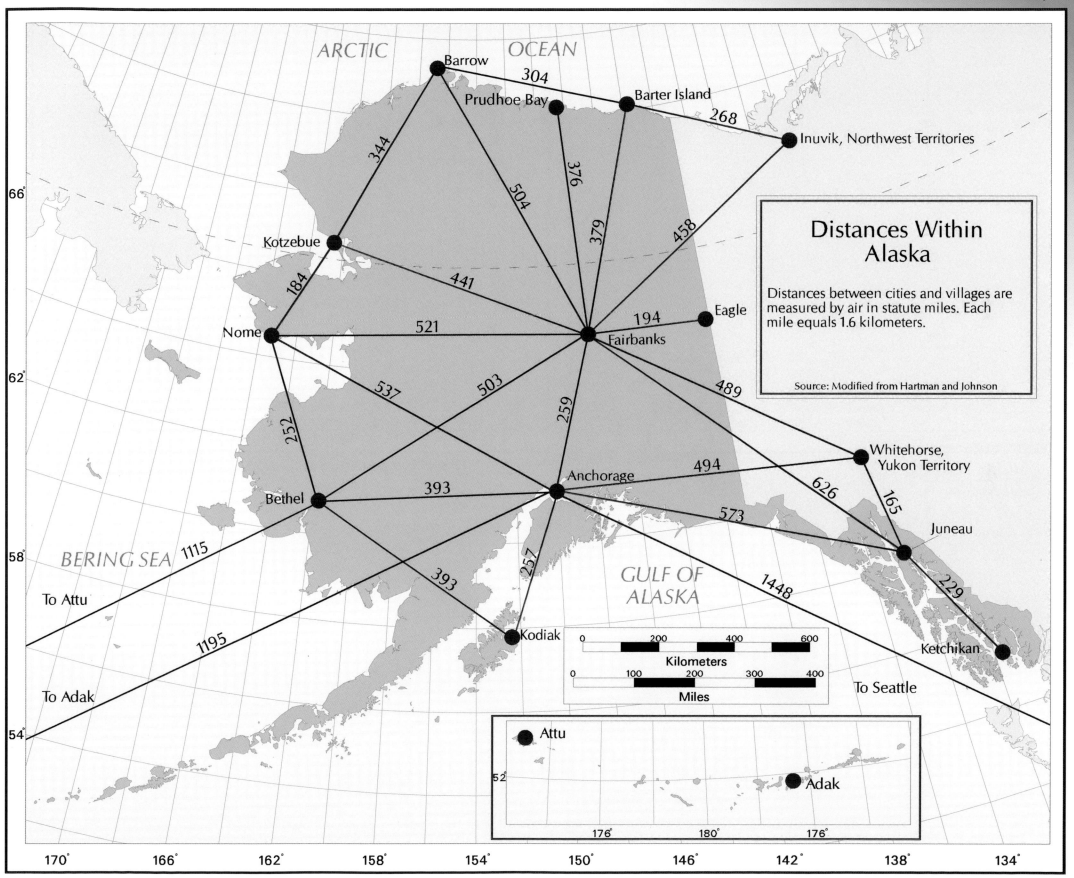

ARCTIC OCEAN

Barrow

304

Barter Island

Prudhoe Bay

268

Inuvik, Northwest Territories

344

504

376

379

458

Kotzebue

441

184

Eagle

521

194

Fairbanks

Distances Within Alaska

Distances between cities and villages are measured by air in statute miles. Each mile equals 1.6 kilometers.

Source: Modified from Hartman and Johnson

Nome

537

503

489

259

494

Whitehorse, Yukon Territory

252

626

Anchorage

393

165

393

573

Bethel

Juneau

257

229

BERING SEA 1115

GULF OF ALASKA

1448

To Attu

1195

Kodiak

To Adak

To Seattle

Ketchikan

0   200   400   600
Kilometers
0   100   200   300   400
Miles

Attu

52

Adak

176°   180°   176°

170°   166°   162°   158°   154°   150°   146°   142°   138°   134°

66°

62°

58°

54°

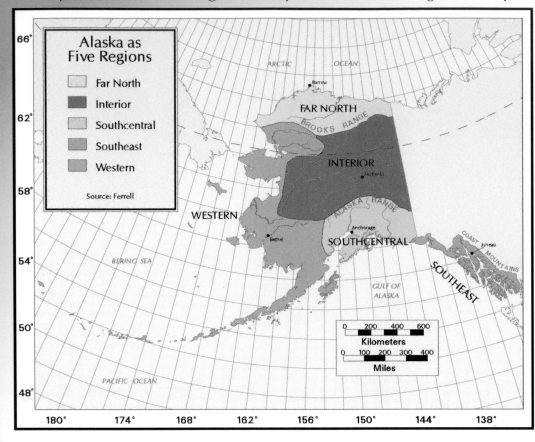

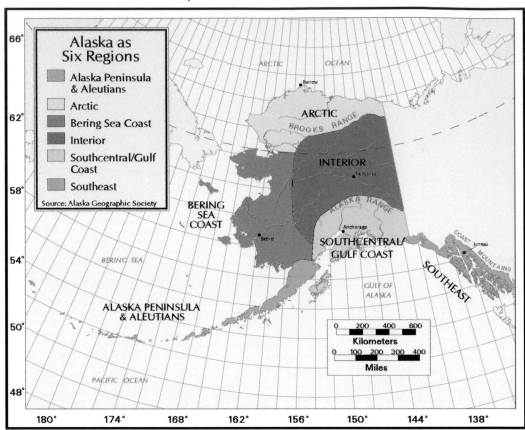

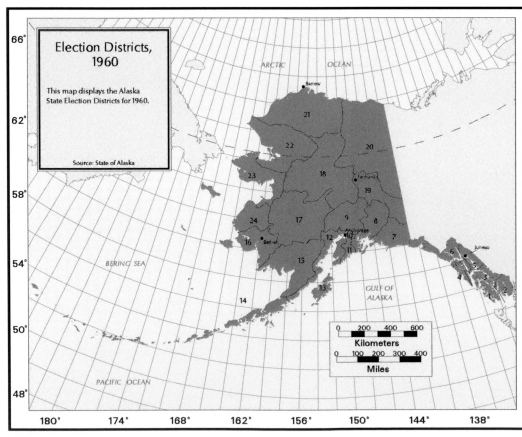

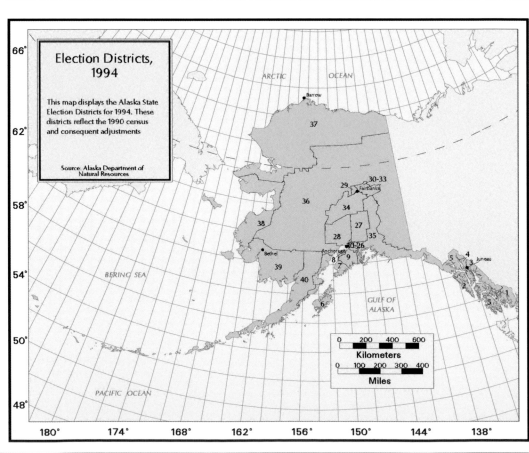

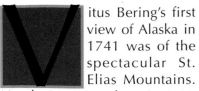

Vitus Bering's first view of Alaska in 1741 was of the spectacular St. Elias Mountains. Nearly 200 years later in 1935 the American explorer Bradford Washburn reported to *National Geographic* magazine his discovery of another complex of glaciated mountains beyond the peaks first seen by Bering. The gap of two centuries between those two discoveries reminds us that until recently large areas of Alaska were difficult to reach and not at all well known. Some parts of Alaska are still very remote, but today satellite imagery, a variety of monitoring devices, and detailed field work are combining to give us a much clearer picture of Alaska's physical geography than ever before.

The physical features depicted in the maps in this section can be grouped into four "spheres" that geographers use in describing the physical world:

- the lithosphere, or the earth's crust, which includes geology and plate tectonics
- the atmosphere, which includes weather and climate
- the hydrosphere, the realm of water, which includes oceans, lakes, and rivers, and
- the biosphere, which includes plant and animal communities, and ecosystems.

The Lithosphere, the Earth's Crust

Map 11 Topography shows the geomorphic landscape, or land surface features, of Alaska. The main map uses digital shading and colors to show large topographic features of Alaska based on their elevations above sea level. This perspective shows the extensive arced mountain systems and the large but interrupted lowlands.

One way geographers categorize landforms is by their surface appearance, or physiography. From this perspective, topography in Alaska can be seen as part of large systems of physiographic divisions extending through western North America. The inset on **Map 11,** and **Figure 3– Physiographic Regions of Western North America** show these divisions. **Map 1 Alaska** shows the locations of mountain ranges in the following description.

The Pacific Mountain System is a continuation of the larger Coastal Mountain System of the U.S. and Canadian west coast. In Alaska it forms two broad arcs. The northern arc includes the Coast Mountains, which form the mainland portion of Southeast Alaska; the Alaska Range, which curves through Southcentral Alaska; the Aleutian Range; and the Aleutian Islands. This system includes the highest peak in the state and North America, Mt. McKinley (20,320 feet; 6,194 meters) in the Alaska Range.

The southern arc, the Pacific Border Ranges, includes the large islands of Southeast Alaska, the Fairweather Range, the St. Elias Mountains, the Kenai Mountains and Chugach Mountains, and Kodiak Island. Between the two arcs is a trough composed of the Inside Passage, the Copper River Lowlands, the Cook Inlet-Susitna Lowlands, and Shelikof Strait.

The largest physiographic division is Alaska's Intermontane Basins and Plateaus, which lie east, north and west of the Alaska Range and south of the Brooks Range. These are comparable to that part of the continental United States bordered by the Rocky Mountains on the east and the Cascade Mountains and Sierra Nevada range on the west. In Alaska these uplands, valleys, and lowland basins house the great river systems: Yukon, Koyukuk, Porcupine, Tanana, and Kuskokwim.

Alaska's Brooks Range is the northern extension of the Rocky Mountain System. In contrast to the Pacific Mountain System, which arcs northward in Alaska, the Brooks Range arcs southward. Mt. Chamberlin (9,020 feet; 2,749 meters) is the highest Alaska peak in this system.

The low-lying Arctic Coastal Plain extends northward from the Brooks Range to the Arctic Ocean. It is an extension of the great Interior Plains that dominate the central United States. Unlike those fertile areas of deep and relatively dry soil, the Arctic Coastal Plain is dominated by wet shallow soils and a vast array of small, shallow lakes.

Alaska's topographic features can also be viewed in profile, as if someone had taken a vertical slice of the earth's surface to reveal its changing shape from north to south. **Figure 4–North-South Transect of Alaska** shows this perspec-tive. From this point of view we can see the striking differences between the high, rugged mountain systems and the low, relatively flat Interior Plateaus and the Arctic Coastal Plain.

While the topographic map and the physiographic divisions describe the surface features of Alaska's terrain, they do not tell us about the nature of the underlying rocks and their geologic history. **Map 12 Terranes of the Bering Region** provides some clues to the processes that helped create today's landforms.

The rock underlying the Wrangell Mountains that so impressed Bradford Washburn have geologic "relatives" in Southeast Alaska, British Columbia (notably Vancouver Island), Washington, and Idaho. The similarity of rock age and structure suggests that over millions of years these mountains have literally been on the move.

Physical Geography 2

Figure 3

Physiographic Regions of Western North America

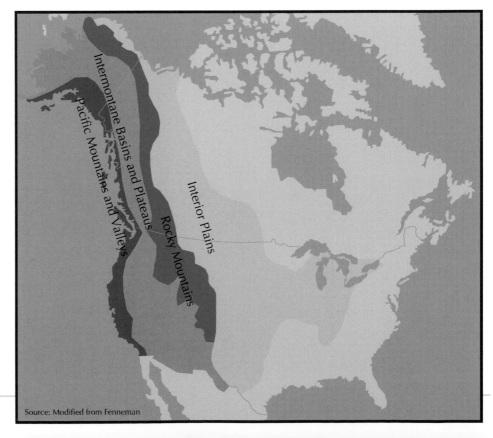

Intermontane Basins and Plateaus

Pacific Mountains and Valleys

Rocky Mountains

Interior Plains

Source: Modified from Fenneman

Theories of plate tectonics are relatively new, and they have been applied to Alaska only since the late 1970s. These theories describe the earth's surface as a collection of gigantic plates, or pieces of crust, floating on the shifting, plastic mantle of the earth. Plates may move as much as a few inches a year. When they collide, the heavier oceanic plates subduct, or drop down under, the lighter continental plates. In Alaska the Pacific Plate is moving northward at about 2 inches (5 centimeters) per year. Its subduction beneath the North American Plate has produced the massive Aleutian Trench, a sudden dropoff of the sea floor that is nearly 5 miles (8 kilometers) deep (See **Map 19 Ocean Basin Topography Around Alaska**).

As with glass or ceramic plates that are shoved around or banged against each other, pieces of tectonic plates can eventually break off. The small, undefined areas on **Map 12 Terranes of the Bering Regions,** show such "broken" pieces, which are not individually named on this map. Tectonic theory suggests that the pieces of plate that make up Alaska's southeast and southcentral coast up to the Alaska Range consist of plate fragments that have drifted northward and accreted, or added on, to the edge of the

continent. This explains how pieces of a large ancient plate called Wrangellia broke off, and over millions of years ended up in Idaho, Canada, and Alaska.

In northwestern Alaska, the Chukotka-Alaska Plate (a portion of the Terranes Originating in the Arctic Ocean, shown on **Map 12**) is part of a much larger system that extends from continental North America into northeastern Russia. This plate, too, has pieces that over the eons have been added to today's Alaska. The northernmost part of Alaska was quite possibly formed when pieces of rock from the Canadian Arctic rotated and joined Alaska from the north.

The wording for the Terranes Originating in the Arctic Ocean Region and Terranes Originating in the Pacific Ocean Region in each case is aligned approximately along the 1,000 meter isobath line indicating terrane divisions.

Map 13 Glaciation shows that over the centuries much of Alaska has been sculpted by ice. Today nearly 5% of Alaska (30,000 square miles, or 78,000 square kilometers) is covered by ice. Frozen in glaciers is nearly three-fourths of all Alaska's fresh water—vastly more than is found in rivers, streams, ponds, and lakes.

As the map shows, most of Alaska's thousands of glaciers are in Southeast and South-central Alaska. Both these regions have high mountain

ranges near the coast. Moisture-laden oceanic air forced up against these mountains rises and is cooled. Since cold air can hold less moisture than warm air, the moisture condenses and falls as precipitation. Often falling as snow, it feeds glaciers and icefields, some of which, like the Bering and Malaspina complexes, are larger than entire states or countries. The mountains of the Alaska Range, farther inland, have numerous glaciers fed by the same process. Mountains in the Brooks Range are tall as well, but because they receive very little precipitation they have relatively few glaciers.

During the peak of the last glacial period some 18,000 to 20,000 years ago, glaciers covered much but not all of Alaska. **Map 13** shows that glaciers did not cover the Arctic Coastal Plain or large portions of the Intermontane Basins and Plateaus. The heavy, slow-moving masses of glacial ice sculpted the mountain landscape beneath them, forming ridges and U-shaped valleys. Behind them they left deep, ocean-flooded valleys, or fjords; scratches, grooves, and striations on bedrock; and deposits of sand and gravel called moraines and eskers. Sometimes lakes formed when water from melting glaciers was blocked from flowing to the sea. The largest of these ancient lakes, Lake Ahtna, was larger in area than modern day Lake Michigan.

A less dramatic feature of Alaska's lithosphere is perma-frost, ground that has remained frozen for two or more years. Permafrost, too, has shaped the landscape of Alaska, and today it is found over a much larger part of the state than are glaciers. More than 20% of the world's landscapes are in permafrost zones. In Alaska, the figure is close to 80%, as shown in **Map 14 Permafrost.**

Permafrost is deepest and most extensive on the Arctic Coastal Plain. Core drillings there have located permafrost as much as 2,000 feet (610 meters) below the surface, and it is found virtually everywhere. As one moves southward, permafrost becomes less common and its depth decreases. Near Fairbanks, permafrost is discontinuous or found only in isolated patches. It extends no more than about 150 feet (46 meters) below the surface. The Anchorage area is generally free of permafrost.

The soil and rocks beneath glaciers are not necessarily frozen. Consequently, on the map even the areas covered by glaciers in Southcentral Alaska are characterized as "generally underlain by isolated masses of permafrost."

Figure 5 shows how permafrost is found in the soil. Freezing and thawing of the upper, or active, layer of permafrost creates a number of characteristic landforms, many of which are common in far northern Alaska.

Figure 4
North-South Transect of Alaska

Source: Adapted from Joint Federal State Land Use Planning Commission

Arctic Coastal Plain   Brooks Range   Interior Basins and Plateaus

These landforms include:

- thaw lakes, which form when water pools in ground surface depressions and begins to thaw the permafrost immediately beneath. As thawing continues, the pools expand. Along the Arctic Coastal Plain, prevailing northeast winds have given thaw lakes a distinctive northwest-southeast orientation due to strong perpendicular wave action.
- ice-wedge polygons, patterns in the ground formed when soil freezes, cracks, and expands, pushing up and out into low ridges. When the areas between ridges collapse and become troughs, the ground is marked by characteristic polygon shapes.
- pingos, rounded hills with ice cores, that form in the centers of drained lakes. When the unfrozen area in the lake basin freezes inward it expands upward, forming a central mound.

Permafrost is of great importance to people because of its potential effect on structures such as buildings, roads, railroads, and pipelines. In northern Alaska most structures are designed to minimize heat transfer to the ground so they will not melt the permafrost and cause the ground to slump. That is why nearly half of the TransAlaska Pipeline was built on aboveground supports. Some scientists now predict a period of climatic warming for

Figure 5

Permafrost in the Soil

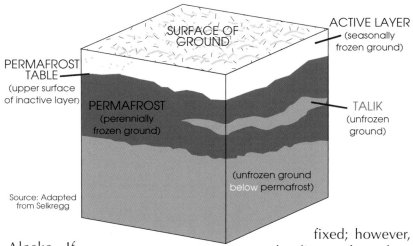

Source: Adapted from Selkregg

Alaska. If that happens, southerly areas of permafrost would likely thaw, causing the ground surface to weaken and become unstable. The impact of such a change could be disastrous for many highways and buildings.

The Atmosphere

Climate, the nature of weather conditions over a long period of time, is a major factor in understanding any place or region. In the past 12,000 years, Alaska has gone from a predominantly glaciated area to one where glaciers cover only 5% of the landscape. Clearly, climate is not something that is

fixed; however, the climate of any place or region can be described in terms of average conditions over a period of time.

Alaska's climatic regions are based on characteristics of temperature and precipitation. **Map 15 Climatic Regions** distinguishes six different climatic types. Lines separating climatic regions are often arbitrary, especially when there are no distinct and dramatic differences over an area. The line separating Interior from West Coast climate is somewhat arbitrary. A person 50 miles (80 kilometers) on either side of the line would not notice much difference in climate. On the other hand, there is a sharp contrast between Arctic and Interior climates on the north and south sides of the

Brooks Range. That boundary line reflects very real differences especially in summer temperatures.

Geographers often talk about climatic controls to explain why climate varies from place to place. One significant climatic control is latitude. Places at high northern latitudes, like most of Alaska, have relatively cold climates for two reasons: because sunlight strikes the earth at a relatively low angle throughout the year, and because hours of daylight are greatly reduced in winter. As the graphs in **Figure 6–Climographs for Six Alaska Locations** show, average temperatures are considerably warmer in Juneau (58° N) than in Barrow (71° N).

A second climatic control, maritime and continental influences, is more complex. Nome and Fairbanks are at the same general latitude, but because Nome faces the Bering Sea and Fairbanks is far inland, Fairbanks is much warmer in summer. Water bodies heat and cool much more slowly than land areas. The Bering Sea is quite cool in the summer, so it keeps Nome cool as well. In contrast, Fairbanks receives long hours of daylight in summer without any cooling from a large water body. Daily temperatures ranging to 90° F (32° C) are not uncommon.

Enjoying a continental influence in summer has its price, however. In Fairbanks, January

Pacific Mountain System

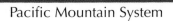

Gulf of Alaska Coast

Figure 6

Climographs for Six Alaska Locations

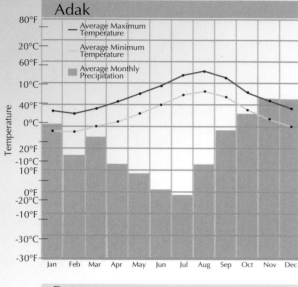

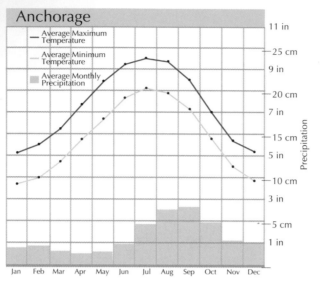

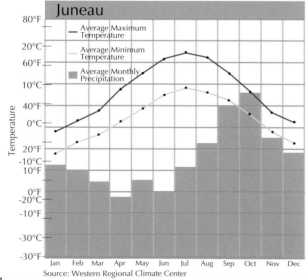

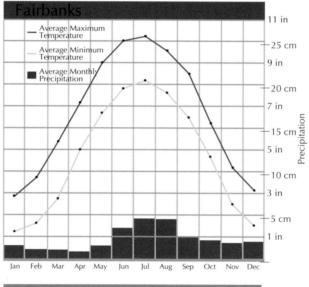

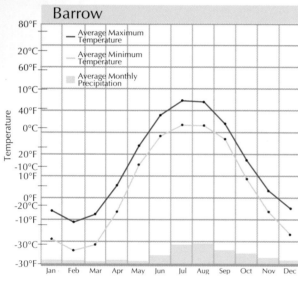

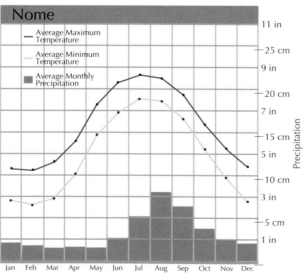

Source: Western Regional Climate Center

temperatures are very low. With no modifying ocean nearby, temperatures in mid-winter can plummet to -60° F (-51° C) or colder. At the same time, Nome is not warmed from the Bering Sea because the sea freezes over for several months (See **Map 20 Extent of Sea Ice–Alaska Coastal Region**).

The Aleutian Islands, the Alaska Peninsula, and Kodiak Island are in the Western Maritime climatic region. The region has virtually no continental influences. During winter this area is subject to severe storms. During summer, the Bering Sea and the North Pacific Ocean have a cooling effect, while clouds often block the sun.

Differences in temperature and precipitation between the Western and Eastern Maritime regions are not great, but they are significant. Eastern Maritime is less windy, somewhat warmer, and has more sunny days than Western Maritime. These factors help explain why luxuriant forests grow in Southeast Alaska, while the Aleutian Islands have no forests. Precipitation in the Eastern Maritime region varies locally because of the rugged topography. Some mountainous areas receive more than 300 inches (760 centimeters) of precipitation a year. In contrast, areas cut off from moist ocean air by mountains ("rainshadow" areas) are often cloudy, but they receive less precipitation.

The Southcentral climatic region has both maritime and continental influences. Extensive mountains capture moisture from air off the Gulf of Alaska and support an enormous area of glaciation. Communities in the region are at low elevations, where they can take advantage of warmer air. Also, depending on a settlement's location, the mountains can offer protection from excessive precipitation. During winter, weather in the Southcentral region is influenced by both the warmer, unfrozen Gulf of Alaska and the frozen continental Interior.

Temperatures and precipitation for Barrow are typical of the Arctic climatic region. At this northerly latitude there is minimal warmth in the sun's rays because they strike the earth at a low angle. For 84 days in winter Barrow receives no direct sunlight, and the frozen Arctic Ocean offers no moderating effect. No maritime influence comes from the south because the Alaska land mass and the Brooks Range block most northerly flows of air.

The Hydrosphere, Fresh and Salt Waters

Alaska has more than three million lakes, more than 12,000 rivers, and uncounted thousands of streams, creeks, and ponds. Together these water bodies hold about one-third of all the fresh water found in the United States.

The five longest rivers in Alaska are the Yukon, Porcupine, Koyukuk, Kuskokwim, and Tanana. The Yukon is nearly three times longer than the next four longest rivers, as shown in **Figure 7–Ten Longest Rivers**. After a roughly 600-mile (965-kilometer) start in Canada, the Yukon winds some 1,400 miles (2,253 kilometers) in a great arc through Alaska's interior. The arc closely

Figure 7

Ten Longest Rivers

Yukon	1,400 mi	(2,253 km)
	plus 600 mi	(965 km) in Canada
Porcupine	555 mi	(893 km)
Koyukuk	554 mi	(891 km)
Kuskokwim	540 mi	(869 km)
Tanana	531 mi	(854 km)
Innoko	463 mi	(745 km)
Colville	428 mi	(689 km)
Noatak	396 mi	(637 km)
Kobuk	396 mi	(637 km)
Birch Creek	314 mi	(505 km)

parallels the arc of the Alaska Range.

The Yukon and Alaska's other great rivers, shown in **Map 16 Major Rivers and Lakes**, provide food, transportation, and recreation for people, as well as habitat for fish and wildlife. Day by day their flowing waters shape the landscape. When they jam with ice or flood their banks they transform valleys, wetlands, and human settlements. Each year they carry millions of tons of silt and debris from land to the sea.

The flow of rivers in northern places such as Alaska changes with the seasons. During winter, water flow in most of Alaska's rivers drops dramatically as glacial melt declines and rivers, lakes, and the ground freeze. Near Stevens Village (66°01′N, 149°06′W), for example, the Yukon River shows discharges of approximately 25,000 cubic feet per second (708 cubic meters per second) in March and April. Once thawing occurs in May, the flow rate can jump to more than 600,000 cubic feet per second (16,992 cubic meters per second). Though other Alaska rivers have less flow than the Yukon, they show a similar wide range in flow levels.

The area encompassing a stream or river system is called a drainage basin, or a drainage region when referring to more than one basin. A basin includes all the land drained by a particular river and its tributary streams. A drainage region, like the ones shown in **Map 17 Drainage Regions and River Discharge**, reflects the geographic patterns streams follow as they flow toward the sea. The Arctic Region encompasses stream systems that flow generally northward into the Arctic Ocean. Streams in the South Central Region flow generally southward into the Gulf of Alaska. Streams in the Yukon Region flow generally westward into the Bering Sea.

The yellow lines on the map indicate drainage "divides." These boundaries between regions are located in high elevation areas, from which water flows downward toward one drainage region or another.

The volume of water in a drainage basin or region is partly influenced by climate. Areas with high precipitation have more runoff to contribute to river flow. Volume of flow is also influenced by the size of a drainage basin. The largest drainage basin in Alaska is, of course, the Yukon River Basin. Including Canada, it drains an area of 330,000 square miles (855,000 square kilometers). In Alaska the Yukon basin occupies one-third of the area of the state.

The next largest river basins in Alaska are the Kuskokwim, the Porcupine, and the Tanana. Because of their smaller size, their discharge is far less than that of the Yukon. The Porcupine River, for example, has an average annual discharge of 23,000 cubic feet per second (651 cubic meters per second), which is less than one-tenth the discharge of the Yukon (225,000 cubic feet per second; 6,372 cubic meters per second).

Drainage basins are important in regional planning studies and assessments of flood hazards.

Alaska's lakes, shown in **Map 16 Major Rivers and Lakes**, are not particularly large, but there are a great many of them. About 100 have surface areas of more than 10 square miles (26 square kilometers). Iliamna Lake is the third largest lake completely within the borders of the United States, and Becharof Lake is among the 10 largest. Lake Minchumina, another large lake, lies near the geographic center of Alaska.

About 20,000 smaller lakes have been counted in the Yukon Flats area, and there are innumerable lakes in the Yukon-Kuskokwim Delta and on the Arctic Coastal Plain.

Alaska's lakes serve as repositories of fresh water, habitat for fish and other wildlife, and focal points for human settlement, recreation, and industry. **Figure 8** lists **Areas of Selected Lakes**.

No less important as part of Alaska's hydrosphere is salt water. In essence, the state is a

Figure 8

Areas of Selected Lakes

Iliamna	1,150 sq mi	(2,979 sq km)
Becharof	458 sq mi	(1,186 sq km)
Teshekpuk	315 sq mi	(816 sq km)
Naknek	242 sq mi	(627 sq km)
Tustemena	117 sq mi	(303 sq km)
Clark	110 sq mi	(285 sq km)
Dall	100 sq mi	(259 sq km)
Upper Ushagik	75 sq mi	(194 sq km)
Lower Ushagik	72 sq mi	(186 sq km)
Kukaklek	72 sq mi	(186 sq km)

Lakes on the Arctic Coastal Plain

U.S. Geological Survey

huge peninsula, since it is surrounded by water on three sides (See **Map 18 Ocean Currents in Waters Around Alaska**). To the south is the Pacific Ocean, which washes the coast of Southeast Alaska and flows into the sheltered bays, straits, and fjords of the Inside Passage. Farther north the Gulf of Alaska forms a large arc that connects to Prince William Sound and Cook Inlet. From there the Pacific curves south and west, along the southern edges of the Aleutian Islands.

The waters of the North Pacific form part of a large spiral, or gyre, that transports water around the ocean. The Kuroshio Current flows northward and eastward from Japan and across the Pacific, where it splits. One part called the California Current moves clockwise, or southward, off the coast of Washington to California. The other part called the Alaska Current flows northward into a smaller gyre that moves counterclockwise and flows southwesterly along the Alaska coast. It was the Alaska Current that in spring 1989 dispersed oil from the leaking supertanker *Exxon Valdez*. The current carried oil more than 600 miles (1,000 kilometers) from Prince William Sound to the Kenai Peninsula, Kodiak Island and the Alaska Peninsula.

Figure 9–Drifting Objects on the Ocean shows and tells about drifting objects and how they reveal the nature of ocean currents off Alaska.

Through several passes among the Aleutian Islands, the Pacific Ocean flows into the Bering Sea. This arm of the Pacific Ocean covers 890,000 square miles (2,300,000 square

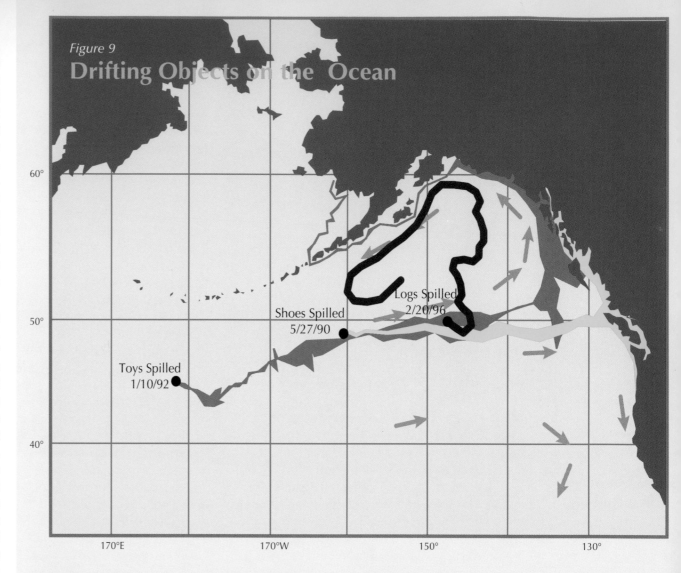

Figure 9
Drifting Objects on the Ocean

Logs Spilled
2/20/96

Shoes Spilled
5/27/90

Toys Spilled
1/10/92

W hat can ocean scientists learn from plastic bathtub toys and soggy sneakers? A great deal, to judge from reports about objects found drifting in the ocean and washed up along Alaska and nearby coasts.

In May 1990, 80,000 Nike athletic shoes washed overboard from a container ship traveling from Korea to the U.S. They were found months later along the coasts of Oregon, Washington, and British Columbia as far north as the Queen Charlotte Islands.

In January 1992, 29,000 children's bathtub toys were washed off a container ship traveling from Hong Kong to Tacoma, Washington. Ten months later, yellow ducks, green frogs, blue turtles, and red beavers started showing up in Sitka, and by January 1994 they were being found in Bristol Bay. Scientists predicted some toys could be trapped in ocean ice and could eventually travel northward, into the Arctic Ocean and on to the North Atlantic.

In 1996, 1,100 Douglas fir logs dropped off a transport ship far offshore in the Gulf of Alaska. The National Marine Fisheries Service used knowledge about ocean currents to predict where the 20-foot-long floating timbers might drift and become hazards to fishing boats and other seagoing vessels.

Scientists at the National Oceanic and Atmospheric Administration study these objects and reports from people who find them to learn more about winds and currents in the ocean off Alaska's coast. Their findings also help predict year-to-year variations in currents that might affect populations of fish such as pollock, whose eggs and larvae are carried on the surface currents that flow like low-salinity rivers in the salty ocean off Alaska's coast.

Objects washed off cargo ships in storms or accidents are a good source of information because shipping routes from Asian ports to North America follow Great Circle routes that intersect ocean currents.

Source: National Marine Fisheries Service

kilometers), an area more than one-third larger than Alaska. Nearly half the sea is underlain by a broad reach of continental shelf, and it is less than 650 feet (200 meters) deep (See **Map 19 Ocean Basin Topography Around Alaska**).

The Bering Sea fosters one of the world's largest bottomfish fisheries, centered primarily on pollock. It is home to massive populations of marine mammals, what may be the world's largest clam population, world-class salmon runs, and some of the world's largest gatherings of breeding seabirds. Its two largest bays, Bristol Bay and Kuskokwim Bay, are highly productive fishing areas fed by the massive systems of rivers and lakes in Alaska's interior. The complex currents in the Bering Sea generally tend to move counterclockwise (See **Map 18 Ocean Currents in Waters Around Alaska**).

Bering Strait, only about 50 miles (80 kilometers) wide between Alaska and Russia, directs the flow of water between the Bering Sea and the Arctic Ocean. About 19% of the water flowing into the Arctic Ocean comes from the Bering Sea. One hundred million years ago, most of the water in the Arctic Ocean was from the Pacific. Today, due to the shifting of tectonic plates, most of the water is from the Atlantic.

The Chukchi Sea, north of Bering Strait, is part of the Arctic Ocean. It is quite shallow for several hundred miles offshore. Warmed by ocean currents from the south, it supports large numbers of marine mammals.

The Beaufort Sea on Alaska's northern coast is deeper and has a narrower continental shelf than the Chukchi or Bering Seas. Influenced mostly by the Arctic Ocean, it is ice-covered for many months of the year. Ocean currents off the Arctic coast move westward. Below the surface near Barrow is the **Barrow Canyon**, shown in **Figure 10**. This deep submarine canyon is occasionally the conduit for upwelling water from the Atlantic Ocean. The Atlantic water travels eastward through the Arctic Ocean from Norway, along the northern coast of Russia, to Alaska. The source of the water has been determined by its temperature and salinity. It is slightly warmer and more saline than the Pacific waters. The Atlantic meets the Pacific at Barrow!

The Bering Sea and the Arctic Ocean display a dramatic seasonal shift in freezing and thawing. This is shown in **Map 20 Extent of Sea Ice (Alaska Coastal Region)**. During a mild winter, the Bering Sea may freeze along a line extending approximately from St. Matthew Island to Nunivak Island and then to the coast near Bristol Bay. In some years severe winter freezes have moved the sea ice southward to the western tip of the Alaska Peninsula, extending beyond the Pribilof Islands of St. Paul and St. George. During summer, sea ice retreats north of the Bering Strait. The permanent ice pack, consisting of multi-year ice, is never far from Barrow.

Because water heats and cools more slowly than land, the maximum extent of sea ice is usually reached in March after many months of winter, while minimums occur in August and September after several months of summer.

Map 21 shows the **Coastline of Alaska,** where land and water meet. Alaska coasts vary from rocky shores, sandy beaches, and high cliffs to offshore pinnacles, river deltas, mud flats, and barrier islands with sheltered lagoons. The state has 6,640 miles (10,700 kilometers) of coastline—more than all the other 49 states together. If the distance around shorelines of islands is added, Alaska has 33,900 miles (54,545 kilometers) of coastline—9,000 miles (14,481 kilometers) more than the distance around the entire earth at the Equator.

Coastlines everywhere change constantly due to wave action, ocean currents, storms, and river deposits. Waves and currents may deposit coarse materials along the coast, forming spits that extend across the mouths of bays, and barrier islands, which are similar to spits but not connected to the mainland. Some of these coastal landforms can be seen in northwestern Alaska.

Waves and currents may also erode the coastline. In the area near Prudhoe Bay, on the Beaufort Sea, the coastal erosion rate is 6.5 to 16.4 feet (2 to 5 meters) per year. That is the highest rate in the world, and it takes place over a period of only three months a year.

Much of Alaska's coastline is affected every winter by sea ice. Tectonic shifts in the earth's crust, volcanic eruptions, and earthquakes can also change the shape and height of areas along the shore. Large areas of coastline around Prince William Sound, for example, changed drastically during the Good Friday Earthquake of 1964. In Southeast Alaska, parts of the coastline are rising more than one inch (2.5 centimeters) a year, partly due to tectonic forces and

Figure 10
Barrow Canyon

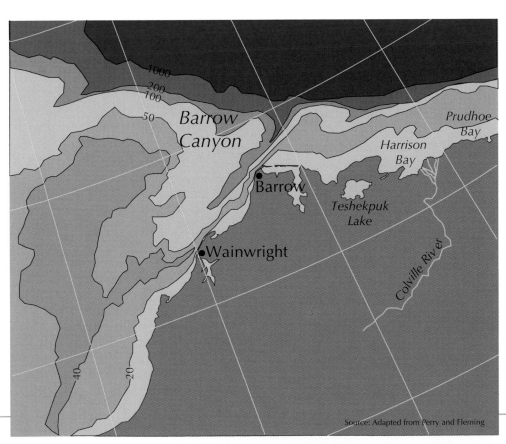

Source: Adapted from Perry and Fleming

partly as large glaciers have retreated and lifted the weight of many cubic miles of ice from the land.

Human activities may change the coastline physically as well. When communities build breakwaters or dredge for harbors, tides and currents almost invariably begin new patterns of erosion and buildup that reshape the coastline.

The Biosphere

Thousands of plant and animal species, along with their nonliving environments, make up the biotic communities and ecosystems of Alaska. Forests are a vegetative type and brown bears are an animal species that illustrate the importance of geographic distribution.

Map 22 Forests shows the coastal and northern forests in Alaska. With no other vegetation types presented on the map, it can be seen that forests occupy less than half, roughly 37%, of Alaska's territory. Alpine and tundra vegetation types occupy much of the remaining area.

Pinned between the ocean and lofty mountains, Coastal Western Hemlock-Sitka Spruce forests dominate coastal areas of Southeast and Southcentral Alaska. Sometimes called "temperate rain forests," these areas are nurtured by a wet, relatively mild maritime climate. They are made up of large trees, some of them 300 to 400 years old, with a generally lush understory. The Sitka spruce, Alaska's official "state tree," often grows to 160 feet (49 meters) in height. Along with the Western hemlock, it has historically provided the

Caribou bull in Denali Park

Alaska Division of Tourism

foundation for Alaska's timber harvest.

Timberline in the coastal forests varies greatly depending in part on local conditions. It occurs at about 2,500 feet (760 meters) near Ketchikan, at 2,000 feet (600meters) in Prince William Sound, and at 500 feet (150 meters) in Cook Inlet.

Alaska's northern forests are often called boreal forests, or *taiga* using the Russian word for "little sticks." Northern forests grow in areas of moderate precipitation with long, cold winters and short, warm summers. Bottomland Spruce-Poplar forests appear on the map as narrow lines close to northern Alaska's major rivers. Specifically, they occur on broad floodplains and river terraces. They are made up of tall, relatively dense white spruce mixed in some areas with cottonwood or balsam poplar.

Upland Spruce-Hardwood forests are fairly dense areas of white spruce, birch, aspen, and poplar. White spruce and poplar trees grow to 80 feet (24 meters) tall, while birch and aspen average 50 feet (15 meters). Black spruce typically grow on north-facing slopes and poorly drained flats.

Lowland Spruce-Hardwood forests are found in large, lowland river valleys like those of the Yukon, Tanana, Koyukuk, Copper, and Susitna rivers. These forests are made up of evergreen and deciduous trees. They include large, pure stands of black spruce and areas of slow-growing, stunted tamarack in wet low lying places.

Alaska's northern forests are subject to several hundred fires every summer, most started by

lightning. In 1990, during a particularly dry summer, more than 900 fires scorched nearly 5,000 square miles (13,000 square kilometers) of forest lands.

Map 23 Brown Bear Density shows how one species of wildlife is distributed throughout most of Alaska but at varying population densities, depending on local environments. The species *Ursus arctos* includes the coastal brown bears of Southeast and Southcentral Alaska and the grizzlies of northern Alaska and the Interior. The absence of brown bears on islands south of Frederick Sound in Southeast Alaska is believed to be a result of glaciation patterns and changes in sea level thousands of years ago.

The density of brown bear populations in Alaska varies immensely from one bear per square mile on some islands in Southeast Alaska to one bear per 300 square miles on the coastal plain south of Barrow. In metric measures that is a variation in density from more than 386 to less than 2 bears every 1,000 square kilometers. The highest densities of bears are on Admiralty, Baranof, and Chichagof Islands in Southeast Alaska, and on Kodiak Island and the Alaska Peninsula. Studies show that bear populations are higher, and bears are generally larger, in these coastal areas where abundant salmon spawning streams provide large quantities of highly nutritious food during summer and fall.

On the Southeast Alaska mainland, especially around Glacier Bay, glaciers inhibit bears' movements and eliminate the foods they depend on. Farther north, around Yakutat,

populations increase. On the Kenai Peninsula and around Anchorage, where bear foods are typically available, the density of human population and activity is a major factor limiting the number of bears.

The physical features that characterize Alaska—terrain, climate, soils, rivers and lakes, plants and animals—do not exist in isolation. The lithosphere, the atmosphere, the hydrosphere, and the biosphere are all interconnected. The U.S. Geological Survey developed **Map 24 Ecoregions of Alaska** to show the importance of these connections and to provide an integrated view of regional patterns in Alaska's physical geography. The map shows 20 ecoregions. Each one is ecologically distinct in its combination of many factors, including climate, land forms, geology, glaciation, permafrost, soils, vegetation, and amount of water present. The regions are useful for studying vegetation, soil erosion, characteristics of surface water, wildlife habitat, potential effects of human activities, and climate changes. They are also helpful in resource exploration and development, community planning, resource management, and efforts to deal with natural hazards or risks of pollution.

Photos and descriptions of representative ecoregions can be found in **Figure 11** on the page opposite **Map 24**.

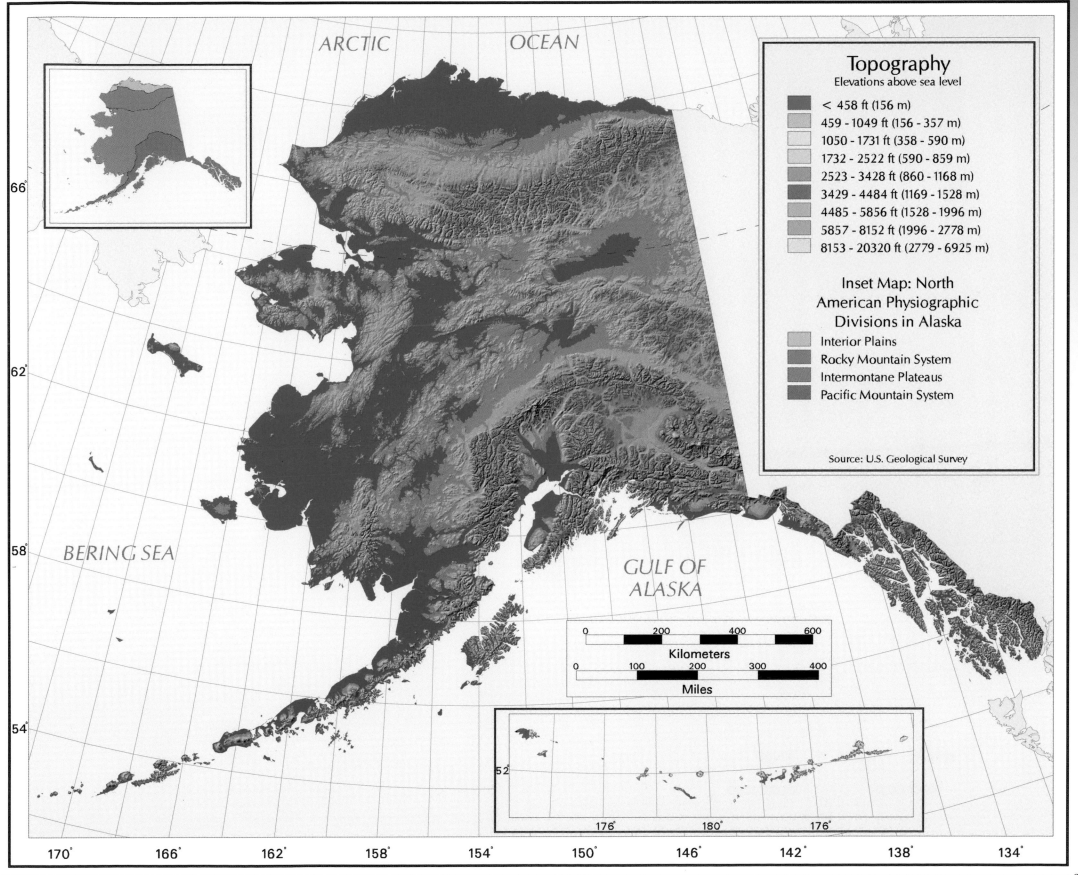

ARCTIC OCEAN

Topography
Elevations above sea level

< 458 ft (156 m)
459 - 1049 ft (156 - 357 m)
1050 - 1731 ft (358 - 590 m)
1732 - 2522 ft (590 - 859 m)
2523 - 3428 ft (860 - 1168 m)
3429 - 4484 ft (1169 - 1528 m)
4485 - 5856 ft (1528 - 1996 m)
5857 - 8152 ft (1996 - 2778 m)
8153 - 20320 ft (2779 - 6925 m)

Inset Map: North
American Physiographic
Divisions in Alaska

Interior Plains
Rocky Mountain System
Intermontane Plateaus
Pacific Mountain System

Source: U.S. Geological Survey

BERING SEA

GULF OF
ALASKA

0   200   400   600
Kilometers
0   100   200   300   400
Miles

66°
62°
58°
54°
52°

170°   166°   162°   158°   154°   150°   146°   142°   138°   134°

176°   180°   176°

Map 12—Terranes of the Bering Region

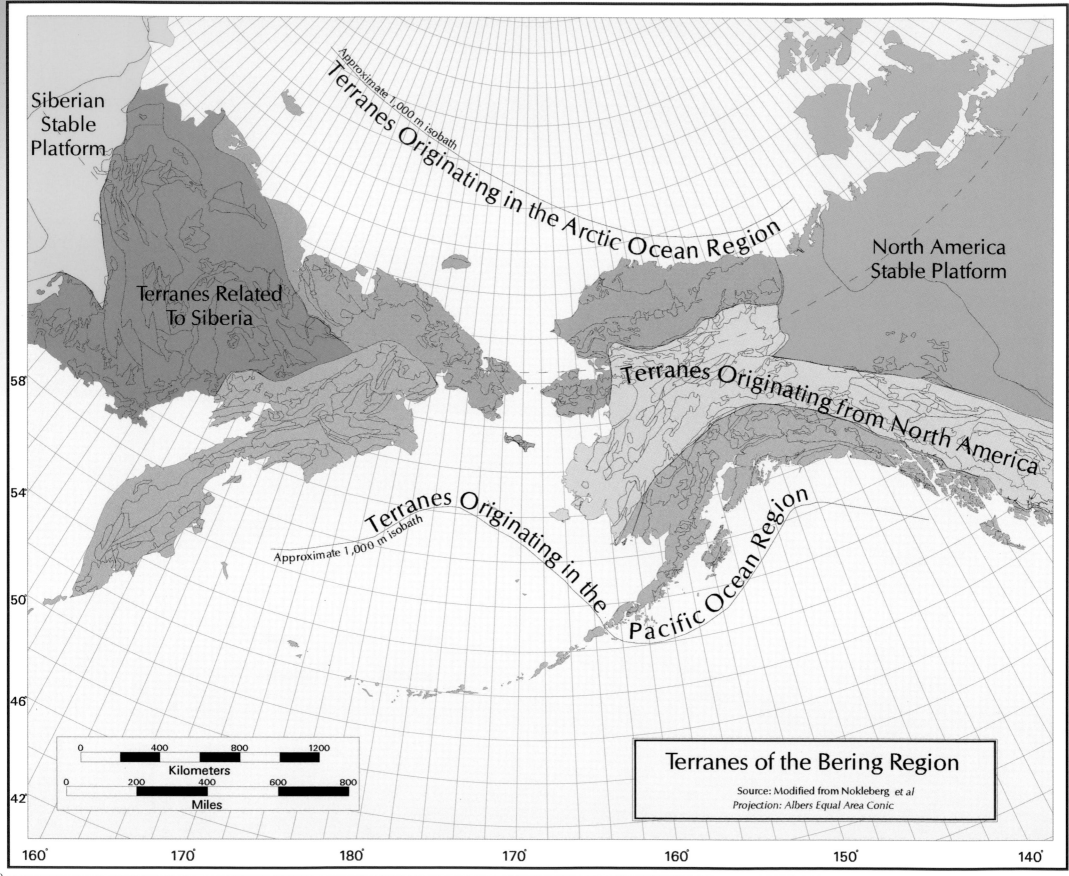

Siberian Stable Platform

Terranes Related To Siberia

Terranes Originating in the Arctic Ocean Region

Approximate 1,000 m isobath

North America Stable Platform

Terranes Originating from North America

Terranes Originating in the Pacific Ocean Region

Approximate 1,000 m isobath

58

54

50

46

42

0   400   800   1200
Kilometers

0   200   400   600   800
Miles

Terranes of the Bering Region

Source: Modified from Nokleberg *et al*
Projection: Albers Equal Area Conic

160°   170°   180°   170°   160°   150°   140°

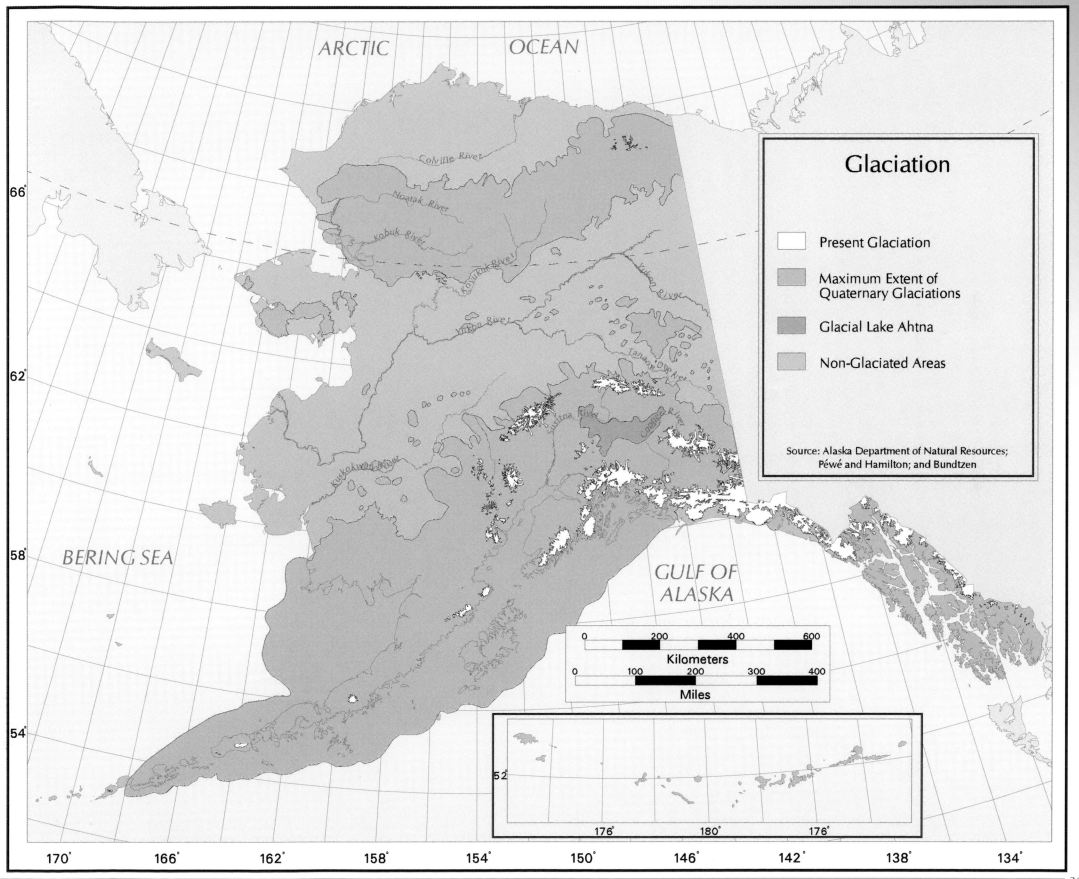

ARCTIC OCEAN

Colville River

Noatak River

Kobuk River

Kobukuk River

Yukon River

Yukon River

Tanana River

66°

62°

58°

54°

BERING SEA

Kuskokwim River

Susitna River

Copper River

GULF OF ALASKA

Glaciation

Present Glaciation

Maximum Extent of
Quaternary Glaciations

Glacial Lake Ahtna

Non-Glaciated Areas

Source: Alaska Department of Natural Resources;
Péwé and Hamilton; and Bundtzen

0   200   400   600
Kilometers

0   100   200   300   400
Miles

52°

176°   180°   176°

170°   166°   162°   158°   154°   150°   146°   142°   138°   134°

Map 14–Permafrost

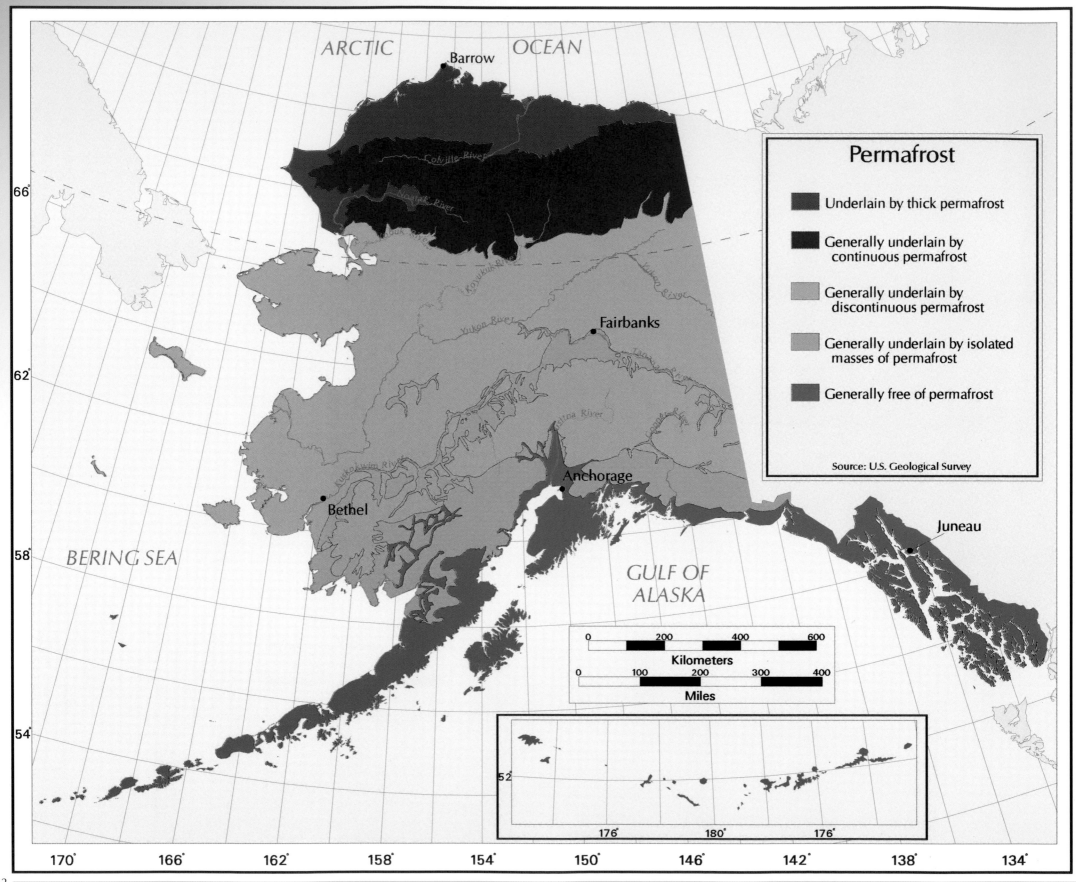

ARCTIC OCEAN

Barrow

Colville River

Noatak River

Kobuk River

Koyukuk River

Yukon River

Fairbanks

Yukon River

62°

66°

Kuskokwim River

Susitna River

Copper River

Anchorage

Bethel

58°

BERING SEA

GULF OF
ALASKA

Juneau

54°

52°

176°   180°   176°

170°   166°   162°   158°   154°   150°   146°   142°   138°   134°

Permafrost

- Underlain by thick permafrost
- Generally underlain by continuous permafrost
- Generally underlain by discontinuous permafrost
- Generally underlain by isolated masses of permafrost
- Generally free of permafrost

Source: U.S. Geological Survey

0   200   400   600
Kilometers

0   100   200   300   400
Miles

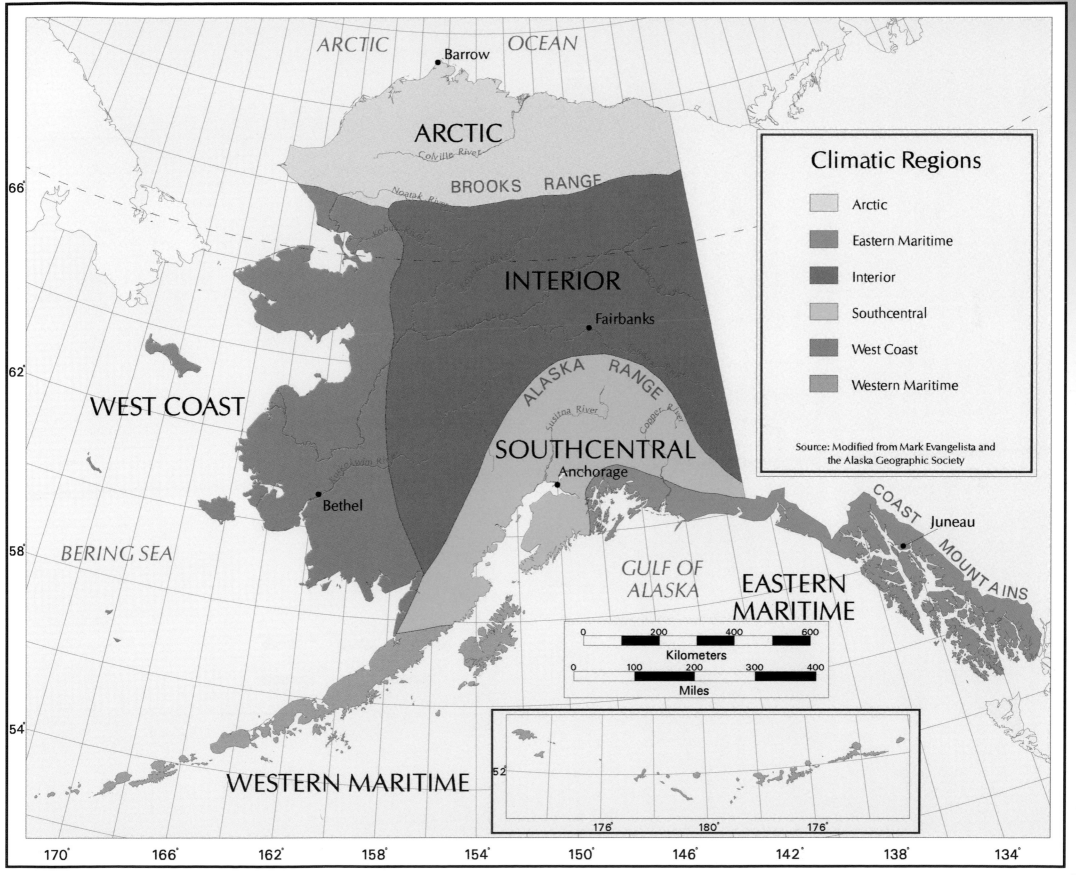

Climatic Regions–Map 15

ARCTIC OCEAN
• Barrow

ARCTIC

Colville River
BROOKS RANGE
Noatak River

INTERIOR

Fairbanks •

ALASKA RANGE
Susitna River
Copper River

SOUTHCENTRAL

Anchorage •

WEST COAST

Bethel •

BERING SEA

GULF OF ALASKA

EASTERN MARITIME

COAST MOUNTAINS
Juneau •

WESTERN MARITIME

Climatic Regions

- Arctic
- Eastern Maritime
- Interior
- Southcentral
- West Coast
- Western Maritime

Source: Modified from Mark Evangelista and the Alaska Geographic Society

0 200 400 600
Kilometers
0 100 200 300 400
Miles

66°
62°
58°
54°
52°

170° 166° 162° 158° 154° 150° 146° 142° 138° 134°
176° 180° 176°

Map 16–Major Rivers and Lakes

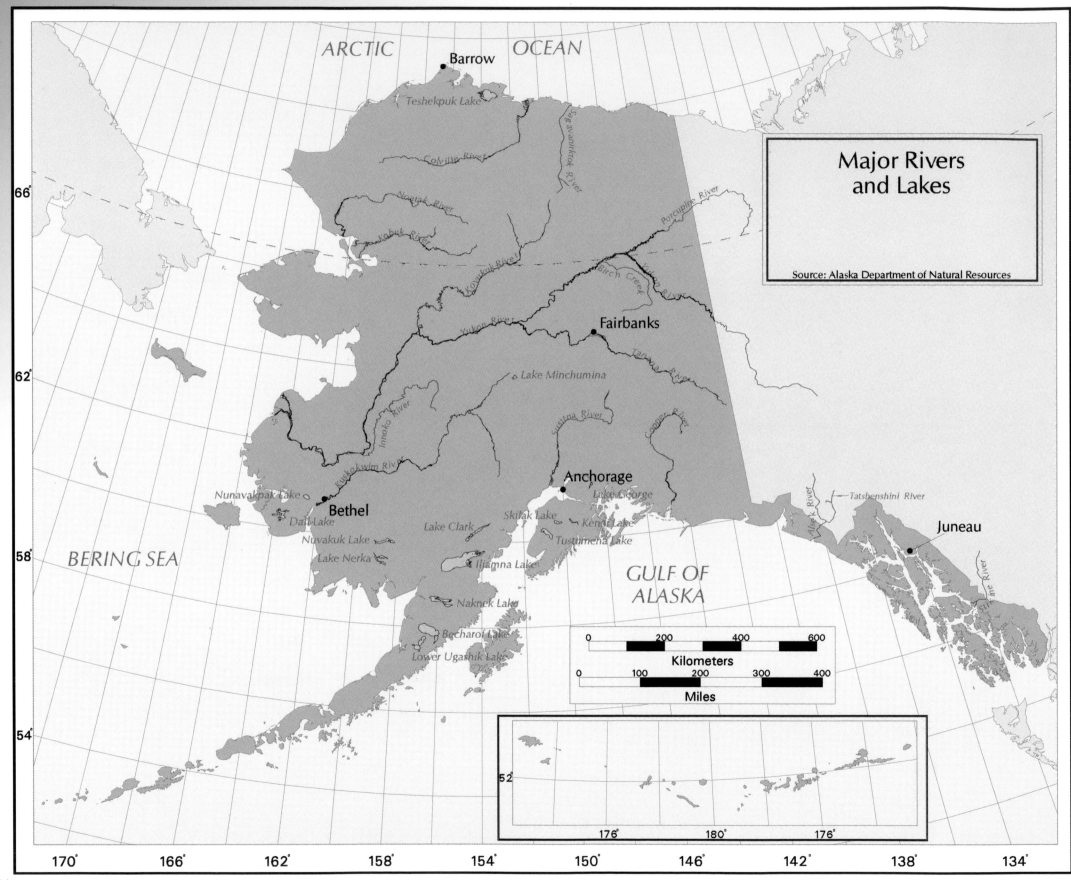

Major Rivers and Lakes

Source: Alaska Department of Natural Resources

ARCTIC OCEAN

Barrow

Teshekpuk Lake

Colville River

Sagavanirktok River

Noatak River

Porcupine River

Kobuk River

Koyukuk River

Birch Creek

Yukon River

Fairbanks

Yukon River

Tanana River

Lake Minchumina

Susitna River

Copper River

Innoko River

Kuskokwim River

Anchorage

Lake George

Nunavakpak Lake

Bethel

Dall Lake

Skilak Lake

Kenai Lake

Lake Clark

Tatshenshini River

Nuvakuk Lake

Tustumena Lake

Lake Nerka

BERING SEA

Iliamna Lake

GULF OF ALASKA

Juneau

Naknek Lake

Becharof Lake

Lower Ugashik Lake

| 0 | 200 | 400 | 600 |
Kilometers

| 0 | 100 | 200 | 300 | 400 |
Miles

66°
62°
58°
54°

52°

176°   180°   176°

170°   166°   162°   158°   154°   150°   146°   142°   138°   134°

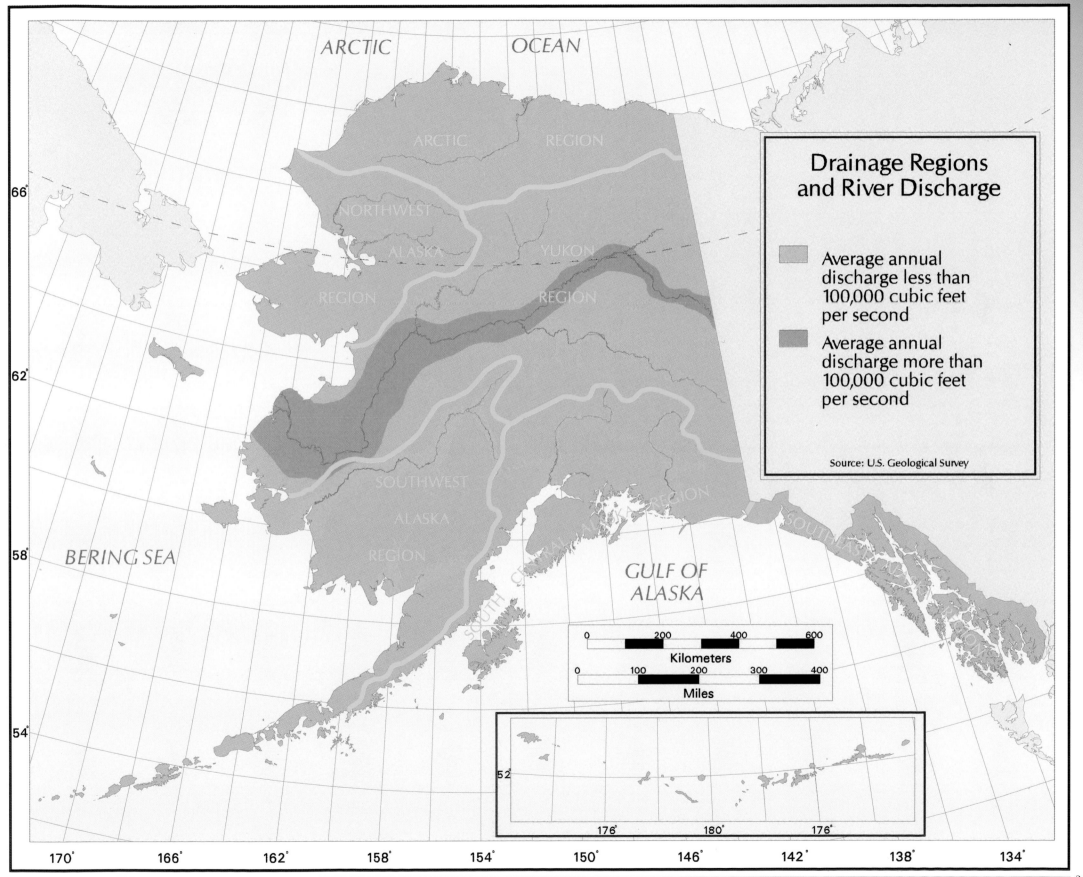

ARCTIC OCEAN

ARCTIC REGION

NORTHWEST ALASKA REGION

YUKON REGION

BERING SEA

SOUTHWEST ALASKA REGION

SOUTH CENTRAL ALASKA REGION

SOUTHEAST ALASKA REGION

GULF OF ALASKA

Drainage Regions and River Discharge

Average annual discharge less than 100,000 cubic feet per second

Average annual discharge more than 100,000 cubic feet per second

Source: U.S. Geological Survey

Kilometers
0   200   400   600

Miles
0   100   200   300   400

Map 18-Ocean Currents in Waters Around Alaska

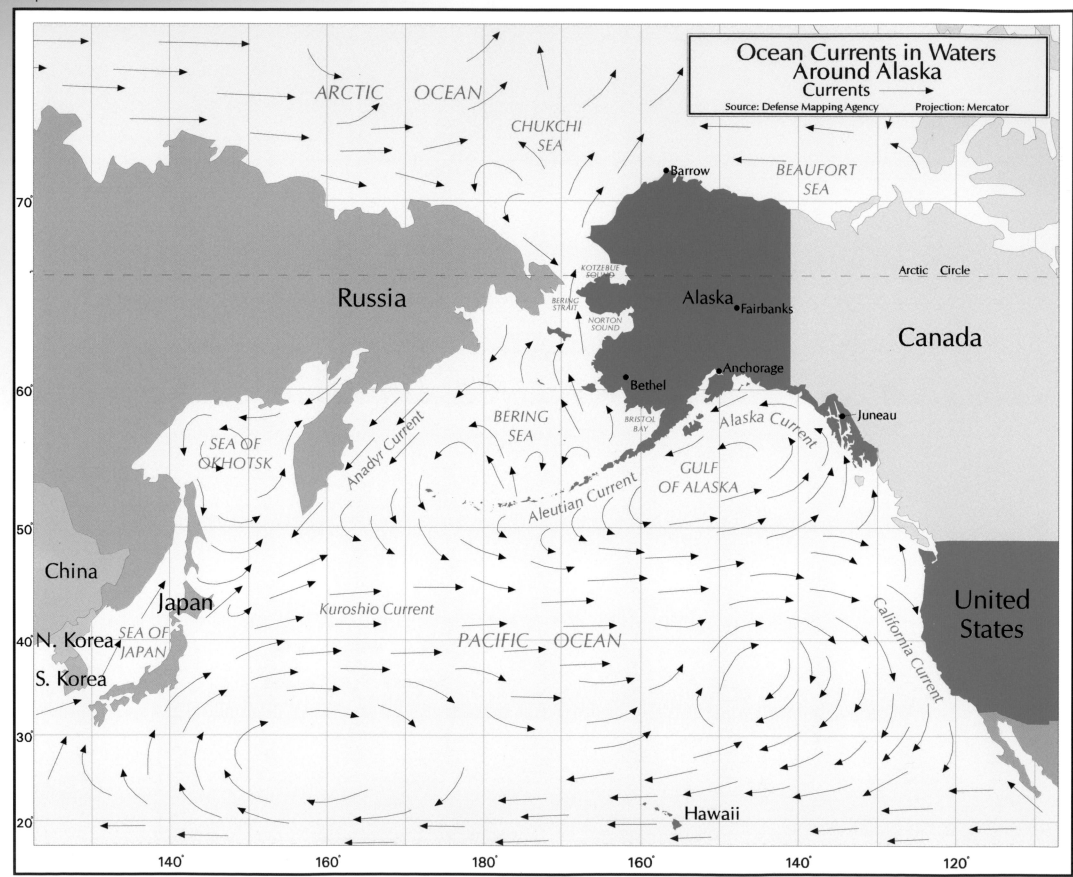

Ocean Currents in Waters Around Alaska

Currents

Source: Defense Mapping Agency   Projection: Mercator

ARCTIC   OCEAN

CHUKCHI
SEA

•Barrow

BEAUFORT
SEA

Russia

KOTZEBUE
SOUND

BERING
STRAIT

NORTON
SOUND

Alaska

•Fairbanks

Arctic   Circle

Canada

•Bethel

•Anchorage

BRISTOL
BAY

Anadyr Current

BERING
SEA

Alaska Current

•Juneau

SEA OF
OKHOTSK

Aleutian Current

GULF
OF ALASKA

China

Japan

Kuroshio Current

PACIFIC   OCEAN

United
States

N. Korea

SEA OF
JAPAN

California Current

S. Korea

Hawaii

140°   160°   180°   160°   140°   120°

70°

60°

50°

40°

30°

20°

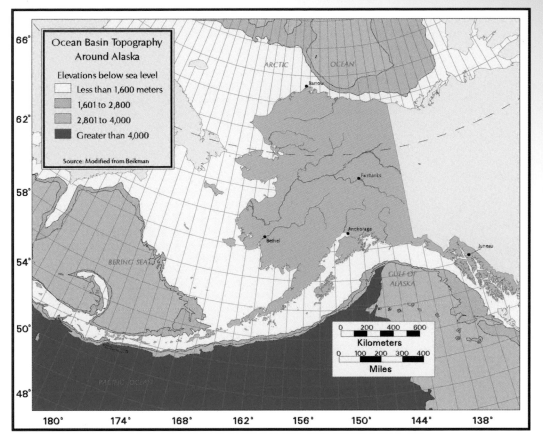

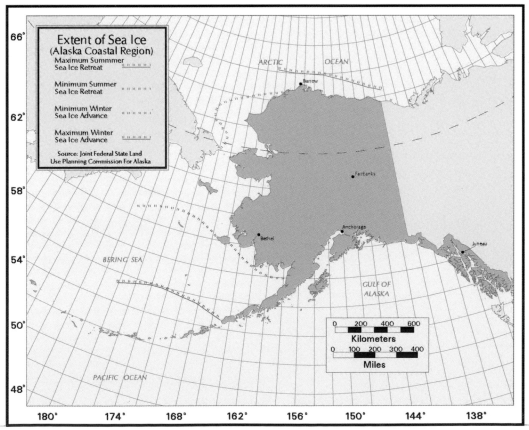

Map 21–Coastline of Alaska

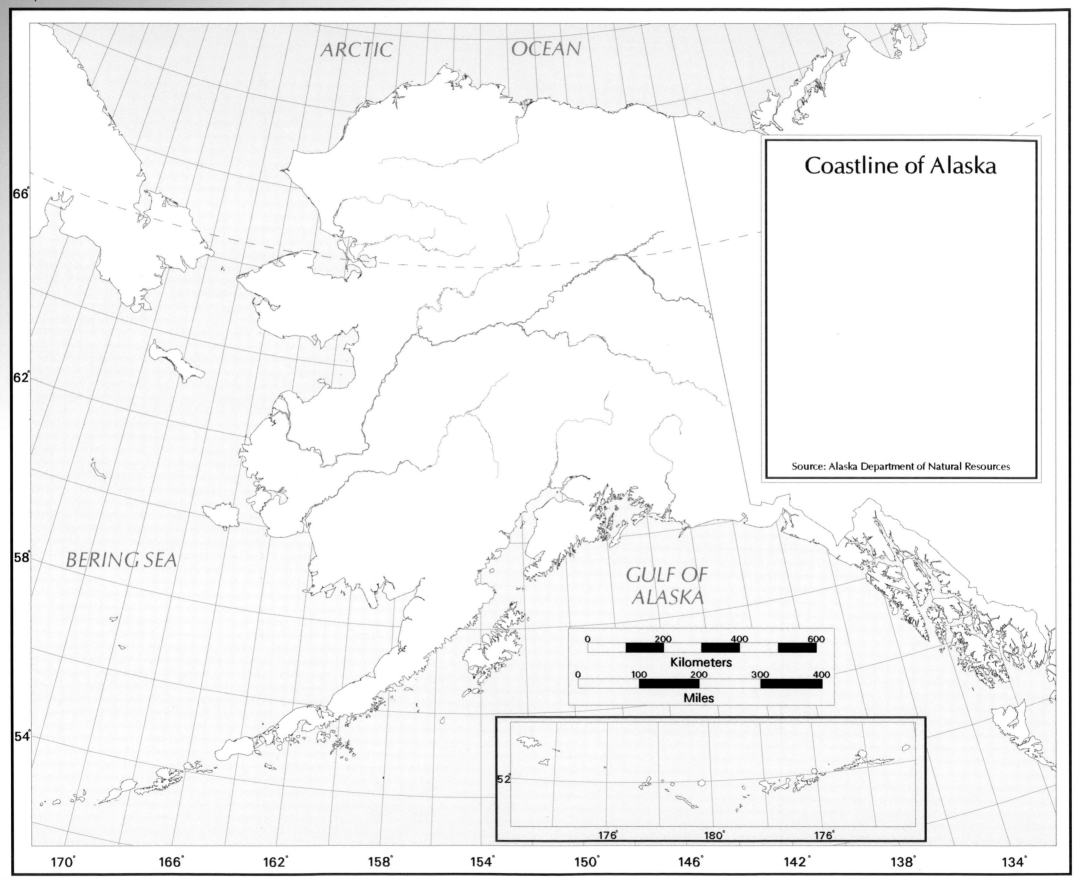

ARCTIC OCEAN

Coastline of Alaska

Source: Alaska Department of Natural Resources

66°
62°
58°
54°

BERING SEA

GULF OF ALASKA

| 0 | | 200 | | 400 | | 600 |
Kilometers
| 0 | 100 | | 200 | | 300 | | 400 |
Miles

52°

176°   180°   176°

170°   166°   162°   158°   154°   150°   146°   142°   138°   134°

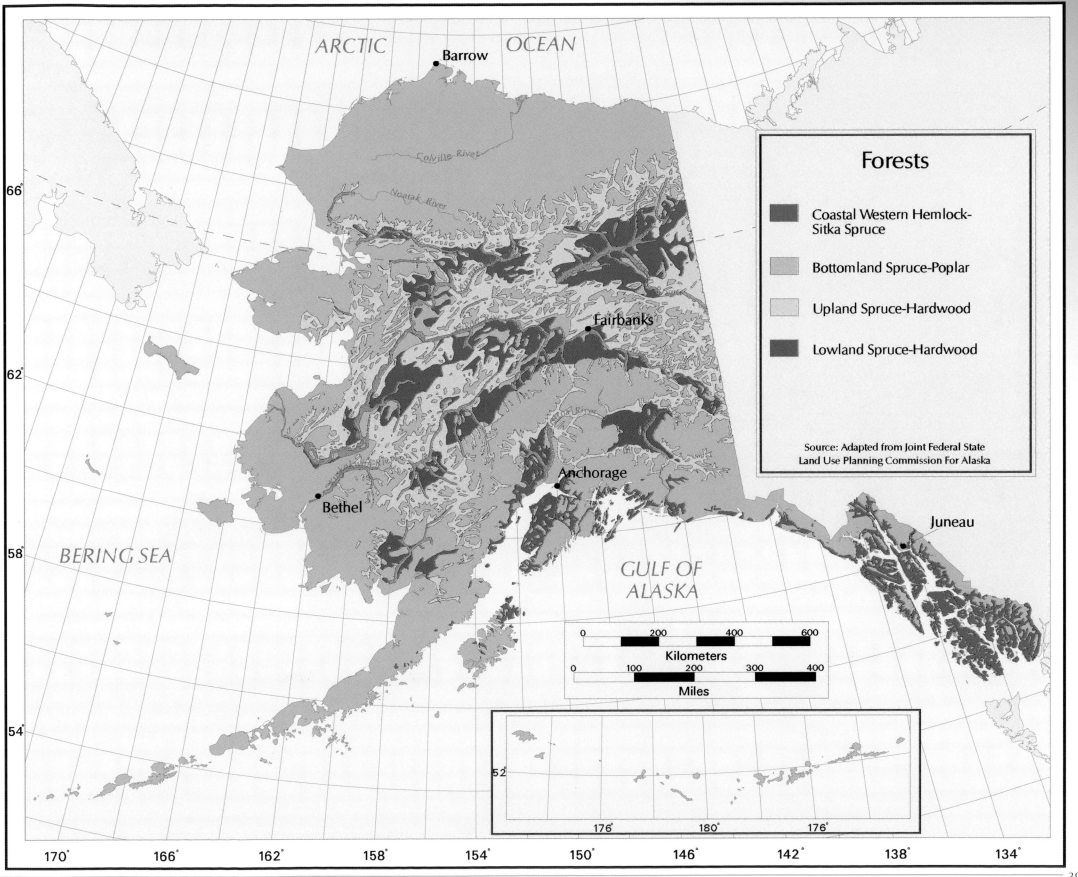

ARCTIC OCEAN

Barrow

Colville River

Noatak River

66°

62°

Fairbanks

58°

BERING SEA

Bethel

Anchorage

GULF OF
ALASKA

Juneau

54°

Forests

- **Coastal Western Hemlock-Sitka Spruce**
- **Bottomland Spruce-Poplar**
- **Upland Spruce-Hardwood**
- **Lowland Spruce-Hardwood**

Source: Adapted from Joint Federal State
Land Use Planning Commission For Alaska

Kilometers
0   200   400   600

Miles
0   100   200   300   400

52°

176°   180°   176°

170°   166°   162°   158°   154°   150°   146°   142°   138°   134°

Map 23–Brown Bear Density

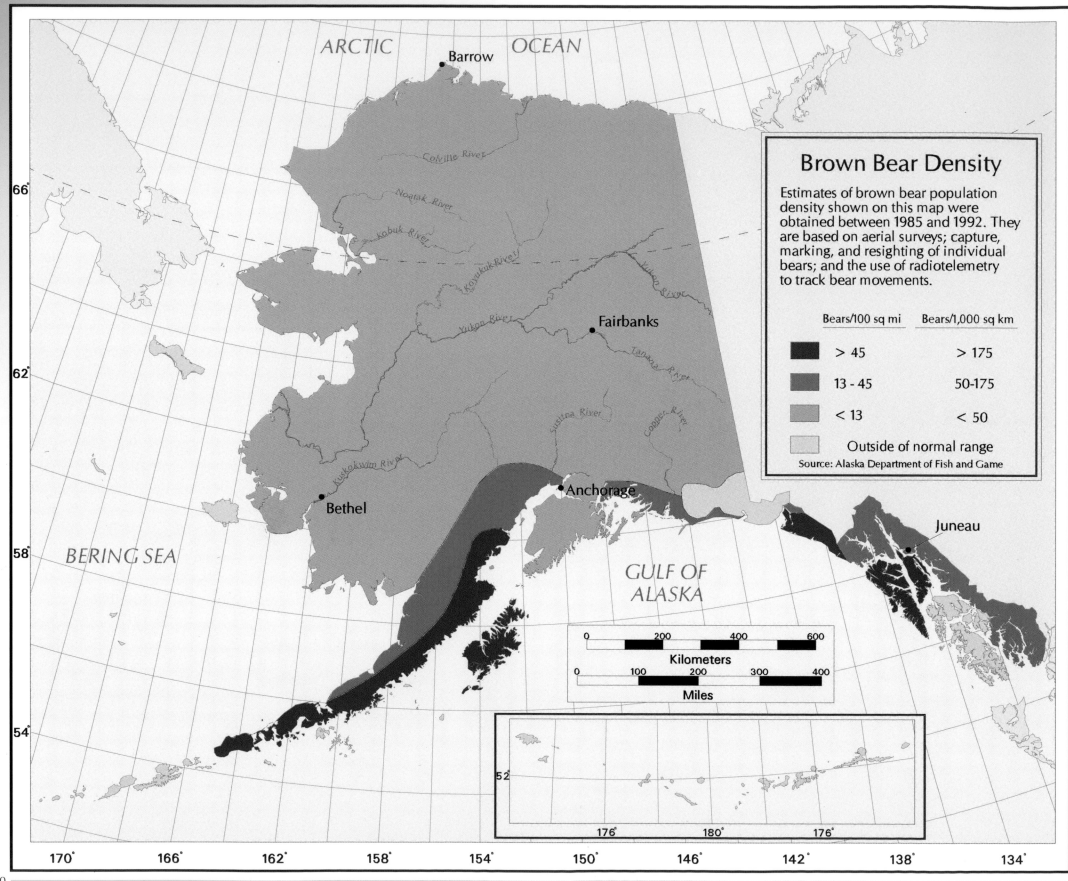

Brown Bear Density

Estimates of brown bear population density shown on this map were obtained between 1985 and 1992. They are based on aerial surveys; capture, marking, and resighting of individual bears; and the use of radiotelemetry to track bear movements.

	Bears/100 sq mi	Bears/1,000 sq km
	> 45	> 175
	13 - 45	50-175
	< 13	< 50
	Outside of normal range	

Source: Alaska Department of Fish and Game

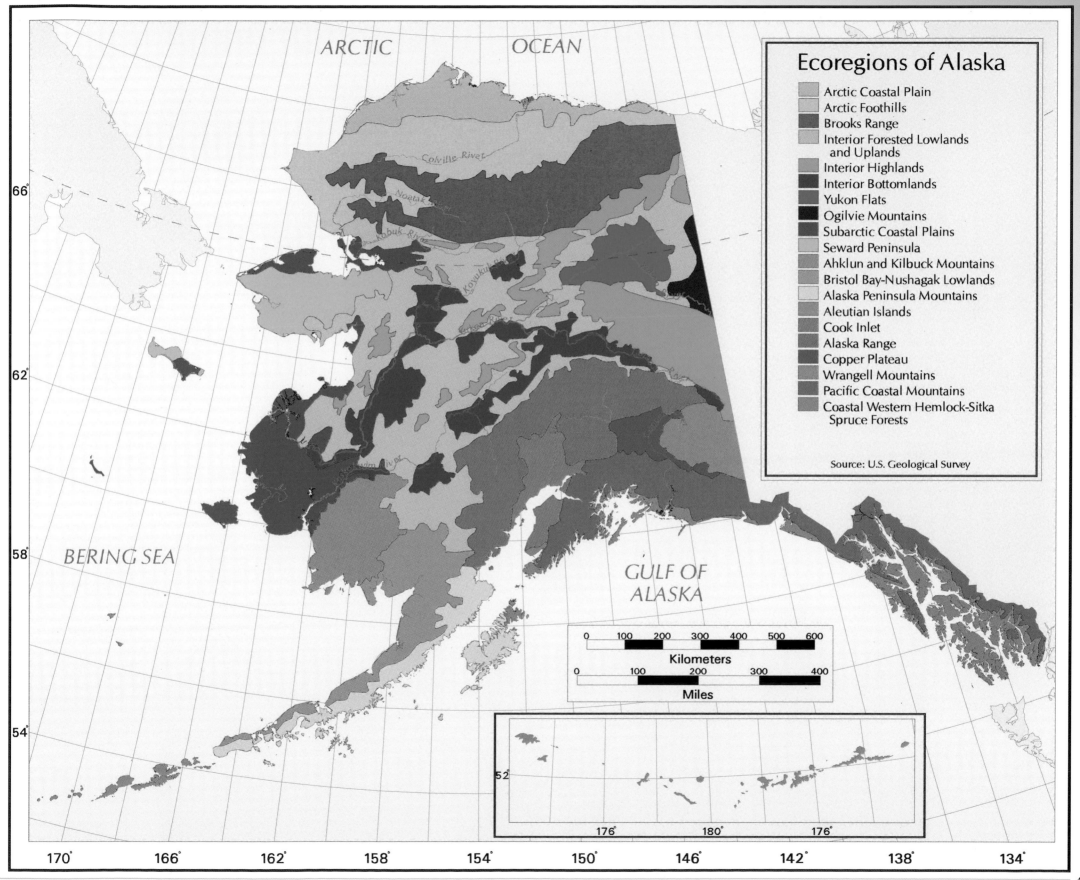

ARCTIC OCEAN

Colville River

Noatak River

Kobuk River

Koyukuk River

Yukon River

BERING SEA

GULF OF
ALASKA

Ecoregions of Alaska

- Arctic Coastal Plain
- Arctic Foothills
- Brooks Range
- Interior Forested Lowlands
  and Uplands
- Interior Highlands
- Interior Bottomlands
- Yukon Flats
- Ogilvie Mountains
- Subarctic Coastal Plains
- Seward Peninsula
- Ahklun and Kilbuck Mountains
- Bristol Bay-Nushagak Lowlands
- Alaska Peninsula Mountains
- Aleutian Islands
- Cook Inlet
- Alaska Range
- Copper Plateau
- Wrangell Mountains
- Pacific Coastal Mountains
- Coastal Western Hemlock-Sitka
  Spruce Forests

Source: U.S. Geological Survey

0 100 200 300 400 500 600
Kilometers

0 100 200 300 400
Miles

Figure 11

Four Ecoregions of Alaska

The **Arctic Coastal Plain** is a poorly drained, treeless coastal plain that rises very gradually from sea level to the foothills of the Brooks Range. The region has an arctic climate, and the entire area is underlain by thick permafrost. Pingos, ice-wedge polygons, oriented lakes, and frost boils are common. Because of poor soil drainage, wet grasses and sedges are the dominant vegetation. Mosses are common. In better drained areas such as old lake basins and river, lake, or coastal bluffs there are dwarf shrub communities, including willows, bearberry, and mountain cranberry. Land animals include caribou, arctic fox, and large populations of migratory birds. Marine mammals include bowhead and beluga whales, polar bears, walrus, and seals. The ecoregion is rich in oil, gas, and coal deposits.

The **Yukon Flats** ecoregion is a relatively flat, marshy basin floor in east central Alaska. It is patterned with braided and meandering streams, numerous thaw lakes, and oxbow lakes. Surrounding the basin floor is a variable band of more undulating topography with fewer water bodies. Mountains surrounding this region isolate it from moderating weather systems. Winters are very cold, summers are very warm, and precipitation averages less than 7 inches a year. Forests dominated by spruce and hardwoods are widespread. Near rivers where there is periodic flooding, tall scrub communities dominated by willows grow, and in wet areas, sedges, highbush cranberry, horsetails, and mosses are found. Several small villages are located near rivers. Animal resources include salmon and freshwater fish, caribou, moose, bears, and small mammals. Millions of migratory waterfowl use wetlands in this region.

The **Alaska Range** ecoregion is made up of very high, steep mountains separated by broad valleys. Many areas are covered by rocky slopes, icefields, and glaciers, and they support no vegetation. The Alaska Range has a continental climate but high annual precipitation at upper elevations. On well drained, windswept sites, dwarf scrub vegetation can be found. Low scrub communities (mostly birch and willows) are found on protected slopes, and tall scrub (mostly willow, alder, and some birch) is found at treeline, along streambanks, in drainages, and on floodplains. Well drained sites in some valleys and lower hillslopes have forests of white spruce, sometimes mixed with black spruce. There are few settlements, but the area is traditionally used for recreation and subsistence hunting and fishing. Animal resources include salmon, freshwater fish, caribou, moose, Dall sheep, and small fur-bearers such as beaver. Many extractable resources occur here, including a variety of metals, coal, and uranium.

Along the southeastern and southcentral coast of Alaska is the **Coastal Western Hemlock - Sitka Spruce Forests** ecoregion. This area shows the results of intense Pleistocene glaciation. The land has deep narrow bays, very irregular coastline, and high sea cliffs. Steep valley walls expose bedrock, and there are many glacial moraine deposits. Near sea level there are floodplains and river deltas. The region has a maritime climate, with cool summers and mildly cold winters. Large amounts of precipitation support widespread forests of western hemlock and Sitka spruce. There are also scrub and wetland communities. Population is concentrated along small stretches of flat coastal areas. Commercial fishing, tourism, timber harvest, and mining are important economic activities. Large mammals include deer and brown bears and in some areas moose and mountain goats. Marine resources include salmon, herring, halibut, seaweed, and clams.

**Photos and detailed descriptions of all ecoregions can be found in the 73-page booklet *Ecoregions of Alaska,* available at a small cost from the U.S. Geological Survey in Anchorage. (Ask for USGS Professional Paper 1567).
In summer 1998 photos and descriptions were also available on the USGS web site, *http://www-erosafo.wr.usgs.gov/ecoreg/ecoregmap.html***

The 1880 Census was the first official U.S. census of Alaska. In charge of gathering the information was Ivan Petroff. His work involved two summers of travel in Alaska. He often relied on locally knowledgeable people for estimates of population. The result of his reconnaissance efforts was a census figure of 33,326 people. Undoubtedly he undercounted.

One hundred and ten years later, the 1990 census was completed in less than a year and involved mailed forms, as well as door-to-door census taking. The results were read into computers, tallied, and made available in printed form and via the Internet. The census reported a total Alaska population of 550,043.

Seven years later in 1997 the state's population was estimated at 611,300 people. That is less than one-fourth of one percent of the total U.S. population. Only Wyoming, Washington, D.C., and Vermont have fewer people.

Human geography is concerned with more than the numbers of people in a region. It also looks at other features such as:

- where and how people are distributed,
- settlement patterns,
- cultural patterns,
- political organization of space, and
- trade and economic organization.

Population

Although Alaska is the largest state in the Union, its population density, or the number of people per square mile, is by far the lowest—just over one person per square mile (0.4 people per square kilometer). In contrast, the average population density of the whole United States is 75 persons per square mile (30 people per square kilometer).

Map 25 Alaska Population by Boroughs and Census Areas shows relative numbers of Alaskans in each of the state's boroughs and census areas, the areas designated for compiling population data. With more than 250,000 people, Anchorage Borough outstrips all other boroughs and census areas in the state. Two neighboring boroughs, Matanuska-Susitna to the north and Kenai Peninsula to the south, are home to another 97,000 people. Together these three boroughs account for 58% of Alaska's population, and they are growing much more rapidly than other parts of the state. From 1990 to 1996 "Mat-Su" grew 28% and Anchorage grew 13%.

Alaska's second largest population concentration is in the Fairbanks North Star Borough, in Interior Alaska. In 1996 the Fairbanks area contained 82,400 people. A larger regional grouping of boroughs and census areas yields a startling result. A population region extending from Fairbanks to the Kenai Peninsula, including Mat-Su and Anchorage, accounts for 72% of Alaska's population. This region is known in Alaska as "the Railbelt" since it extends from the southern terminus of the Alaska Railroad at Seward to the northern terminus in the Fairbanks North Star Borough. The one census area of low population density between the Fairbanks and Mat-Su boroughs, the Denali Borough, reflects the presence of rugged highlands encompassed by Denali National Park.

Outside of the Railbelt region, Southeast Alaska has the only other large concentration of people in the state. It accounts for 12% of the state's population. The district encompassing the City and Borough of Juneau has 29,000 people and includes the state capital. The rest of Southeast includes several population centers, the largest of which are Ketchikan, Alaska's fourth largest city, and Sitka, the fifth largest. The Bethel and Kodiak Boroughs are the only other boroughs with populations of more than 12,000.

Alaska's population is younger on average than the U.S. population. In 1996 the median age in Alaska was 30.8 years compared with a U.S. median of 34.8. The number of older Alaskans, people over 65, has increased by one-third since 1990; yet Alaska still has by far the smallest proportion of older people in the nation.

There are more men than women in Alaska—about 109 men for every 100 women. In fact, Alaska has the lowest overall percentage of women of any state. This figure reflects the impact of the military and the numbers of men who come north for seasonal work in construction and fishing.

Figure 12–Population by Age and Gender shows the distribution of Alaska's population and how it compares with population distribution in the United States overall.

Historically, members of the military have been an important part of Alaska's population. In 1960 33% of Alaska's labor force was military. By the 1990s, however, military personnel had dropped to 7% of the labor force. By 1997 closure of several military bases and reductions in personnel at others had reduced full-time military and their dependents to 44,400 people. Effects of such changes are felt most strongly in communities such as Fairbanks, Adak, and Delta Junction, where military personnel and their dependents are, or were, a large proportion of the population.

Alaskans are people from all races and hundreds of ethnic and national groups. According to the ways people classify themselves in the census, about 74% of Alaskans are White, 16.5% are Alaska Native, 4.5% are African American, and 4.4% are Asian or Pacific Islander. As **Map 26 Ethnic Groups by Region** shows, people from these groups are

Homes in the village of Angoon, in Southeast Alaska

Alaska Division of Tourism

distributed differently in different parts of the state. The percentage of White people is high in urban regions, especially the Railbelt, while the percentage of Native Alaskans is higher in the northern and western parts of the state.

Figure 12

Population by Age and Gender, 1996

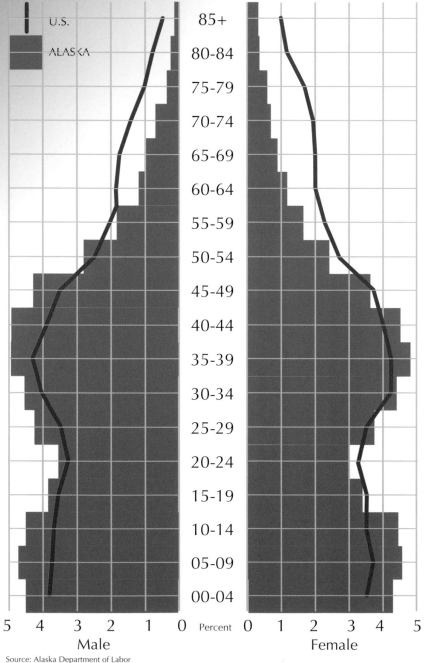

Source: Alaska Department of Labor

Some 20 different Native groups have traditionally lived in Alaska. Customary Native homelands and associated languages are shown in **Map 27 Alaska Native Languages.** Many Native Alaskans continue to live in places long inhabited by their people. Others now live in different communities, particularly the larger urban centers. In 1996 nearly one-fifth of all Native Alaskans lived in Anchorage, Alaska's largest urban center.

Exactly how many people lived in Alaska before the Russian arrival is not known. The general consensus is that the Native population witnessed a significant and tragic decline in the wake of disease, conflict, and other effects of contact. Starting with the 1880 census, however, the state's population has shown long-term growth, largely associated with natural resource development and military activities (See **Figure 13–Population of Alaska, 1880-2000).**

Between 1890 and 1900, when gold rushes in many parts of Alaska brought thousands of people north, Alaska's population almost doubled. After that period and during World War I the total number of Alaskans declined. All that changed with World War II and the national realization of Alaska's military significance. The military population swelled during the war years. After the war many who had served in the military stayed and became residents of the Alaska Territory. Since then more and more people have come to the state. Many came as part of the U.S. military buildup during the Cold War, as workers

Figure 13

Population of Alaska, 1880-2000

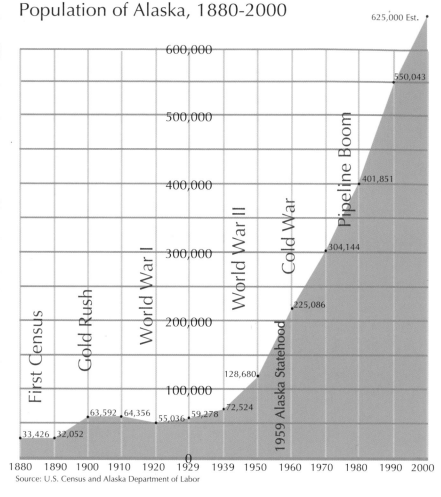

Source: U.S. Census and Alaska Department of Labor

on North Slope oil fields and the TransAlaska Pipeline, and as workers on construction projects funded by government and private industry.

In addition to people coming into the state, more people have been born in Alaska. These two factors combined gave Alaska 611,000 residents in 1997—18 times its population in 1880. The birth rate in Alaska has been declining since 1991. This is associated with a decline in people aged 18 to 24, the prime age group for family formation and child-bearing, and the age group most affected by the closure or cut-back of military bases. Nevertheless, the birth rate

has been sufficient to allow for a continued growth in population despite greater out-migration than in-migration from 1993 to 1997. In this regard, Alaska has one of the highest rates of migration—people moving in or out—of any state. According to the 1990 census, 66% of all Alaskans were born elsewhere.

Most newcomers settle in urban areas, that is, communities of 2,500 people or more. The dramatic trend toward urbanization can be seen in **Figure 14– Urban Population of Alaska, 1910-1997.** This graph shows that in 1950 less than 30% of the population was urban, whereas by 1997, 70% of all Alaskans

Figure 14

Urban Population of Alaska, 1910-1997

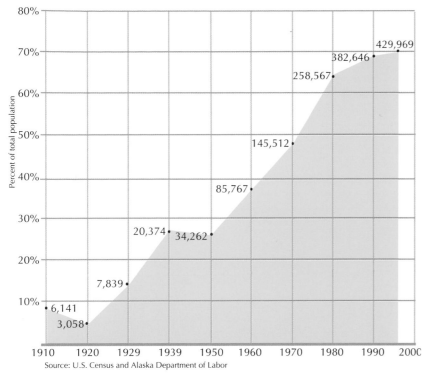

Source: U.S. Census and Alaska Department of Labor

Figure 15

Urban* and Rural Places of Alaska, 1996

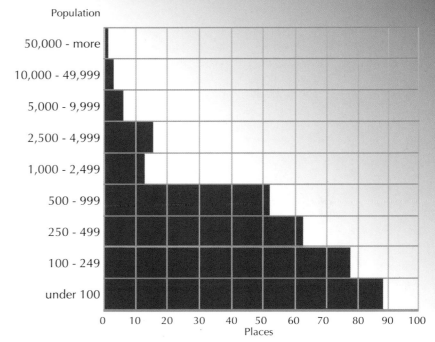

Percent of Population in Places of Various Sizes, 1996

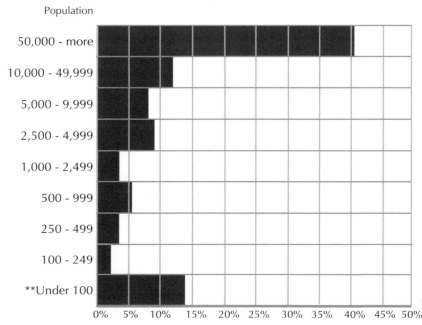

* Urban places are cities and other census designated units with populations of 2,500 or more.
** Includes population living outside of census designated places

Source: Alaska Department of Labor

lived in urban areas. This pattern of settlement can be seen in **Map 28 Communities**, which expands on the general distribution of population shown in **Map 25 Alaska Population by Boroughs and Census Areas.**

The extent to which Alaska's population is concentrated in only a few of the 26 places designated as urban is shown in the two graphs **Urban and Rural Places of Alaska** and **Percent of Population in Places of Various Sizes (Figure 15).** Alaska has several smaller urban places, but their total population is dwarfed by population in the largest settlements—especially Anchorage, which accounts for 42% of all Alaska's people. These two graphs illustrate Alaska's *hierarchy of settlement:* many small places, a few large places,

and the domination of the largest city.

In contrast to the trend toward urbanization, about 30% of Alaska's people, including both Natives and newcomers, live in small villages or away from large population centers. Some families live miles from their nearest neighbors. Others live in villages separated from other settlements by rugged mountains, soggy tundra, or large expanses of water. All these settlement patterns are very much related to other aspects of the physical and human geography of the state.

Government

Alaska's large physical size, small population, and uneven distribution of population

together raise an interesting geographic problem: how to efficiently provide people with goods and services. In some northern countries, such as Greenland and the former Soviet Union, people were encouraged to abandon small settlements so that services could be provided more easily and cheaply in a few select places. Alaska has not had such a policy and instead has directed its efforts toward providing services to people whether they are clustered in urban areas or widely dispersed.

Alaska laws and the state constitution allow for several types of local government. In 1997, about one-third of Alaska was made up of 16 organized boroughs, units of local government that are similar to the counties found in many other states. The remaining two-thirds of the state, made up of large areas of sparsely populated land, is considered a single "unorganized borough." It is subdivided into Regional Educational Attendance Areas (REAAs) that administer schools. Alaska's boroughs and REAAs are shown on **Map 29 Regional Governments,** as are three Unified Home Rule Municipalities, organized boroughs that include all cities within them as a single unit of local government.

The Alaska Constitution allows for the formation of first class and second class cities. In 1997 there were 21 first class and 114 second class cities. They are shown on **Map 28 Communities,** as are unincorporated communities throughout the state.

Traditional governing bodies often coexist with these governments. There are more than 200 federally recognized tribal governments in Alaska. All but five of them are associated with particular villages.

Federal, state, and local government agencies provide Alaskans with a wide array of services. Government agencies build and operate schools, provide social services, manage natural resources, construct and maintain facilities such as roads and airports, and administer legal services. In 1996 about 34% of Alaska's labor force was directly employed by federal, state, or local government, including the military services. The distribution of employees in regions of Alaska is shown in **Map 30** **Government Employees by Region**.

In parts of Alaska, government agencies provide more jobs than any other sector of the economy.

Northern and Southwest Alaska, which are predominantly rural, illustrate the importance of local government jobs. Urban areas have a more balanced distribution of local, state, and federal jobs.

There is a large presence of federal employees in Alaska because many federal agencies are responsible for federal lands and waters. Many Alaskans work for the Forest Service, the Bureau of Land Management, the National Marine Fisheries Service, the Fish and Wildlife Service, and other federal offices. The dominance of state workers in Southeast Alaska reflects the presence of the state capital in Juneau.

The size of the work force in each region is also important, as shown in the total numbers of employees listed in the legend of

The Port of Anchorage handles almost 80% of all cargo entering Alaska. That included a total of 3.1 million tons in 1997.

Aeromap U.S.

Figure 16

Air Routes in the Nome and Kotzebue Area

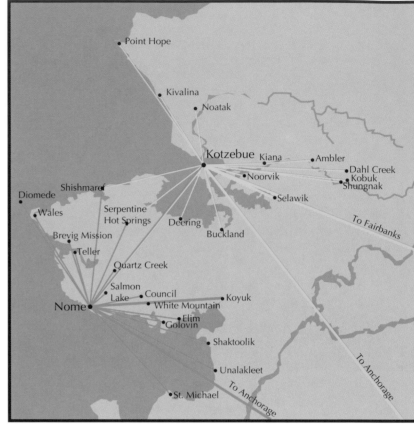

Source: Alaska Department of Transportation and Public Facilities

Map 30. Southcentral Alaska has a lower percentage of state workers than Southeastern; however, the total number of state workers in Southcentral is much larger than the total in Southeastern. This is a reflection of the large population in and around Anchorage and its functional importance to the entire state.

Health Care

Even before Statehood, one of the highest priorities of Alaska government and community leaders was providing people with adequate health care. This was often difficult because

people were spread out over vast distances, and travel for both patients and medical personnel was difficult. Today a network of hospitals, clinics, and rural health aides makes health care available to people in virtually every part of the state.

Map 31 **Health Care Facilities** shows hospitals and rural health clinics certified or licensed by the Alaska Department of Health and Social Services in 1998. Alaskans also receive health care at nursing homes, private physicians' offices, birth centers, outpatient clinics, and other facilities. In more isolated settlements, nurses and health aides can communicate directly with doctors in large centers such as Anchorage, Fairbanks, and Juneau. Patients needing special medical care including emergency evacuation are commonly flown to the large regional hospitals.

Transportation

Airline, water, and highway routes connect Alaskans with the rest of the United States and other parts of the world. **Map 32** shows major **Transportation** facilities within the state.

Virtually every community in Alaska has an airport or landing strip. In remote areas without such facilities, Alaska's famous "bush planes" make do with what is available, landing on salt water, lakes or ponds, frozen lakes or rivers, sandbars, or beaches.

Communities with larger airports often serve as regional centers. Scheduled jet service connects these places with the state's air transportation centers, Anchorage, Fairbanks, and Juneau. Smaller scheduled airlines and charter services transport passengers and freight between outlying villages and isolated locations (See **Figure 16–Air Routes in the Nome and Kotzebue Area**).

Alaska has no road system connecting all communities as most other states do. A number of highways, however, link settlements in Southcentral Alaska and the Interior. These vary from six-lane divided highways to unpaved roads. The Alaska, Klondike, and Taylor Highways connect this road system with highways in Canada and the Lower 48 states. There are road systems in cities, and

many small communities have local roads, snowmobile trails, and seasonal "ice roads" over frozen rivers. Travel by road has proved less practical than air or water travel in many parts of Alaska because of great distances, bodies of water, rugged terrain, freezing weather, sparse population, and heavy snowfall.

Water routes are extremely important for transporting freight and passengers in Alaska. The Alaska Marine Highway is made up of two ferry systems serving two different areas separated by the stormy, open water of the Gulf of Alaska. The Southeast system serves Southeast Alaska port cities from Ketchikan to Skagway, and connects Alaskan ports with Bellingham, Washington, and Prince Rupert in British Columbia, Canada. The Southwest and Southcentral system serves many coastal communities from Prince William Sound to the Aleutian Islands. In 1998 a new ocean-going ferry was scheduled to begin monthly trips connecting the two routes. Ferry travelers can connect with highways at Haines and Skagway in Southeast Alaska and at Valdez, Homer, and Seward in Southcentral Alaska. At Whittier in Southcentral Alaska the Alaska Railroad provides a car shuttle to the central highway system.

Barges from Seattle and other ports outside the state transport tons of freight every year to the Port of Anchorage and other distribution centers such as Juneau, Bethel, Kotzebue, and Barrow. Many of Alaska's rivers are navigable for small barges and skiffs, and when frozen in

winter they may be traveled by snowmachine, dogsled, or motor vehicles.

The 470-mile (756-kilometer) Alaska Railroad connects Fairbanks, Nenana, Anchorage, and the ports of Seward and Whittier. It also forms a link with rail barges traveling between Whittier and the port of Seattle. In 1996 the railroad carried 518,000 passengers and 5.5 million tons (5 million metric tons) of freight. That included 763,000 tons (692,000 metric tons) of coal and 21,011 carloads (15 million barrels) of petroleum.

Visible even on some satellite photos of Alaska is the Trans-Alaska Pipeline, a marvel of engineering that carries oil from Prudhoe Bay to the port of Valdez. From Valdez the oil is transported by ship to ports outside the state. The pipeline extends 798 miles (1,284 kilometers) across mountains, tundra, permafrost, and hundreds of rivers and streams. In 1996 it transported an average 1.4 million barrels of crude oil a day. That was about one-fourth the total U.S. oil production that year.

Communication

Just as people use transportation systems to move passengers and freight, they use communication systems to exchange ideas and information. Modern Americans expect to have access to television, telephones, fax transmissions, the Internet, cable television, and worldwide telecommunications. People want up-to-date newspapers, magazines, and books. They want to contact

government agencies and take part in political decisions. They want to get job training and high quality education without having to leave home. All those things are possible only if communication systems are in place.

For many reasons establishing such communication systems in Alaska has not been easy. The state is far from Lower 48 and world population centers. It is an area of great distances and

Great distances, severe weather, and rugged terrain often challenge efforts to provide utilities and services to Alaskans.

rugged terrain. Equipment must often be installed and maintained under extremely difficult conditions of climate and weather. Costs of labor and material shipments are often high. Yet nearly every community in Alaska has some level of local and inter-state telephone service. Urban Alaskans use cell phones and personal communication devices. Nine out of ten Alaskans have access to live or same-day television. Internet connections and global telecommunications are available in urban areas, and in rural areas more and more residents are acquiring this advanced communications technology.

Alaskans enjoy the benefits of communication primarily because of a statewide system based largely on satellite communication. More than 20 local exchange carriers serve customers in specific geographic areas. Long distance carriers provide statewide and out-of-state service. Both types of carriers tie into a complex network that includes more than 220 earth stations, 160 microwave stations, fiber optic cables both on land and undersea to the Lower 48, and the *Aurora II* communications satellite.

Alaska's communication network grew out of the U.S. Army/Air Force's "White Alice" Alaska Communications System that was installed after Alaska's strategic importance became obvious during World War II. Since then federal and state funding have promoted expansion of statewide com-munications by commercial enterprises.

Many Alaska communities have commercial and public radio and television stations (See **Map 33** **Newspapers, Television Stations, Radio Stations**). State funding supports the Alaska Rural Communication System, which distributes educational and general interest programming to more than 250 communities. Newspapers, books, and special interest publications are published within many communities, and publications from around the world are distributed statewide through mail and freight networks.

A great deal of state and federal funding has been devoted to creating educational and health care networks in Alaska. The State Library Electronic Doorway (SLED) makes library and information services available statewide. For more than 8 out of 10 Alaskans the service is offered free through local telephone exchanges. The Alaska Telemedicine Project allows health care professionals to teleconference between large urban facilities and rural centers. It promises many advances in diagnosing and planning treat-ment of patients and in offering advanced training in rural areas.

Since the 1970s educational telecommunications in Alaska has been a model for places with similar communications challenges, such as Australia. Programs through the Star Schools Partnership, school district consortiums, and the University of Alaska allow students, teachers, and townspeople in hundreds of communities to take television and computer classes that originate hundreds or thousands of miles away.

Alaskans put a high priority on including citizens from even the most remote areas in government activities and decision making. **Map 34** shows the network of **Legislative Information Offices** that spans the state. The offices provide nonpartisan government infor-mation, electronic mail, and teleconferencing facilities. Three offices—in Anchorage, Fairbanks, and Juneau—had videoconference capability in 1997.

Government- and industry-sponsored projects continue to bring advanced communication

Figure 17

Export Partners, 1996

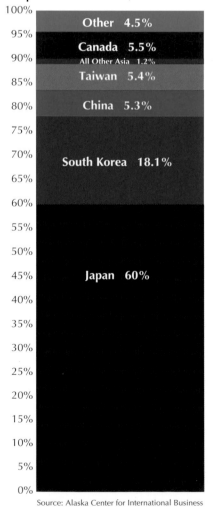

Source: Alaska Center for International Business

to more and more areas of the state. In remote areas, advanced technologies are supplemented by traditional networks such as VHF radio, citizens band radio, and personal messages relayed over local radio programs.

Trade and Economic Organization

Every day Alaskans enjoy products shipped in from all over the world: gourmet coffee from Tanzania, strawberries from Mexico, apples and kiwi fruit from New Zealand. Alaskans drive cars and all-terrain vehicles manufactured in Japan. Even people in remote areas use products from the global marketplace. Much of the money to buy those products comes from resources and products sold to people outside the state—products such as salmon and shellfish, timber, petroleum, and minerals.

Alaska is in a prime location to ship natural resources and manufactured products to Pacific Rim countries. In 1996 products produced in Alaska and shipped outside the state were valued at $2.72 billion. As **Figure 17– Export Partners** shows, 60% of these products were shipped to Japan, Alaska's primary trading partner. Large quantities of Alaska products also were shipped to South Korea (18.1%), Taiwan (5.4%), China (5.3%), and Canada (5.5%).

Location is the key to another sector of international trade that is growing rapidly in Alaska—the air freight business. Located approximately equidistant along important air routes linking East Asia, North America, and

Europe, Anchorage is now a major distribution center for international cargo. Air freight exports in 1996 were valued at $3.2 billion. Japan, Korea, and Taiwan were the three main destinations. Most of the shipments were products manufactured in the continental United States.

Figure 18 shows the **Value of Alaska Resource Exports** in 1996. Alaska has traditionally been the largest exporter of seafood in the United States. In 1995, in fact, the state accounted for nearly half the U.S. total of seafood exports. World markets are constantly changing, however, and Alaska seafood, timber, and minerals compete with products from other places where people are equally eager to capture a share of the world market.

In 1971, Alaska's economic organization took on a dramatic new appearance. The U.S. Congress passed the Alaska Native Claims Settlement Act (ANCSA), calling for the creation of 13 regional, 4 urban, and more than 200 village corporations to manage money and land received under the Act. The boundaries of 12 Native regional corporations are shown on **Map 35 Alaska Native Regional Corporations**. The thirteenth corporation, headquartered in Seattle, represents Natives living outside of Alaska. The corporations received $962.5 million and 44 million acres (17.8 million hectares) of land. Native regional corporations . have since become important centers for economic activity in the state.

The Native corporations were derived primarily from major language divisions within Alaska, as can be seen by comparing **Map 35** with **Map 27 Alaska Native Languages**. Seven Native village corporations chose to take title to reservation land and are not served by regional corporations. The people of Metlakatla and Annette Island in Southeast Alaska chose to maintain the status of a federal Indian reservation, as shown in the single gold dot on **Map 28 Communities**.

Figure 18

Value of Alaska Resource Exports, 1996

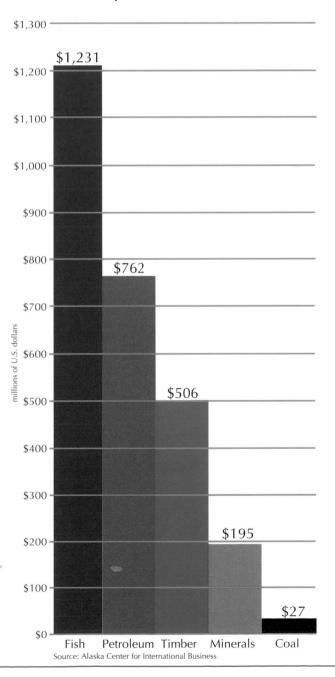

Source: Alaska Center for International Business

Map 25–Alaska Population by Boroughs and Census Areas

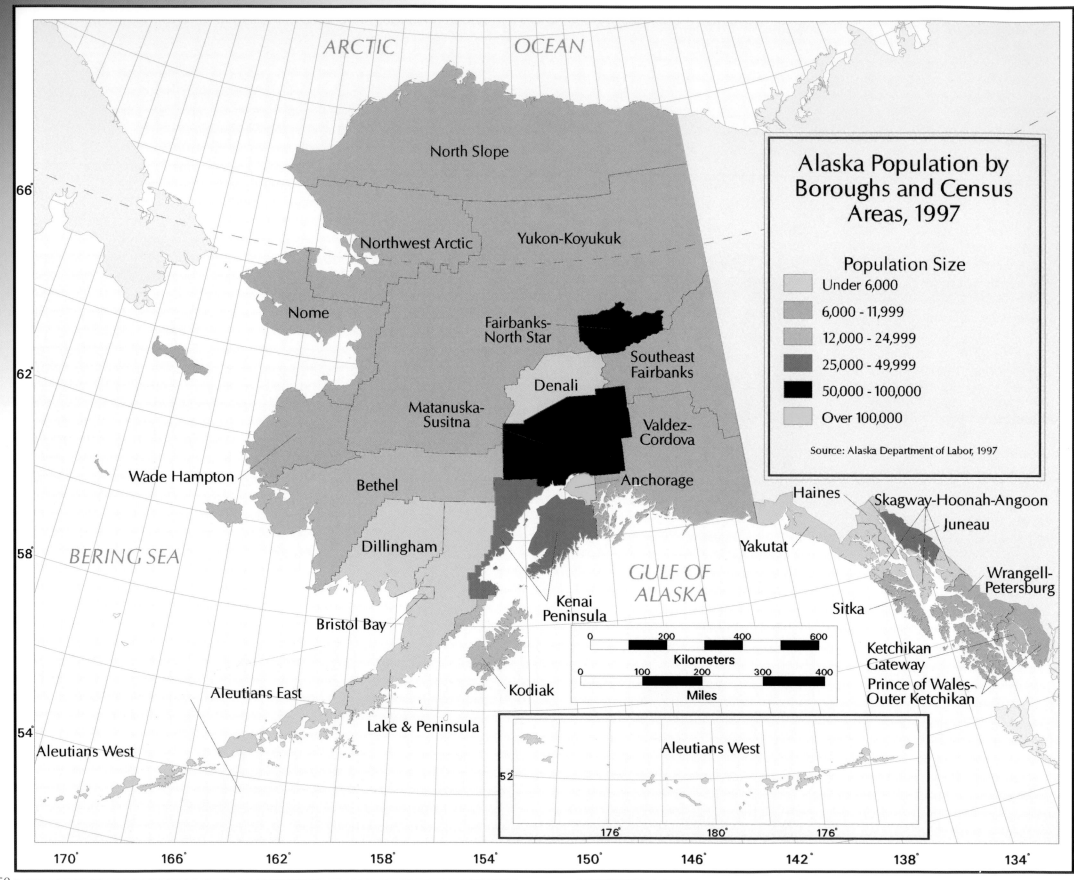

ARCTIC OCEAN

North Slope

Northwest Arctic

Yukon-Koyukuk

Nome

Fairbanks-North Star

Southeast Fairbanks

Denali

Matanuska-Susitna

Valdez-Cordova

Wade Hampton

Bethel

Anchorage

Haines

Skagway-Hoonah-Angoon

Juneau

Yakutat

Dillingham

BERING SEA

GULF OF ALASKA

Wrangell-Petersburg

Kenai Peninsula

Sitka

Bristol Bay

Ketchikan Gateway

Aleutians East

Kodiak

Prince of Wales-Outer Ketchikan

Lake & Peninsula

Aleutians West

Alaska Population by Boroughs and Census Areas, 1997

Population Size

- Under 6,000
- 6,000 - 11,999
- 12,000 - 24,999
- 25,000 - 49,999
- 50,000 - 100,000
- Over 100,000

Source: Alaska Department of Labor, 1997

Aleutians West

200   400   600
Kilometers
0   100   200   300   400
Miles

66° 62° 58° 54°

52°

176°   180°   176°

170°   166°   162°   158°   154°   150°   146°   142°   138°   134°

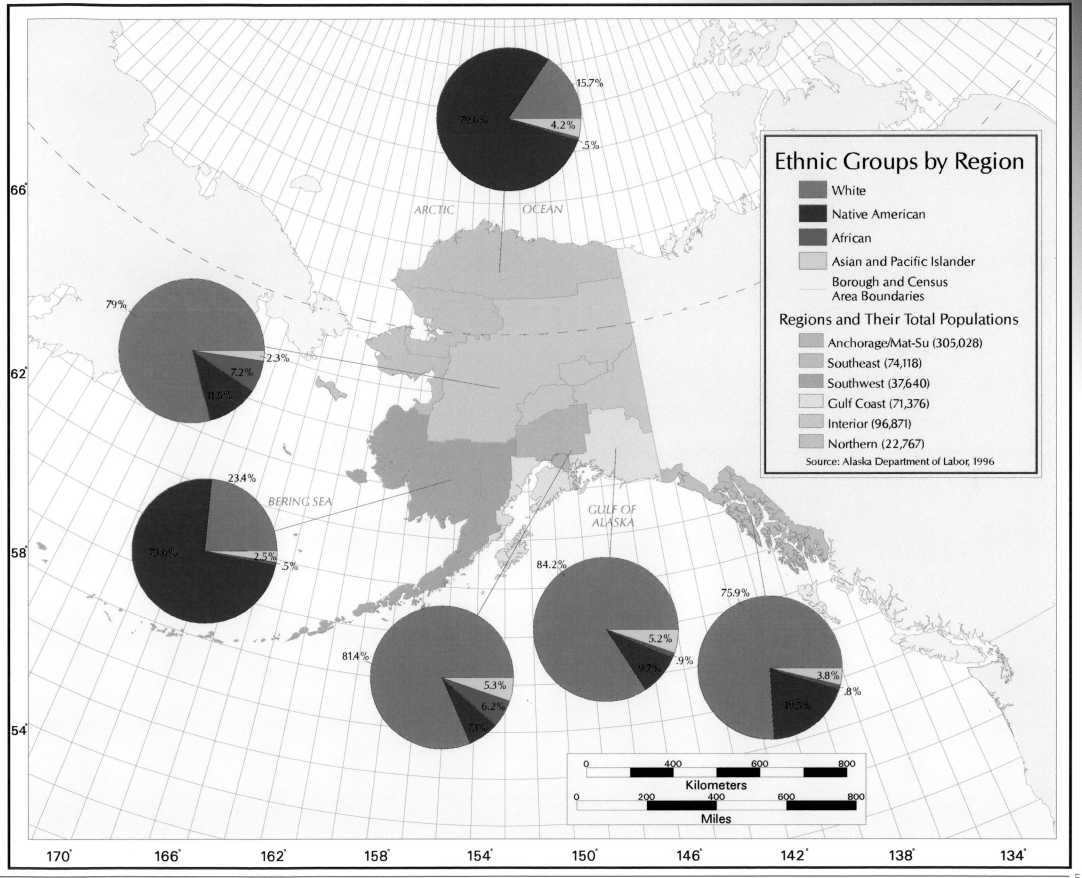

ARCTIC OCEAN

79.6%
15.7%
4.2%
.5%

Ethnic Groups by Region

- White
- Native American
- African
- Asian and Pacific Islander
- Borough and Census Area Boundaries

Regions and Their Total Populations

- Anchorage/Mat-Su (305,028)
- Southeast (74,118)
- Southwest (37,640)
- Gulf Coast (71,376)
- Interior (96,871)
- Northern (22,767)

Source: Alaska Department of Labor, 1996

79%
2.3%
7.2%
11.5%

BERING SEA

GULF OF ALASKA

23.4%
73.6%
2.5%
.5%

84.2%
5.2%
9.7%
.9%

75.9%
3.8%
.8%
19.5%

81.4%
5.3%
6.2%
7.1%

0   400   600   800
Kilometers

0   200   400   600   800
Miles

170° 166° 162° 158° 154° 150° 146° 142° 138° 134°

66°
62°
58°
54°

Map 27–Alaska Native Languages

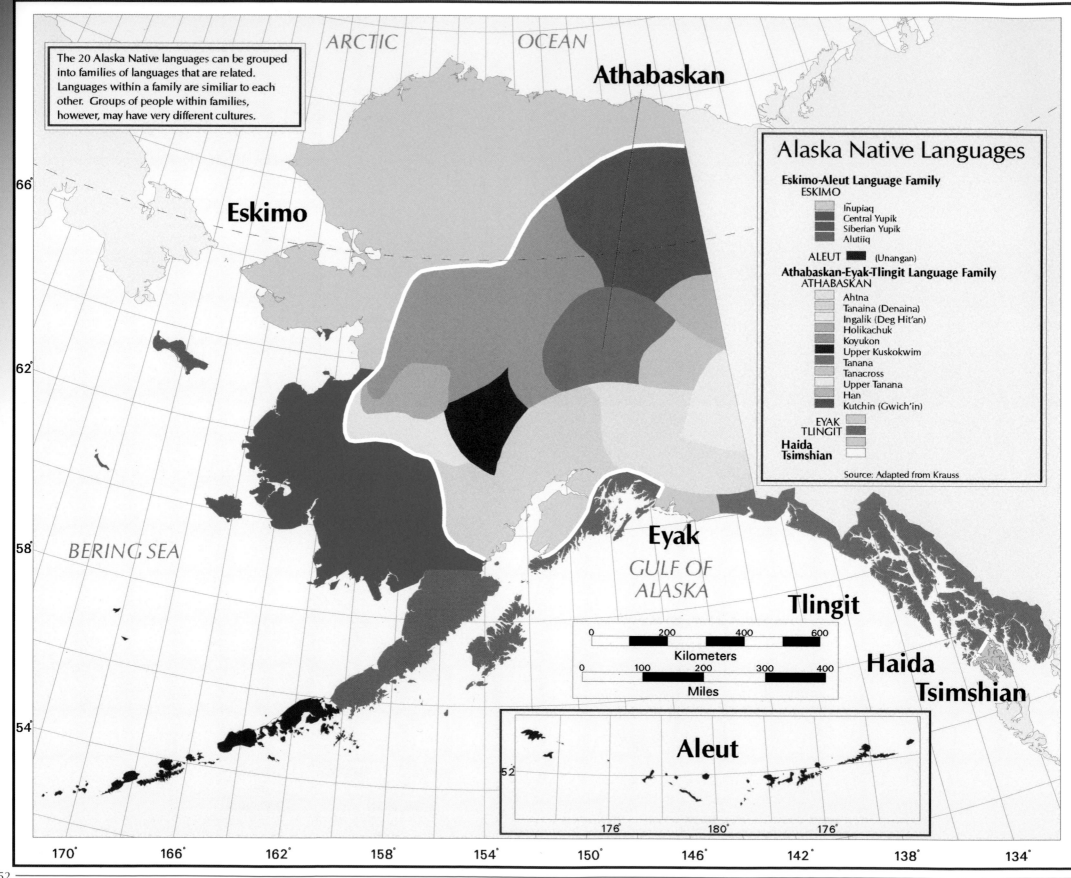

The 20 Alaska Native languages can be grouped into families of languages that are related. Languages within a family are similiar to each other. Groups of people within families, however, may have very different cultures.

ARCTIC OCEAN

Athabaskan

Eskimo

66°

62°

58°

BERING SEA

54°

Alaska Native Languages

Eskimo-Aleut Language Family
ESKIMO
- Iñupiaq
- Central Yupik
- Siberian Yupik
- Alutiiq

ALEUT (Unangan)

Athabaskan-Eyak-Tlingit Language Family
ATHABASKAN
- Ahtna
- Tanaina (Denaina)
- Ingalik (Deg Hit'an)
- Holikachuk
- Koyukon
- Upper Kuskokwim
- Tanana
- Tanacross
- Upper Tanana
- Han
- Kutchin (Gwich'in)

EYAK
TLINGIT
Haida
Tsimshian

Source: Adapted from Krauss

Eyak

GULF OF ALASKA

Tlingit

Haida

Tsimshian

| 0 | 200 | 400 | 600 |
Kilometers
| 0 | 100 | 200 | 300 | 400 |
Miles

Aleut

52

176°   180°   176°

170°   166°   162°   158°   154°   150°   146°   142°   138°   134°

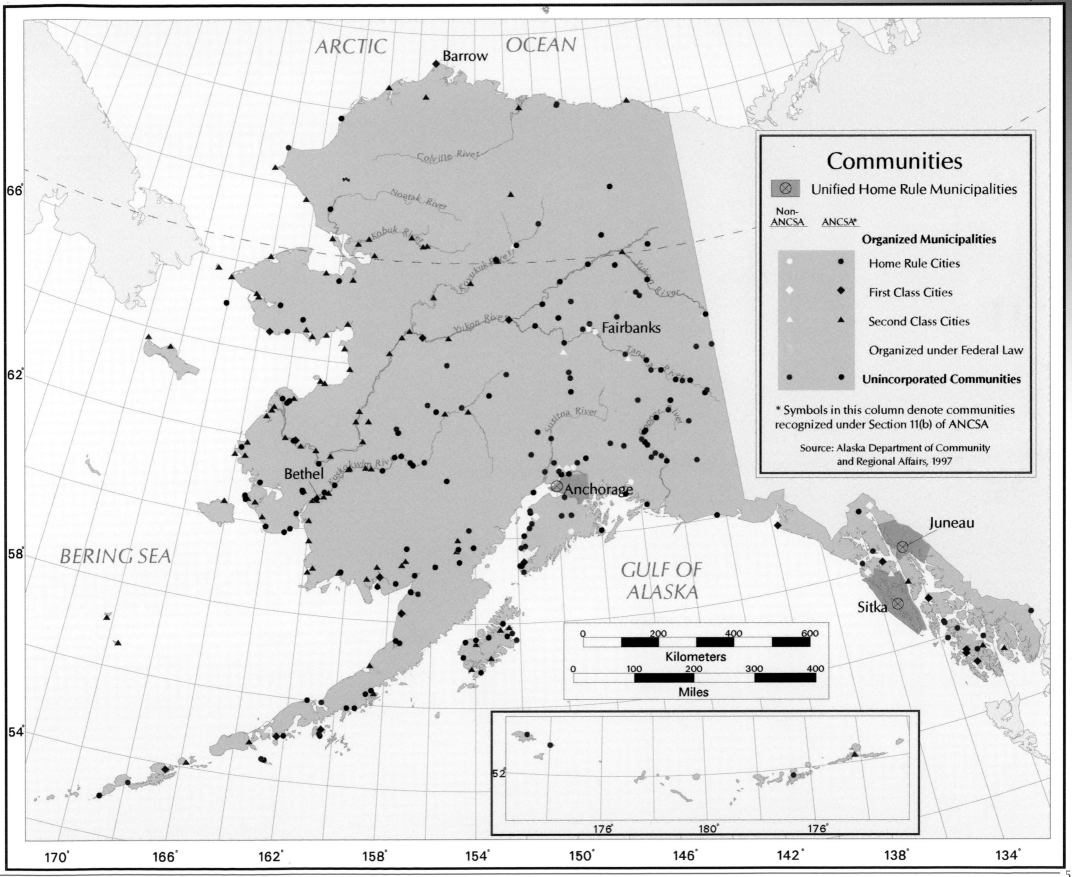

ARCTIC OCEAN

Barrow

Colville River

Noatak River

Kobuk River

Kowukuk River

Yukon River

Fairbanks

Tanana River

Yukon River

Susitna River

Bethel

Kuskokwim River

Anchorage

Juneau

BERING SEA

GULF OF ALASKA

Sitka

Communities

⊗ Unified Home Rule Municipalities

Non-ANCSA	ANCSA*	
		Organized Municipalities
○	●	Home Rule Cities
◇	◆	First Class Cities
△	▲	Second Class Cities
		Organized under Federal Law
●	●	**Unincorporated Communities**

* Symbols in this column denote communities recognized under Section 11(b) of ANCSA

Source: Alaska Department of Community and Regional Affairs, 1997

Kilometers
0   200   400   600

Miles
0   100   200   300   400

Map 29–Regional Governments

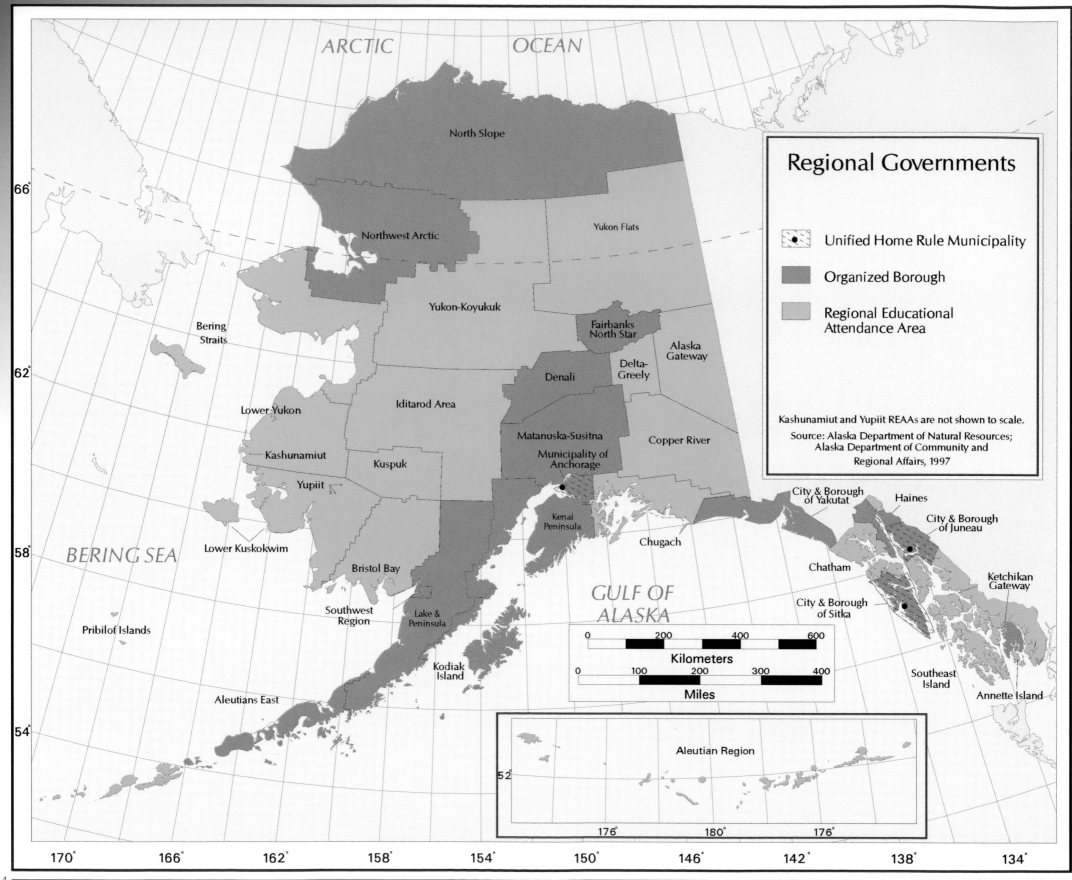

ARCTIC OCEAN

North Slope

Northwest Arctic

Yukon Flats

Yukon-Koyukuk

Bering Straits

Fairbanks North Star

Alaska Gateway

Denali

Delta-Greely

Iditarod Area

Lower Yukon

Kashunamiut

Kuspuk

Matanuska-Susitna

Copper River

Yupiit

Municipality of Anchorage

Lower Kuskokwim

Kenai Peninsula

Chugach

BERING SEA

Bristol Bay

City & Borough of Yakutat

Haines

City & Borough of Juneau

Chatham

GULF OF ALASKA

Southwest Region

Lake & Peninsula

City & Borough of Sitka

Ketchikan Gateway

Pribilof Islands

Kodiak Island

Southeast Island

Aleutians East

Annette Island

Regional Governments

Unified Home Rule Municipality

Organized Borough

Regional Educational Attendance Area

Kashunamiut and Yupiit REAAs are not shown to scale.

Source: Alaska Department of Natural Resources; Alaska Department of Community and Regional Affairs, 1997

Kilometers

| 0 | 200 | 400 | 600 |

Miles

| 0 | 100 | 200 | 300 | 400 |

Aleutian Region

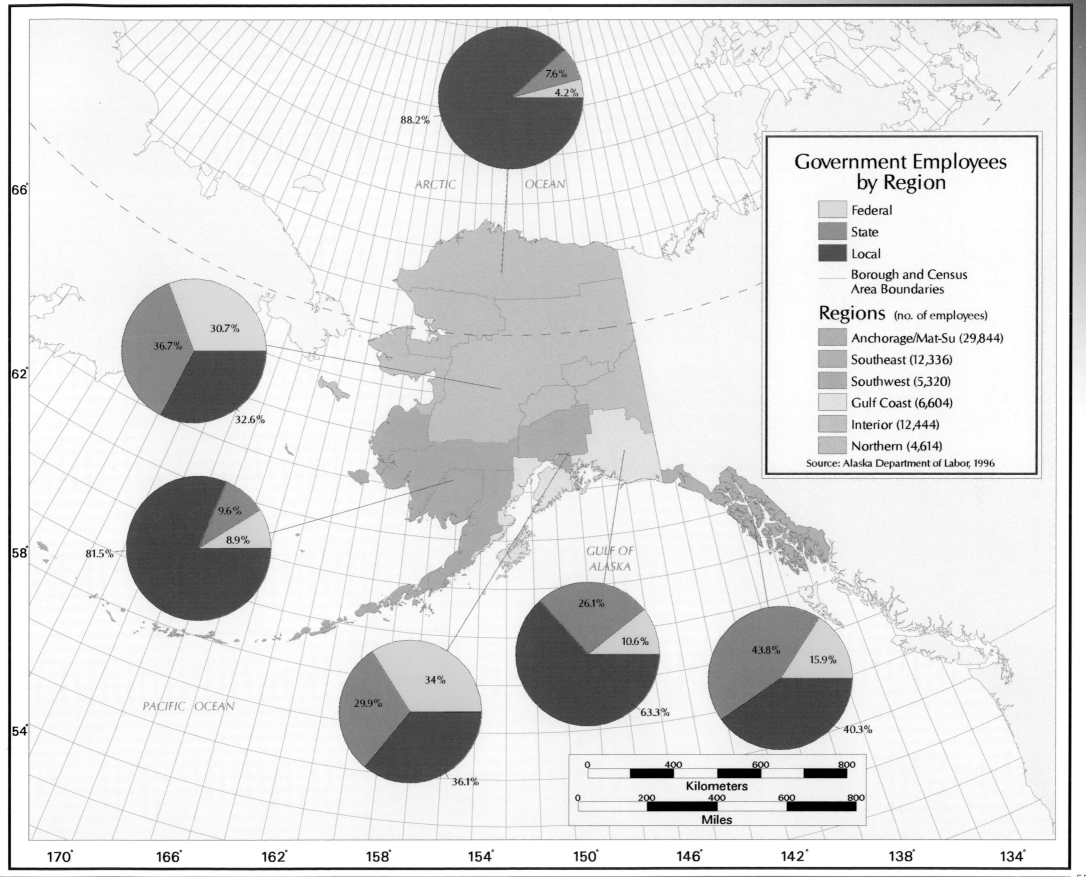

Government Employees
by Region

- Federal
- State
- Local

— Borough and Census
  Area Boundaries

Regions (no. of employees)

Anchorage/Mat-Su (29,844)

Southeast (12,336)

Southwest (5,320)

Gulf Coast (6,604)

Interior (12,444)

Northern (4,614)

Source: Alaska Department of Labor, 1996

Map 31–Health Care Facilities

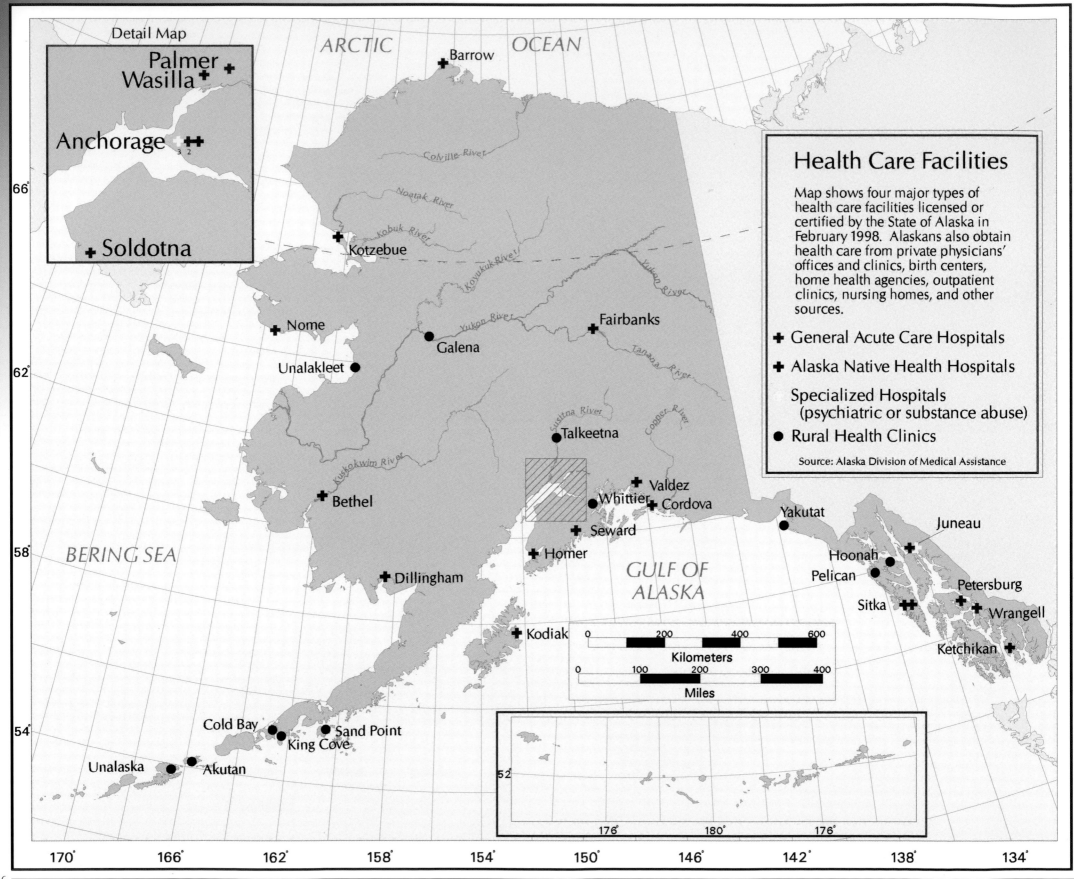

ARCTIC OCEAN

Detail Map

Palmer
Wasilla

Anchorage
3 2

Soldotna

Barrow

Colville River

Noatak River

Kobuk River

66°

Kotzebue

Koyukuk River

Yukon River

62°

Nome

Unalakleet

Galena

Fairbanks

Tanana River

Susitna River

Copper River

Talkeetna

Kuskokwim River

Bethel

Valdez

Whittier
Cordova

Yakutat

Juneau

Seward

58°

Homer

GULF OF
ALASKA

Hoonah

Pelican

BERING SEA

Dillingham

Petersburg

Sitka

Wrangell

Kodiak

Ketchikan

54°

Cold Bay

Sand Point

King Cove

Unalaska

Akutan

Health Care Facilities

Map shows four major types of
health care facilities licensed or
certified by the State of Alaska in
February 1998. Alaskans also obtain
health care from private physicians'
offices and clinics, birth centers,
home health agencies, outpatient
clinics, nursing homes, and other
sources.

✚ General Acute Care Hospitals

✚ Alaska Native Health Hospitals

  Specialized Hospitals
  (psychiatric or substance abuse)

● Rural Health Clinics

Source: Alaska Division of Medical Assistance

0   200   400   600
Kilometers

0   100   200   300   400
Miles

52°

176°   180°   176°

170°   166°   162°   158°   154°   150°   146°   142°   138°   134°

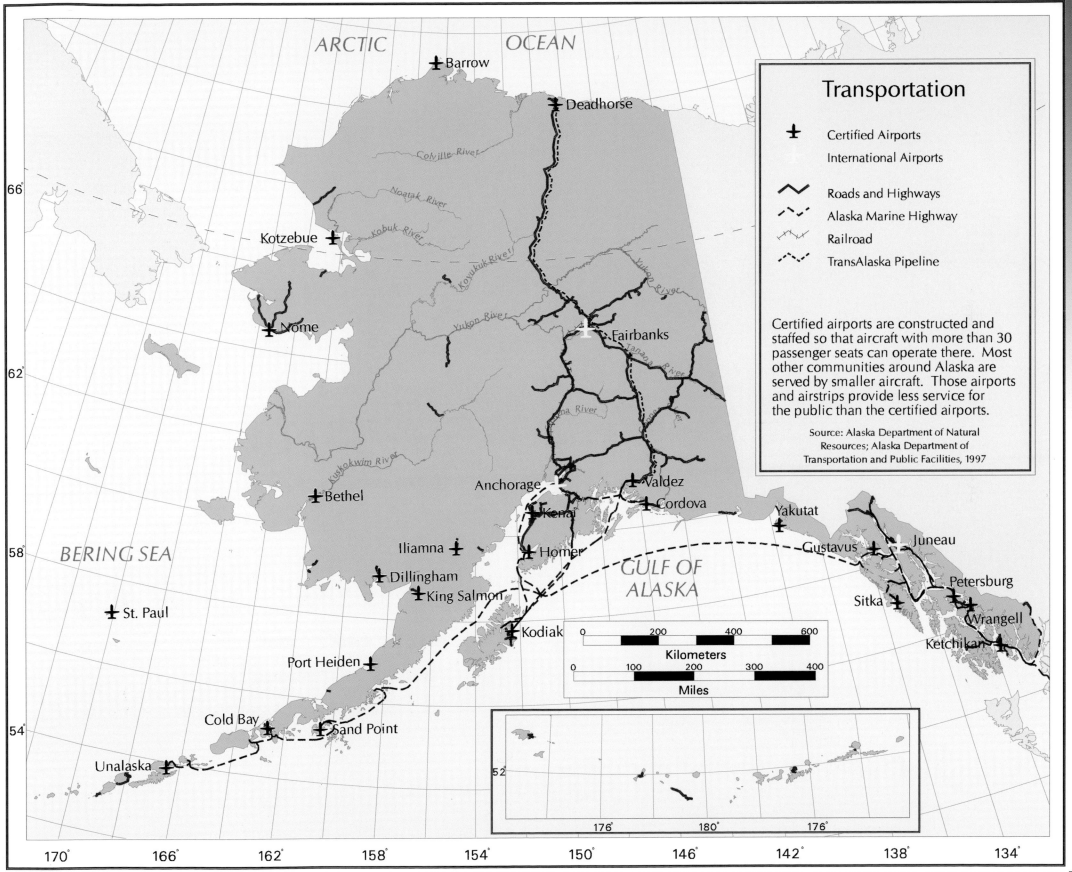

ARCTIC OCEAN

✈ Barrow

✈ Deadhorse

Colville River

Noatak River

Kobuk River

Kotzebue ✈

66°

Kovukuk River

Yukon River

✈ Nome

Yukon River

Fairbanks

62°

BERING SEA

Kuskokwim River

Tanana River

✈ Bethel

Susitna River

Anchorage ✈ Valdez

✈ Kenai ✈ Cordova

Iliamna ✈

58° ✈ Homer

✈ Dillingham

GULF OF ALASKA

Yakutat ✈

✈ St. Paul

King Salmon

Gustavus ✈ Juneau

Sitka ✈ Petersburg

Wrangell

✈ Kodiak

Ketchikan

Port Heiden ✈

Cold Bay ✈ Sand Point

54°

Unalaska ✈

52°

Transportation

✈ Certified Airports

International Airports

∿ Roads and Highways

∿ Alaska Marine Highway

∿ Railroad

∿ TransAlaska Pipeline

Certified airports are constructed and staffed so that aircraft with more than 30 passenger seats can operate there. Most other communities around Alaska are served by smaller aircraft. Those airports and airstrips provide less service for the public than the certified airports.

Source: Alaska Department of Natural Resources; Alaska Department of Transportation and Public Facilities, 1997

| 0 | 200 | 400 | 600 |
Kilometers

| 0 | 100 | 200 | 300 | 400 |
Miles

170° 166° 162° 158° 154° 150° 146° 142° 138° 134°

176° 180° 176°

Map 33–Newspapers, Television Stations, Radio Stations

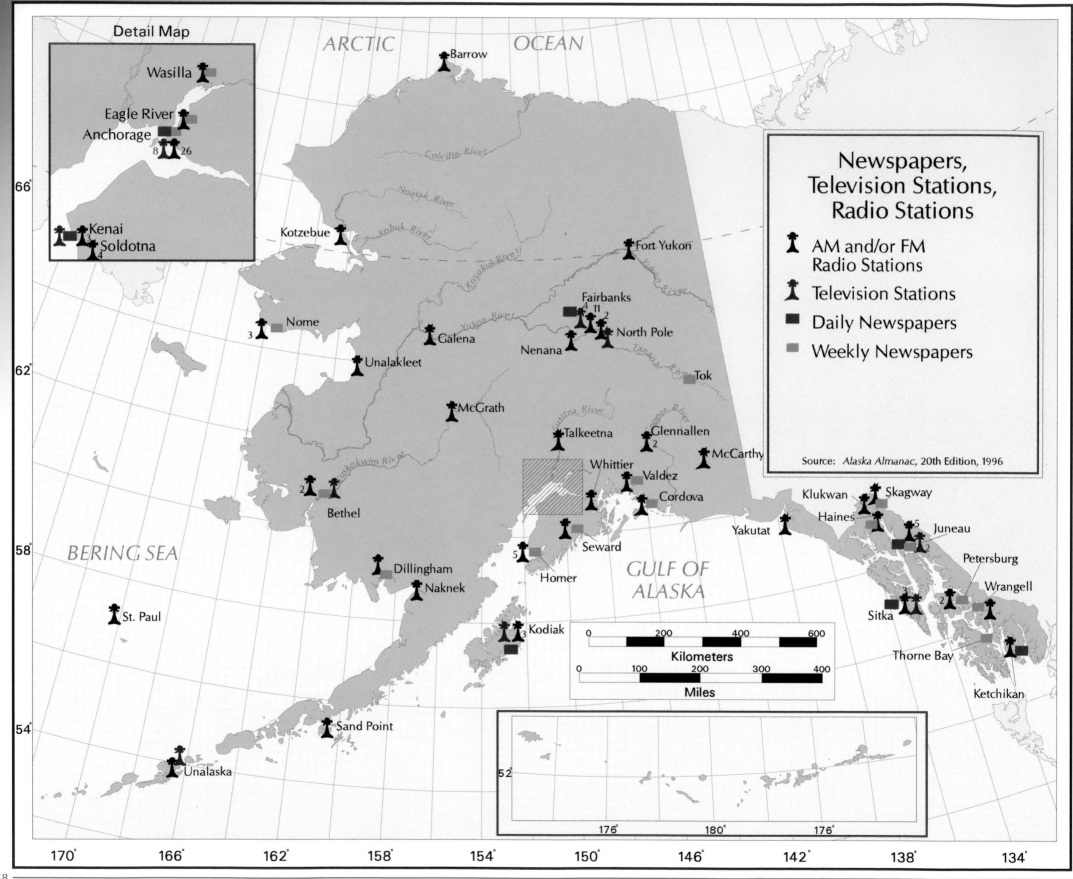

Newspapers, Television Stations, Radio Stations

- ♟ AM and/or FM Radio Stations
- ♟ Television Stations
- ■ Daily Newspapers
- ■ Weekly Newspapers

Source: *Alaska Almanac*, 20th Edition, 1996

Detail Map

Wasilla
Eagle River
Anchorage
8   26
Kenai
3
Soldotna
4

ARCTIC OCEAN

Barrow

Colville River

Noatak River

Kotzebue

Kobuk River

Fort Yukon

Yukon River

Nome
3

Galena

Fairbanks
4 11
2
North Pole
Nenana

Tok

Tanana River

Unalakleet

McGrath

Susitna River

Talkeetna

Glennallen
2

McCarthy

Copper River

Whittier
Valdez
Cordova

Klukwan   Skagway
Haines
Juneau
5
2

Yakutat

Petersburg

Kuskokwim River

Bethel
2

Seward

GULF OF ALASKA

Wrangell

Dillingham

Homer
5

Naknek

Sitka
3

Thorne Bay

St. Paul

Ketchikan

Kodiak
3

BERING SEA

0   200   400   600
Kilometers
0   100   200   300   400
Miles

Sand Point

Unalaska

52

176°   180°   176°

170°   166°   162°   158°   154°   150°   146°   142°   138°   134°

66°
62°
58°
54°

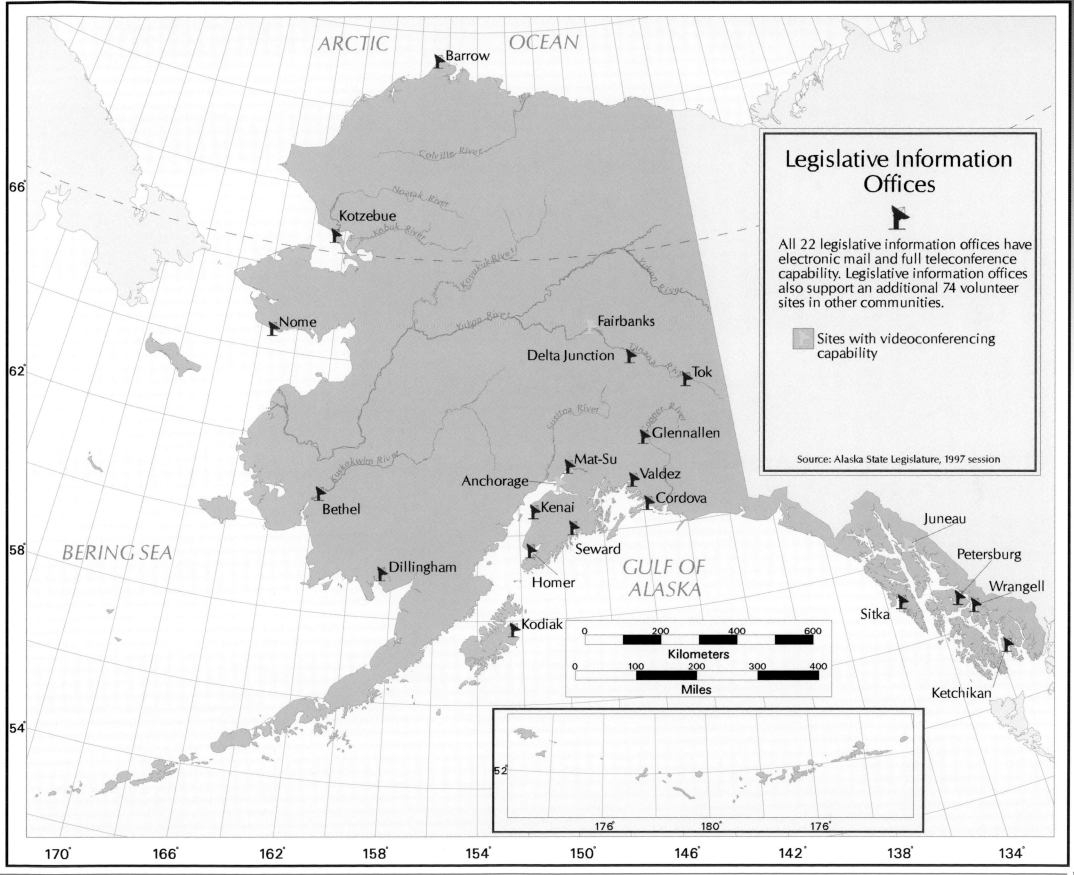

ARCTIC OCEAN

Barrow

Colville River

Noatak River

Kotzebue

Kobuk River

Koyukuk River

Yukon River

Legislative Information Offices

All 22 legislative information offices have electronic mail and full teleconference capability. Legislative information offices also support an additional 74 volunteer sites in other communities.

Sites with videoconferencing capability

Source: Alaska State Legislature, 1997 session

Nome

Fairbanks

Delta Junction

Tanana River

Tok

66°

62°

Susitna River

Copper River

Glennallen

Mat-Su

Valdez

Anchorage

Cordova

Bethel

Kenai

Kuskokwim River

Juneau

58°

BERING SEA

Dillingham

Homer

Seward

GULF OF ALASKA

Petersburg

Wrangell

Sitka

Kodiak

| 0 | 200 | 400 | 600 |

Kilometers

| 0 | 100 | 200 | 300 | 400 |

Miles

Ketchikan

54°

52°

176°   180°   176°

170°   166°   162°   158°   154°   150°   146°   142°   138°   134°

Map 35–Alaska Native Regional Corporations

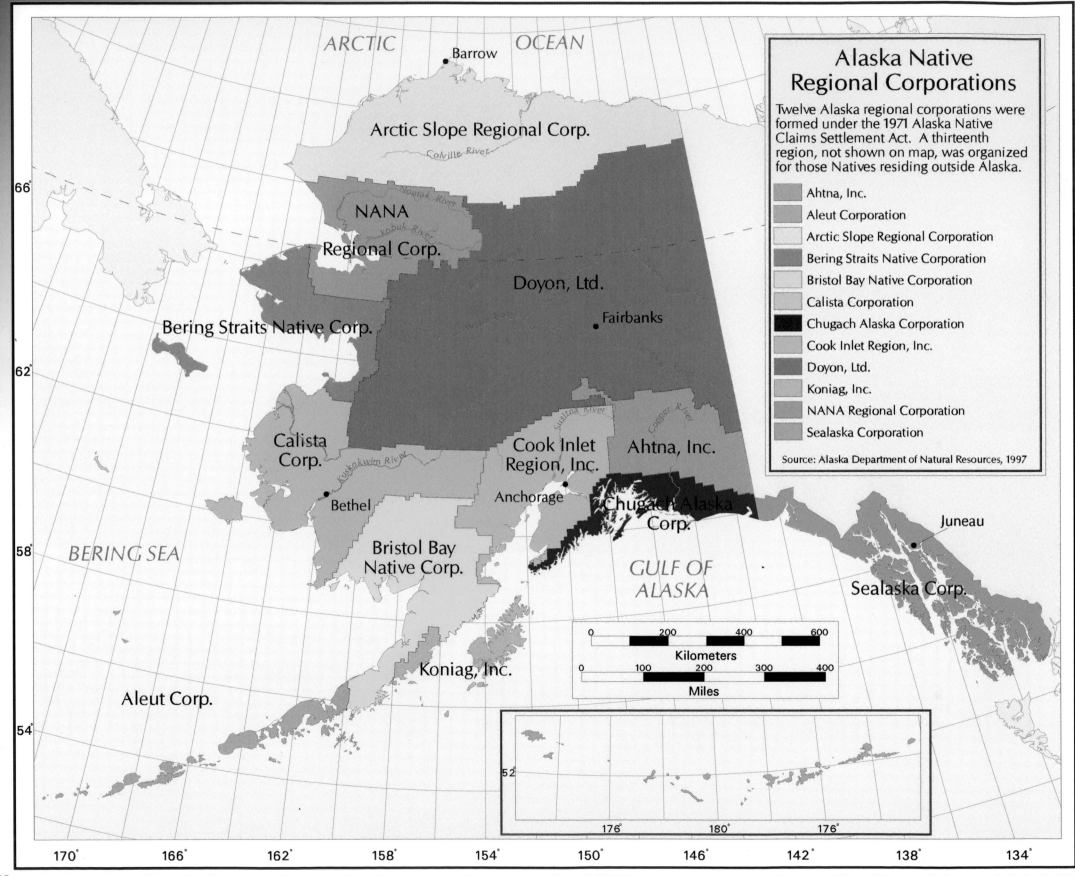

ARCTIC OCEAN

Barrow

Arctic Slope Regional Corp.

Colville River

NANA

Noatak River

Regional Corp.

Kobuk River

Doyon, Ltd.

Bering Straits Native Corp.

Fairbanks

62°

66°

Calista Corp.

Kuskokwim River

Susitna River

Copper River

Cook Inlet Region, Inc.

Ahtna, Inc.

Bethel

Anchorage

Chugach Alaska Corp.

BERING SEA

58°

Bristol Bay Native Corp.

GULF OF ALASKA

Juneau

Sealaska Corp.

Koniag, Inc.

Aleut Corp.

54°

Alaska Native Regional Corporations

Twelve Alaska regional corporations were formed under the 1971 Alaska Native Claims Settlement Act. A thirteenth region, not shown on map, was organized for those Natives residing outside Alaska.

- Ahtna, Inc.
- Aleut Corporation
- Arctic Slope Regional Corporation
- Bering Straits Native Corporation
- Bristol Bay Native Corporation
- Calista Corporation
- Chugach Alaska Corporation
- Cook Inlet Region, Inc.
- Doyon, Ltd.
- Koniag, Inc.
- NANA Regional Corporation
- Sealaska Corporation

Source: Alaska Department of Natural Resources, 1997

| 0 | 200 | 400 | 600 |
Kilometers
| 0 | 100 | 200 | 300 | 400 |
Miles

52

176°   180°   176°

170°   166°   162°   158°   154°   150°   146°   142°   138°   134°

Alaska Native fish camps have always been more than just places for gathering food. They are also learning centers where children are taught about practical matters of survival and their society's view of the world. Native cultures traditionally see the natural, human, and spiritual worlds as intricately related. Humans are an integral part of the physical and biological environment. Modern technology, natural resource demands, and accelerating population growth have accentuated another awareness —that people can greatly impact the environment. This section looks at these interconnections between Alaskans and the world around them. It looks at how environment affects people in Alaska, and how Alaskans use, and in various ways impact, their environment.

Seasonality

Seasonal changes in daylight and temperature influence people, vegetation, animal life, seas and rivers, and weather everywhere in Alaska. They affect people's ability to gather food, to work, to travel, to socialize, and to conduct business.

Seasonal changes influence everything from bird migrations and caribou movements to construction, barge schedules, and employment in tourism, teaching, and fishing. They affect how successfully people are able to garden, which foods they can harvest at particular times of the year, how they must design their homes, and the ease with which

they can travel from place to place.

In modern Alaska large insulated buildings, heating systems, and electric lighting reduce the impacts of natural changes in temperature and hours of daylight. Still, many outdoor activities are dependent on qualities of weather and daylight, and even modern transportation systems cannot escape the effects of extreme conditions. Alaskans in many ways adjust their lives around patterns of seasonal change.

Seasonal changes in hours of daylight—the time from sunrise to sunset—are quite large in Alaska because of the state's generally high latitude. The amount of change varies in different parts of the state because of Alaska's great latitudinal extent. (See **Figure 19– Hours of Daylight**).

On December 21, the direct rays of the sun are at 23.5° south latitude, the Tropic of Capricorn. Any area in Alaska that is at or north of 66.5° latitude will receive no daylight. Barrow, in fact, has 65 days without any direct sunlight. Nome receives 4 hours of daylight then, but the sun angle is very low. Valdez and Juneau, located at lower latitudes, receive more hours of daylight. One compensating

Figure 19

Hours of Daylight

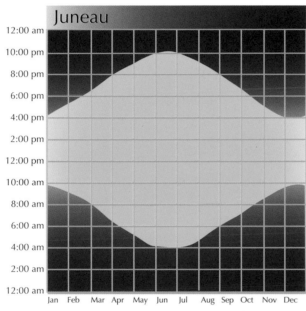

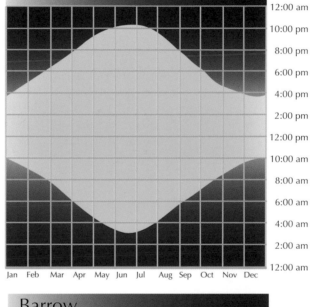

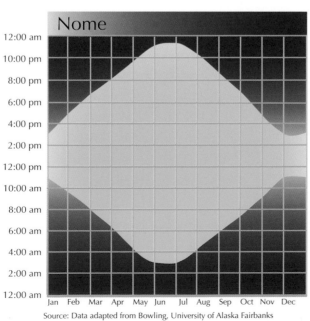

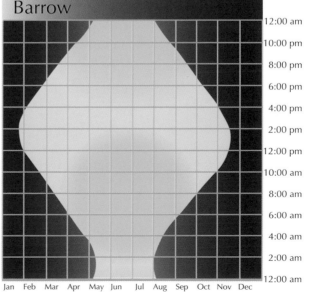

Source: Data adapted from Bowling, University of Alaska Fairbanks

factor is that high latitude areas receive more twilight than low latitude areas. This is true throughout the year.

By summer the situation changes dramatically. Barrow receives 83 days of daylight without any sunset. Nome receives more than 21 hours of daylight on the longest day, June 21. The sun is also considerably higher in the sky, as the direct rays now fall on the Tropic of Cancer at 23.5° north latitude.

Figure 20–Seasonal Changes in the Lower Kuskokwim Region shows how seasonality affects the human and physical environment in another part of Alaska. Average monthly temperatures vary considerably in the Lower Kuskokwim region—from nearly 6° F (-14.4° C) to 55° F (12.7° C) at Bethel. Hours of daylight also vary—from about 5 in winter to more than 19 in summer at Bethel. Seasonal ice on lakes, rivers, and the sea prohibits some types of transportation and opens possibilities for others. People's lives change dramatically from winter to summer.

Figure 21–Subsistence Harvest Cycle in Tununak shows the seasonality of subsistence harvests of plants and animals in one village in southwestern Alaska. In this Central Yup'ik village, residents depend on wild foods and other natural resources such as wood, grasses, and furs for their livelihood. Seasonal changes in fish and game

Figure 20

Seasonal Changes in the Lower Kuskokwim Region

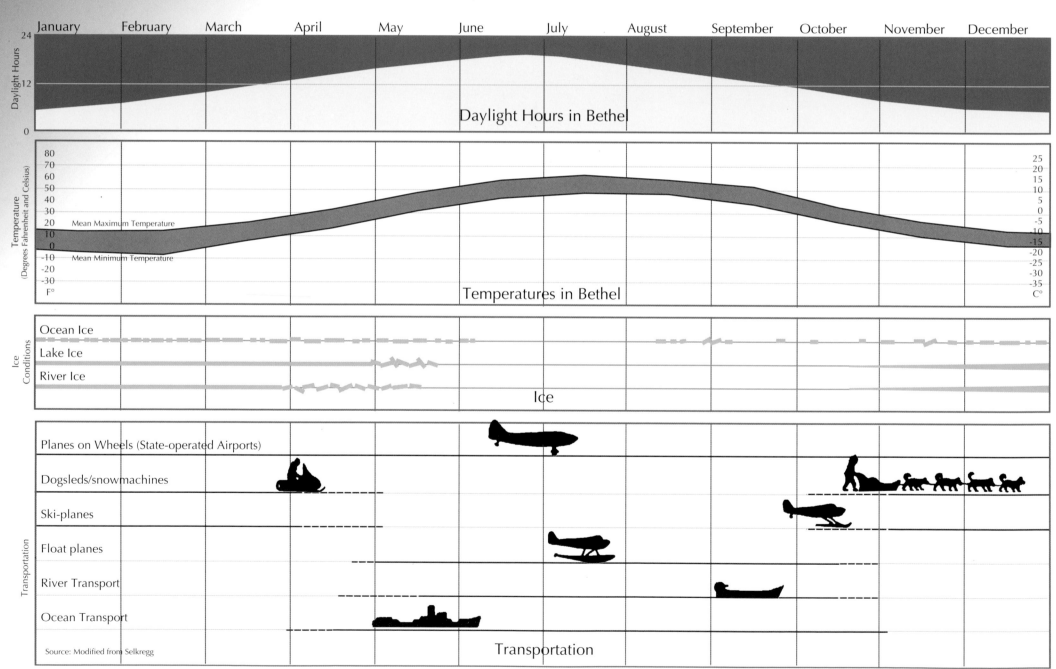

62

Figure 21

Subsistence Harvest Cycle in Tununak, 1985

Source: Pete, Alaska Department of Fish and Game

	Jan	Feb	Mar	Apr	May	Jun	Jul	Aug	Sep	Oct	Nov	Dec
Whitefish												
Tom cod												
Firewood												
Seals												
Hare												
Ptarmigan												
Beaver												
Mink												
Land otter												
Fox												
Alaska blackfish												
Burbot												
Needlefish												
Musk ox												
Walrus												
Waterfowl/seabirds												
Sea lion												
Beluga whale												
Crabs												
Other invertebrates												
Clams/mussels												
Sculpin												
Cod												
Starry flounder												
Eggs												
Pacific herring												
Herring, roe-on-kelp												
Halibut												
Chinook salmon												
Chum salmon												
Capelin												
Sockeye salmon												
Coho salmon												
Pink salmon												
Smelt												
Northern pike												
Dolly Varden												
Berries												
Grasses												

abundance influence the community's economy, work cycle, and family work groups over the course of the year.

Natural Hazards

From time to time, in every part of the world, natural forces and events threaten people and other life forms. Alaskans and agencies of government and society put a great deal of energy into trying to understand where and when these hazards might occur and how best to respond to them.

Volcanoes

Map 36 shows where approximately 100 Alaska volcanoes are located. Currently 53 of them are considered active. Most Alaska volcanoes are located along the Aleutian Peninsula and the Aleutian Islands; however, a number of them are found relatively close to Anchorage and the Kenai Peninsula, major population centers. The Aleutian Islands are actually the peaks of submarine volcanoes rising more than 30,000 feet (9,100 meters) above the ocean floor.

In 1912 Novarupta Volcano near Mt. Katmai on the Alaska Peninsula exploded in what has been the world's largest eruption in the 20th century. Fiery ash flows and steam transformed the landscape for miles around. Ash covered an area of several thousand kilometers. Explosions were heard 900 miles (1,450 kilometers) away in Ketchikan, and acid rain from the eruption reached Vancouver, British Columbia. The explosion affected world weather cycles for three to four years. Temperatures in the Northern Hemisphere dropped because volcanic dust reduced sunlight entering the earth's atmosphere.

More recently, eruptions of Mt. Spurr (in 1953 and 1993), Mt. Iliamna (in 1953), Mt. Augustine (in 1986), and Redoubt Volcano (in 1989-90) dropped ash over Anchorage and the Kenai Peninsula, interrupted air traffic, and sent debris flowing over nearby landscapes. Those eruptions were small, however, compared to the 1912 Katmai event.

Earthquakes

Much of Alaska rests on an unstable part of the earth's crust. Strong pressures build up as the Pacific Plate slides slowly under the adjacent and less-dense North American Plate. When a sudden slippage occurs along the fault separating the plates, earthquakes are generated. This action gives Alaska one of the highest rates of earthquake activity in the world. Earthquakes in the Alaska-North Pacific region account for about one-fourth of the energy released from earthquakes in the entire world.

Figure 22–Top Ten Earthquakes in the World rates earthquakes using the Moment-Magnitude Scale, a complex measure of the total energy released by a quake. It shows that 3 of the 10 largest earthquakes recorded worldwide since 1904 have taken place in the Alaska region. That is a sizable share of severe earthquakes for a region that represents a very small percentage of the world's area. **Map 37 Earthquakes in Alaska** shows that the most seismically active parts of Alaska are in and around the Aleutian Islands, Alaska Peninsula, and Southcentral regions. A smaller clustering of earthquakes can be seen extending from the Cook Inlet and Prince William Sound areas northward to Fairbanks, thus affecting nearly three-fourths of the state's population. The earthquakes on this map have been measured according to the Richter Scale, which records seismic waves, the form of energy generated by disruptions of rock deep in the earth.

The Good Friday Earthquake of 1964 was the strongest earthquake ever recorded in North America and one of the largest in recorded history. Centered near College Fjord, approximately 75 miles (120 kilometers) east of Anchorage, it caused 115 deaths and millions of dollars in damage. Associated with the earthquake were massive tsunamis, huge ocean waves that traveled at hundreds of miles an hour and were felt as far away as Hawaii, Japan, and the Antarctic Peninsula. The tsunamis, in fact, caused 90% of the deaths attributed to the earthquake, including drownings of 4 people in Oregon and 12 in California.

In Anchorage, port facilities, power lines, many businesses, and homes were destroyed by ground shifts and landslides. Along the southcentral Alaska coast, people were killed and villages suffered severe damage. Three coastal villages—Chenega, Kaguyak, and Old Harbor—were completely destroyed. Harbor facilities in Seldovia dropped to below high tide level. The dock and harbor in Cordova were raised up six feet (1.8 meters). Most of the downtown area and the port of Valdez were destroyed, and the city had to be relocated.

Floods

Two other kinds of hazards in Alaska are closely related to seasonality—floods and wildfires. As discussed in Section 2, water levels in Alaska's rivers and streams vary dramatically during different months of the year. Ice jams, rapid snow melt, and extensive rainfall can increase flow or divert huge quantities of water, causing rivers to wash over their banks. In 1967 late summer rains caused flooding in Interior Alaska. Fairbanks, on the Chena River, was almost entirely under water as was Nenana, downstream on the Tanana River. In 1986 the Seward area, the Susitna River Valley, and some areas along Cook Inlet were flooded, and in 1994 the Koyukuk River flooded and inundated a number of villages, including Allakaket, Alatna, and Hughes.

People who live along Alaskan rivers (See the number of settlements along rivers on **Map 28 Communities**) have learned to watch water levels carefully. A retention dam and levee system have been built to protect Fairbanks from potential floods, and in Interior Alaska all or parts of a number of villages have been relocated to eliminate the threat of flooding.

Floods threaten people in coastal settlements when sea ice stacks up, storms generate large waves and surges, or tides are unusually high. Nome, which was flooded by storm waves in 1974, now has a sea wall for protection. Shishmaref was

Figure 22

Top Ten Earthquakes in the World, 1904-1997

Mw = total energy released (Moment-Magnitude Scale)

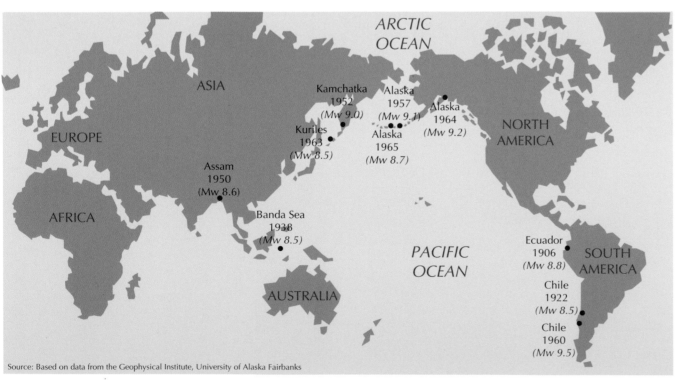

Source: Based on data from the Geophysical Institute, University of Alaska Fairbanks

severely damaged in 1997. In 1998 the people of that settlement were considering ways to protect the community.

Wildfires

Interior Alaska, with its Continental climate, receives little rainfall, and summers are generally warm and dry. Every year thunderstorms generate thousands of lightning strikes a day, and some strikes ignite massive wildfires. Wildfires burn thousands of square miles of Alaska every year. For centuries fires have been a part of Alaska's natural ecology. Over time they can be a constructive force of change, invigorating soils, plant life, and ultimately wildlife populations. When they threaten human lives, property, or valuable natural resources, however, state and federal agencies call in firefighters and heavy equipment to fight them.

Wildfires are most frequent in three areas shown on **Map 24 Ecoregions of Alaska**: Interior Forested Lowlands and Uplands, Interior Highlands, and Interior Bottomlands. Fire season usually lasts from June through early August in these regions. During those months many Alaskans, particularly from Native villages in the Interior, are employed to combat fires.

Land Ownership and Specially Managed Places

Ever since the first people crossed the Bering Land Bridge, life in Alaska has centered on the land and on the region's rich natural resources, including wild foods, furs, fish, sea mammals, forest resources, minerals, and mineral fuels.

How people use a particular piece of land is determined by the qualities of the land and the decisions of those who own or manage it. Control of Alaska's land—all 591,004 square miles or 1,530,700 square kilometers of it—is of vital concern to both Alaskans and citizens and decision makers from through-

Figure 23

State Parks

8 state parks and 3 specially managed areas* shown on Map 39–Selected State and National Parks

Southwest Area
Wood-Tikchik State Park

Kodiak Area
Afognak Island State Park
Shuyak Island State Park

Kenai Peninsula Area
Kachemak Bay State Park
Kachemak Bay State
    Wilderness Park*
Kenai River Special
    Management Area*

Chugach Area
Chugach State Park

Mat-Su Copper Basin Area
Denali State Park

Southeast Area
Alaska Chilkat Bald Eagle
    Preserve*
Chilkat State Park
Point Bridget State Park

The map also shows 34 marine parks. Historical sites, recreation areas, and other specially managed sites are not shown.

Figure 24

National Interest Lands
shown but not named on Map 40

National Wildlife Refuges
1 Alaska Peninsula NWR
2 Arctic NWR
3 Becharof NWR
4 Innoko NWR
5 Izembek NWR
6 Kanuti NWR
7 Kenai NWR
8 Kodiak NWR
9 Koyukuk NWR
10 Nowitna NWR
11 Selawik NWR
12 Tetlin NWR
13 Togiak NWR
14 Yukon Delta NWR
15 Yukon Flats NWR

The Alaska Maritime National Wildlife Refuge is named on the map.

Bureau of Land Management Recreation and Conservation Areas
16 Steese National
    Conservation Areas
17 White Mountains
    National Recreation

out the nation. **Map 38 Land Ownership** shows Alaska's primary landholders: the federal government (approximately 58%), the state (28.8%), and regional and local Native corporations (11.8%). About 1% is privately owned.

The map of land ownership shows distinctive "squared" patterns. These result from the land survey pattern that was developed in the U.S. Land Ordinance of 1785. The "township and range" system is based on surveyed townships that are six square miles by six square miles in extent. Federal,

state, and Native land boundaries in Alaska have been defined using township lines. Thus, straight lines and squared areas rule the land system amid the irregular features of the natural environment.

Alaska has much more public land than any other state. State and national forests, parks, and other specially designated areas are managed for a variety of uses. Each area's specified purposes determine whether precedence will be given to recreation, protection of wildlife or historic features, resource extraction, or multiple uses.

Hiking the Chilkoot Trail near Skagway, in Southeast Alaska

Figure 25

Historic and Archaeological Landmarks

shown on Map 41

▲ Archaeological sites　　● Historic sites

1　Adak Army Base, Naval
　　Operating Base
2　Onion Portage
　　Archaeological District
3　Attu Battlefield, U.S.
　　Army & Navy Airfields
4　Birnik Site
5　Palugvik Archaeological
　　District
6　Eagle Historic District,
　　Fort Egbert
7　George C. Thomas
　　Memorial Library
8　Sternwheeler Nenana
9　Ladd Field,
　　Fort Wainwright
10　Dry Creek
　　Archaeological Site
11　Fort Durham Site
12　Holy Assumption Church
13　Japanese Occupation Site
14　Three Saints Site
15　Russian-American
　　Company Magazin
16　Kodiak Naval Operating
　　Base, Fort Greely, Fort
　　Abercrombie
17　Cape Krusenstern
　　Archaeological District
18　Iyatayet
19　Anvil Creek Gold
　　Discovery Site
20　Cape Nome Discovery
　　Sites
21　Gallagher Flint Station
　　Archaeological Site
22　Chaluka Site

23　Anangula Site
24　Cape Field at Fort Glenn
25　Yukon Island Main Site
26　Alaska Native
　　Brotherhood Hall
27　American Flag Raising
　　Site
28　Old Sitka Site
29　Russian Bishop's House
30　St. Michael Archangel
　　Cathedral
31　Tilson Bldg.
32　Sitka Naval Operating
　　Base
33　Fort William H. Seward
34　Skagway/White Pass
　　Historical District
35　Chilkoot Trail/Dyea
36　Wales Sites
37　Holy Ascension Church
38　Sitka Spruce Plantation
39　Dutch Harbor Naval
　　Operating Base,
　　Fort Mears
40　Leffingwell Camp
41　Kennecott Mines
42　Bering Expedition
　　Landing Site
43　Brooks River
　　Archaeological District
44　Ipiutak Site
45　Seal Islands Historical
　　District
46　New Russia
　　Archaeological Site
47　Kake Cannery
48　Kijik Archaeological Site

◆ 49 World Heritage Site
Wrangell/St.Elias National Park and Glacier Bay National
Park are part of a World Heritage Site in conjunction with
Tatshenshini-Alsek/Kluane National Park in Canada.

Map 39 shows **Selected State and National Parks in Alaska**. **Figure 23** lists **State Parks** shown but not named on the map.

Map 40 **Selected National Interest Lands** shows National Wildlife Refuges, National Forests, two Bureau of Land Management Recreation and Conservation Areas, and the National Petroleum Reserve. **Figure 24** identifies the land areas numbered on the map.

Some places in Alaska have been named as special landmarks because they were important in the state's history. These sites are listed in the National Register of Historic Places. Besides the sites shown on **Map 41** **Historic and Archaeological Landmarks**, Alaska has many locally recognized landmarks and a number of other places designated as National Historic Landmarks. **Figure 25** identifies the **Historic and Archaeological Landmarks** numbered on the map.

Some public and private lands in Alaska receive special protection and management because they are wetlands, a type of landscape the federal government has designated especially valuable and fragile in all states. In wetlands saturated ground is the dominant factor determining both the nature of soil development and the types of plant and animal communities living in the soil or on its surface. Wetlands in Alaska include bogs, muskegs, wet and moist tundra, fens, marshes, swamps, and mud flats. Many Alaska wetlands, such as salt marshes or the flood plains of rivers, are covered with shallow water for at least part of each day or year. Other wetlands, particularly on the Arctic Coastal Plain, are created because permafrost beneath the thin surface layer keeps water from draining so that it collects on top of the ground or saturates the soil.

Map 42 shows **Wetlands** in Alaska. They cover about 273,000 square miles (707,000 square kilometers). "Deepwater habitats" are certain fresh and saltwater areas managed in conjunction with wetlands. On **Map 42** these are lacustrine and palustrine wetlands—lakes and ponds classified as deepwater habitats.

Alaska wetlands such as the Arctic Coastal Plain, the Yukon-Kuskokwim Delta, the Copper River Delta, and the Yukon and Stikine Flats are tremendously important to millions of shorebirds and waterfowl that migrate north each spring and summer. The birds, which may come from as far away as South America and Antarctica, travel north each year to find plentiful food, undisturbed nesting sites, and long daylight hours in which to feed, nest, and raise their young. In fall adults and young birds stop in wetlands as they travel south to winter in warmer climates.

Muskrats and beavers live in wetlands. Moose feed in them. Caribou feed in them, migrate across them, and use them as calving areas. Many types of fish, including all five species of salmon found in Alaska, feed in wetlands or on food produced by wetlands such as estuaries or marshes.

Wetlands are no less important to people. They are some of the most productive areas for hunting, trapping, fishing, and gathering plants such as blueberries, cranberries, willow, and beach greens. They are popular destinations for wildlife viewing and photography, and many have been set aside as refuges to preserve these qualities.

About half the wetlands in the Lower 48 states have been replaced by homes, farms, industrial sites, and other types of human development. Some have been flooded or dried out by the construction of dams and levees. According to the U.S. Fish and Wildlife Service, Alaska now contains 63% of the total wetland acreage in the United States, excluding Hawaii.

Many acres of Alaska wetlands remain untouched by development. Some others, however, are located in areas where people want to use the land for homes, resource development, and other purposes. Federal wetland policies, which favor preservation, conflict with such plans. Debate is intense over how a national policy should be applied in the distinctive geographic setting of Alaska.

Wild Harvests

The people of Alaska harvest more wild foods than people anywhere else in the United States. In 1998 the Alaska Department of Fish and Game estimated that Alaskans harvest about 53.4 million pounds (24 million kilograms) of wild foods annually. For many Alaska Natives, harvesting traditional wild foods is a central part of daily life. It promotes economic well-being and social and spiritual connections integral to

their heritage and their identity. For many other Alaskans, hunting, fishing, and trapping foster important economic, social, and personal values as well, whether they are the focus of daily life or are integrated with urban living.

According to the Alaska Department of Fish and Game, about 60% of the rural food harvest by weight is fish, 20% is game, 14% is marine mammals, and 2% each are birds, shellfish, and plants. Major fish varieties harvested include salmon, halibut, herring, whitefish, and sheefish. Major game species include caribou, moose, deer, bear, and beaver. The most important marine mammals eaten are sea lion, beluga, walrus, bowhead whale, and four types of seal.

Map 43 Subsistence Harvests in Seven Villages shows how the mix of wild foods varies in different parts of the state. In Manokotak, a Central Yup'ik community, salmon is the largest part of the wild foods harvested. In Tanacross, an inland Athabaskan community, land mammals (moose and caribou) are the largest part of the harvest. Kaktovik, an Iñupiat community, harvests a large percentage of marine mammals, including bowhead whale, ringed seal, and bearded seal.

The opportunity to hunt and fish brings thousands of visitors to Alaska from other states and countries. Their visits provide income for Alaskans who sell them food, lodging, guide services, handicrafts, and entertainment.

Map 44 shows the intensity of **Sportfishing** in various management areas of Alaska in

1995. Figures include fishing by Alaska residents and non-residents who did not designate their catch for subsistence use or sell it commercially. Most notably, the number of anglers in the Kenai Peninsula area was four times the number of those in the next highest management area. The intensity of sportfishing overall correlates strongly with population density shown in **Map 25** and transportation systems shown in **Map 32.**

In 1996, an estimated 478,000 people bought sport fishing licenses in Alaska. About half of those were Alaska residents and nearly half were nonresidents. That is testimony to the importance of this activity to Alaskans and nonresidents alike.

In the 10 years between 1985 and 1995, the number of people fishing in Alaska increased by more than a third, and the number of people from outside

the state who sport fished in Alaska more than doubled. These increases are a substantial source of income to the people and industries who serve visiting anglers, and they bring added income to state government from the sale of licenses. At the same time they affect the availability of fish for commercial and subsistence use, and planning by state agencies working to manage fish populations for long-term health and sustainability.

The importance of hunting and trapping is another characteristic that sets Alaska apart from many other states. **Map 45 Hunting and Trapping** shows the numbers of large mammals and furbearers harvested in various regions of Alaska during 1994-95. Harvests in each region vary, partly because the species available vary with local environments and partly because

Steve Henrikson

Harvesting spruce roots in Southeast Alaska

people's lifestyles and interests vary.

Not as many Alaskans or visitors hunt and trap as fish. During 1994-95, however, 79,000 Alaska residents and 11,000 nonresidents bought hunting licenses, while nearly 20,000 residents bought trapping licenses.

Major Resource Industries

Alaskans have long harvested and extracted natural resources for use at home and for export to other parts of the world. Early Native peoples are known to have traded along the Yukon and with people in northeastern Russia. Over the past 250 years furs, whales, fish, minerals, wood products, coal, and petroleum have all been the focus of extensive economic efforts.

Extraction and use of natural resources are still extremely important in Alaska. Resource industries provide the economic base that supports state services. They provide jobs and income to people in service businesses, transportation, construction, education, communication, and finance.

At present, Alaska's primary resource industries include mineral fuels (oil, gas, and coal); seafood; the visitor industry; forest products; minerals, including zinc, gold, silver, lead, and copper; and some agriculture and grazing.

Mineral Fuels— Oil, Gas, and Coal

Map 46 **Mineral Fuels** shows oil basins and coal deposits in Alaska. In 1996 Alaska produced about 23% of the nation's oil. Oil fields on the North Slope were the top producing fields in the United States, and taxes and royalties from oil production generated about 85% of state revenues. **Figure 26–Oil Production and Value** shows how revenues for mineral fuels, as for other natural resources, fluctuate as prices increase and decrease on the world market.

Oil is produced in two regions of Alaska. About 97% of the state's oil comes from fields on the North Slope, which produced about 540 million barrels of oil in 1996. The remainder comes from oil fields on Cook Inlet, many of which operate from platforms offshore.

The 798-mile (1,284-kilometer) TransAlaska Pipeline moves the crude oil from the North Slope to Valdez. From there, tankers carry the oil to U.S. and foreign ports. Only since 1996 has federal law allowed Alaska to export North Slope petroleum to foreign countries. A small amount of the North Slope crude oil is processed at North Pole near Fairbanks, and Valdez. The oil and gas products of Cook Inlet are processed near Kenai in an oil refinery, a urea (fertilizer) plant, and a natural gas plant. From there they are shipped to destinations in Alaska and other parts of the United States as well as to Japan and the Russian Far East.

Markets have not yet been developed for natural gas from the North Slope. Instead the gas is injected back into reservoirs to enhance oil production. Construction of a gas pipeline from the North Slope was approved in 1977 by the federal government; but financing the project, at an estimated cost of $40 billion, has not yet proved feasible. That is largely because gas is readily available at lower costs elsewhere in North America and the world.

Alaska may hold as much as half of the nation's coal reserves—an estimated 5 trillion tons, with the energy equivalent of more than 1,000 Prudhoe Bays. Yet, only a tiny portion of these reserves has been developed because coal has a low unit value, and is cheaper and more readily available elsewhere in the world.

Figure 26

Oil Production and Value, 1978-1997

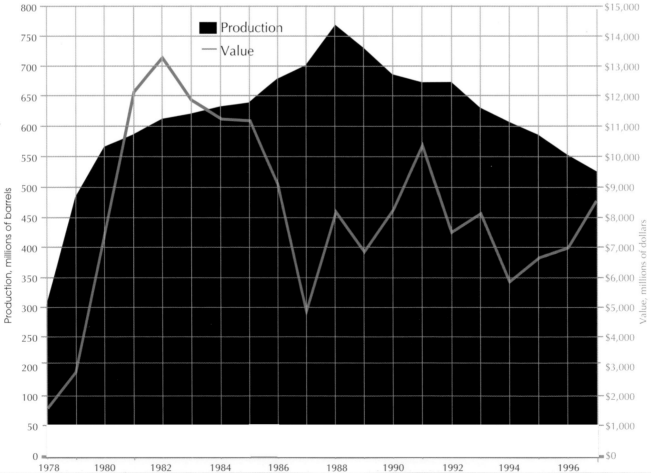

Production, millions of barrels

Value, millions of dollars

Source: Alaska Department of Revenue

Figure 27

Fishery Landings of the Top Five U.S. States, 1995

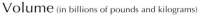

Volume (in billions of pounds and kilograms)

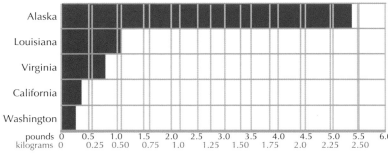

Value (in millions of U.S. dollars)

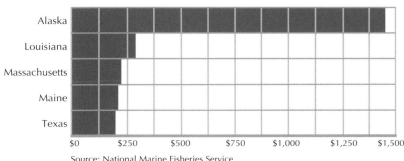

Source: National Marine Fisheries Service

Alaska's only producing coal mine, the Usibelli Mine near Healy, has been operating since 1918. In 1995 the mine produced 1.6 million tons of coal, about half of which was used to fuel power plants in nearby Fairbanks and the Railbelt region. The other half was transported on the Alaska Railroad to Whittier then shipped to a coal-fired power plant in South Korea.

Commercial Fisheries

Map 47 shows **Commercial Fisheries** in Alaska. If Alaska were an independent country, it would rank among the top 10 seafood producers in the world. In 1995 nearly 6 billion pounds (2.7 billion kilograms) of seafood were harvested in Alaska. Seafood exports totaled more than $1.3 billion, and commercial fishing and seafood processing directly and indirectly employed more than 74,000 people.

For years Alaska's seafood harvest has been nearly five times as large and nearly five times as valuable as that of any other U.S. state (See **Figure 27–Fishery Landings of the Top Five U.S. States**). Yet the Alaska seafood industry is facing challenges on many fronts. Farmed salmon is competing with Alaska's wild salmon in traditional world markets, and the quantities of fish available vary from year to year. In 1997, disputes with Canada added extra stress to the situation. Further complicating matters, prices fluctuate with changes in supply and demand. Nevertheless, commercial fishing continues to be an economic mainstay in many parts of Alaska.

In recent years, groundfish have surpassed other Alaska species, including salmon and king crab, in total value and number of pounds landed. Groundfish, or bottomfish, include primarily pollock, blackcod, rockfish, and Pacific cod. Most are caught offshore beyond the three-mile limit of state jurisdiction and are managed by the federal government. According to the National Marine Fisheries Service, 3.8 billion pounds (1.7 billion kilograms) of groundfish were caught off Alaska in 1995. They were valued at more than $511 million. As **Figure 28– Seafood Harvests and Value** shows, more groundfish must be caught to equal the value of an equal quantity of salmon or shellfish. **Figure 28** also shows how the volume and value of seafood caught varies considerably even from one year to the next.

Figure 28

Seafood Harvests and Value, 1995-1996

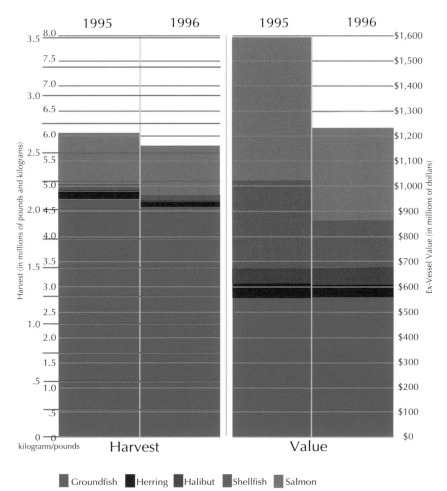

Source: Department of Commerce and Economic Development. Data on groundfish from National Marine Fisheries Service, on halibut from International Pacific Halibut Commission, on all others from Alaska Department of Fish and Game.

The Visitor Industry

After oil and gas and the seafood industry, the Alaska visitor industry contributes the greatest revenues to the state economy. The visitor industry, like most other major industries, is built around the use of natural resources. People from all over the world visit Alaska to see its dramatic landscapes and wildlife, to fish or hunt, to see relics of Alaska's history, and to learn about Alaskans' lifestyles and cultural heritage.

Approximately 1.2 million people visited Alaska in 1997. That is an influx of people twice the state's entire population of about 600,000. As **Figure 29– Summer Visitor Arrivals in Alaska** shows, that is also twice as many visitors as came to Alaska just 10 years ago.

According to the National Park Service, 1.9 million visits were made to national parks in Alaska during 1997. The office of State Parks logged 4,055,318 visits to Alaska state parks between July 1996 and June 1997. While these figures include visits by residents as well as tourists, most visitors to parks are from other states and countries.

Figure 30–Visitors by Mode of Arrival shows how visitors arrived in Alaska in 1996. Visitors arriving by cruise ship and by air enter the state in Southeast or Southcentral Alaska, and that is where most income from the visitor industry is concentrated. Just over 40% of visitor spending has been in Southcentral Alaska while about 25% has been in Southeast. In recent years more and more visitors are traveling to rural areas and remote locations.

Providing for that many visitors, most of whom come during summer, has a substantial influence on public facilities, transportation, communities, personal incomes, wildlife, and wilderness areas. It also brings to the state millions of dollars paid for visitor services, and it provides valuable opportunities to teach people from outside the state about Alaska and the variety of lifestyles found among Alaskans.

Forest Products

In 1995 Alaska exported $548 million worth of forest products. That included lumber, pulp, chips, unprocessed logs, and partially processed logs called *cants*. In 1996 more than half of Alaska's forest products were shipped to Japan. Other important markets were Taiwan, South Korea, and Canada.

Figure 31–Wood Exports in Alaska shows how the harvest and sale of forest products from Alaska is constantly changing. Rising and falling world markets for wood products affect prices and demand. Political and economic decisions affect how much timber will be harvested from public and private lands at any time. Modernization of facilities and equipment is costly yet necessary to meet environmental regulations and remain competitive as industry technology changes. The forest industry must also compete with other uses of the forests, including recreation, tourism, and fish and wildlife habitat. One consequence of the problems besetting the industry was closure in the 1990s of Alaska's only two pulp mills, in Sitka and Ketchikan.

Over the years, most of Alaska's timber harvest has

Figure 29

Summer Visitor Arrivals in Alaska, 1985-1996

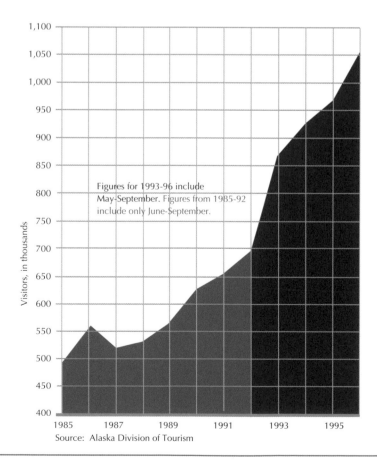

Figures for 1993-96 include May-September. Figures from 1985-92 include only June-September.

Source: Alaska Division of Tourism

Figure 30

Visitors by Mode of Arrival, 1996

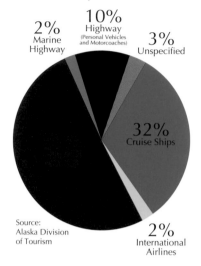

2% Marine Highway
10% Highway (Personal Vehicles and Motorcoaches)
3% Unspecified
32% Cruise Ships
2% International Airlines

Source: Alaska Division of Tourism

Figure 31

Wood Exports in Alaska, 1985-1996

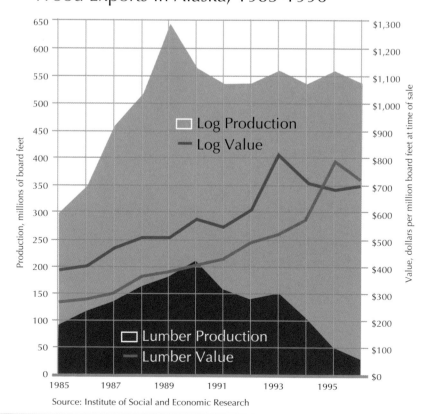

Source: Institute of Social and Economic Research

been taken from the coastal rainforest. That has included primarily the Tongass National Forest and, more recently, Native corporation lands in Southeast and Southcentral Alaska.

Timber that could be of commercial value also is found in parts of the boreal forest in Alaska's Interior. Harvest of this timber has been limited because land ownership is fragmented, transportation costs are high, and there has been strong political opposition to logging on a large scale.

People inside and outside the industry have proposed changes to make timber harvest more compatible with other uses of the forest. Efforts have also intensified to increase the value of harvested timber to Alaskans by processing it more fully into products such as lumber, furniture, souvenirs, and musical instruments.

Minerals

Map 48 shows the distribution of major Minerals deposits and producing mines in Alaska. The state is richly endowed with a variety of mineral resources. In 1997 nearly 200 mines and quarries were operating throughout the state.

Many people are aware of Alaska's colorful gold mining industry, which produced approximately 34 million ounces (1,057 metric tons) of gold between 1880 and 1997 (See **Figure 32—Gold Production and Value in Alaska**). About 70% of that total was derived from placer deposits. About 30% was recovered from hardrock, or lode, deposits. In 1997 Alaska miners recovered about 550,000 ounces of gold worth $176

million. The newly opened Fort Knox Gold mine near Fairbanks produced 366,000 ounces of gold, two-thirds of the total, and became the sixth largest gold mine in North America.

Gold, however, is only part of the Alaska mineral industry story. Before 1940, the rich Kennecott mines in the Chitina Valley and Prince William Sound regions supplied substantial quantities of copper to American industry. The mines were especially active during the critical copper shortages of World War I.

In 1995 zinc accounted for more than half the value of Alaska's mineral production. In 1997 the giant Red Dog Mine, 90 miles (145 kilometers) north of Kotzebue, was the largest zinc mine in the world. It accounted for 7% of all the world's mined

zinc. That same year the Greens Creek Mine on Admiralty Island was one of the largest silver mines in the United States. It also produced gold, and concentrates yielding lead, zinc, and copper.

Certain minerals considered "strategic"—that is, crucial to the national defense—have been mined in Alaska during times of critical shortage. These include tin, asbestos, chromium, platinum group elements, graphite, antimony, mercury, and tungsten. Placer deposits at Goodnews Bay in southwest Alaska were the largest source of platinum group elements (PGE) in the United States during the 40 years between 1935 and 1975. During World War II, much of Alaska's PGE production from Goodnews Bay went into military aircraft production in both the United States and Great Britain.

Alaskan jade is of international quality. Most of it is found in the Jade Mountains of northwestern Alaska, where the Native corporation NANA mines and processes it. Industrial minerals such as limestone, gypsum, ornamental stone, and minor gemstones have all been recovered during times when markets were favorable.

There are thousands of individual mineral deposits in Alaska. Only a small percentage of them, however, has been developed. Their remote locations, Alaska's high labor and energy costs, and harsh climatic conditions make retrieving minerals difficult and expensive. As a result, mineral development in Alaska will probably always be limited to deposits of exceptional quality during periods when market demand is favorable.

Figure 32

Gold Production and Value in Alaska, 1880-1997

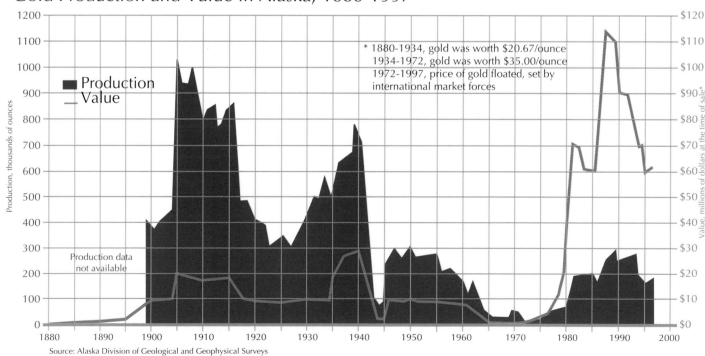

* 1880-1934, gold was worth $20.67/ounce
1934-1972, gold was worth $35.00/ounce
1972-1997, price of gold floated, set by international market forces

Source: Alaska Division of Geological and Geophysical Surveys

Agriculture and Grazing

Map 49 **Potential Agricultural Lands** shows areas in Alaska with potential for agriculture and grazing. Despite Alaska's large size, only a small amount of land, about 7,800 square miles (20,202 square kilometers) in a few river valleys, is capable of producing cultivated crops in quantity. Commercial agriculture is limited to areas near existing transportation lines, which reduces the potential area to about 800 square miles (2,072 square kilometers) (See **Map 32 Transportation**). These lands include the state's two major agricultural areas, the Tanana Valley, especially around Fairbanks and Delta, and the Matanuska Valley and Point Mackenzie, near Anchorage.

In 1997, there were 510 farms and ranches in Alaska that produced food used by Alaskans. Actual cropland for commercial vegetable production and feed crops on these farms amounted to 48 square miles (124 square kilometers). Nearly all of this land was in animal feed crops such as barley, grass, and oats.

Despite their small size, Alaskan farms manage to produce approximately 10% of the food needs of state residents. They supply fresh milk through dairies located in Anchorage and Delta from some 900 dairy cattle in the state. Meat is supplied mostly from beef cattle but also from hogs and sheep. Most of the livestock is found in the Tanana Valley and to a lesser extent in the Matanuska Valley. Vegetables most commonly grown are beans, broccoli, cabbage, carrots, cauliflower, cucumbers, lettuce, potatoes, and zucchini. While the growing season is short, the long hours of daylight allow rapid growth. Indeed, Alaska is well-known for its exceptionally large cabbages.

Much of Alaska's agriculture has nothing to do with producing food and fiber. Some farmers concentrate on producing grass seed for revegetation, while some earn income from raising and stabling horses and dogs. Farmers with greenhouses may grow tomatoes, cucumbers, and other vegetables for the fresh market, but more money can be earned growing bedding plants and flowers.

Reindeer were introduced into Alaska in the late 1800s by Sheldon Jackson, who was then Alaska's Commissioner for Education. Jackson believed that the introduction of these domesticated caribou would provide a significant source of food for the Eskimo populations of Western Alaska. Today, reindeer can still be found in Alaska, with the herds concentrated primarily on the Seward Peninsula, Nunivak Island, and Umnak Island. Numbers of reindeer are small, approximately 27,000 in all.

Harvesting barley near Delta in Interior Alaska

Cathy Birklid, Agricultural and Forestry Experiment Station and Alaska Cooperative Extension, University of Alaska Fairbanks

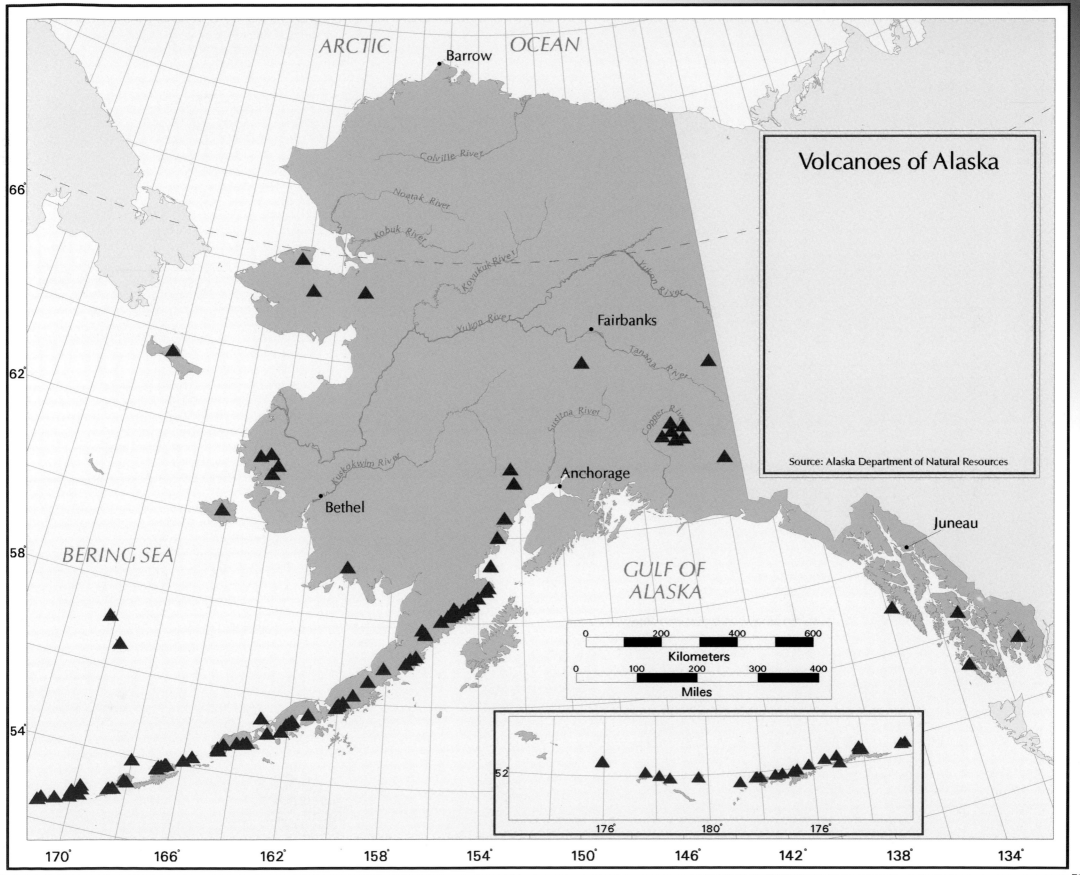

ARCTIC OCEAN

Barrow

Colville River

Noatak River

Kobuk River

Koyukuk River

Yukon River

Yukon River

Fairbanks

Tanana River

66°

62°

Susitna River

Copper River

Anchorage

Kuskokwim River

Bethel

58°

BERING SEA

GULF OF
ALASKA

Juneau

Volcanoes of Alaska

Source: Alaska Department of Natural Resources

0	200	400	600

Kilometers

0	100	200	300	400

Miles

52°

176°   180°   176°

54°

170°   166°   162°   158°   154°   150°   146°   142°   138°   134°

Map 37–Earthquakes in Alaska

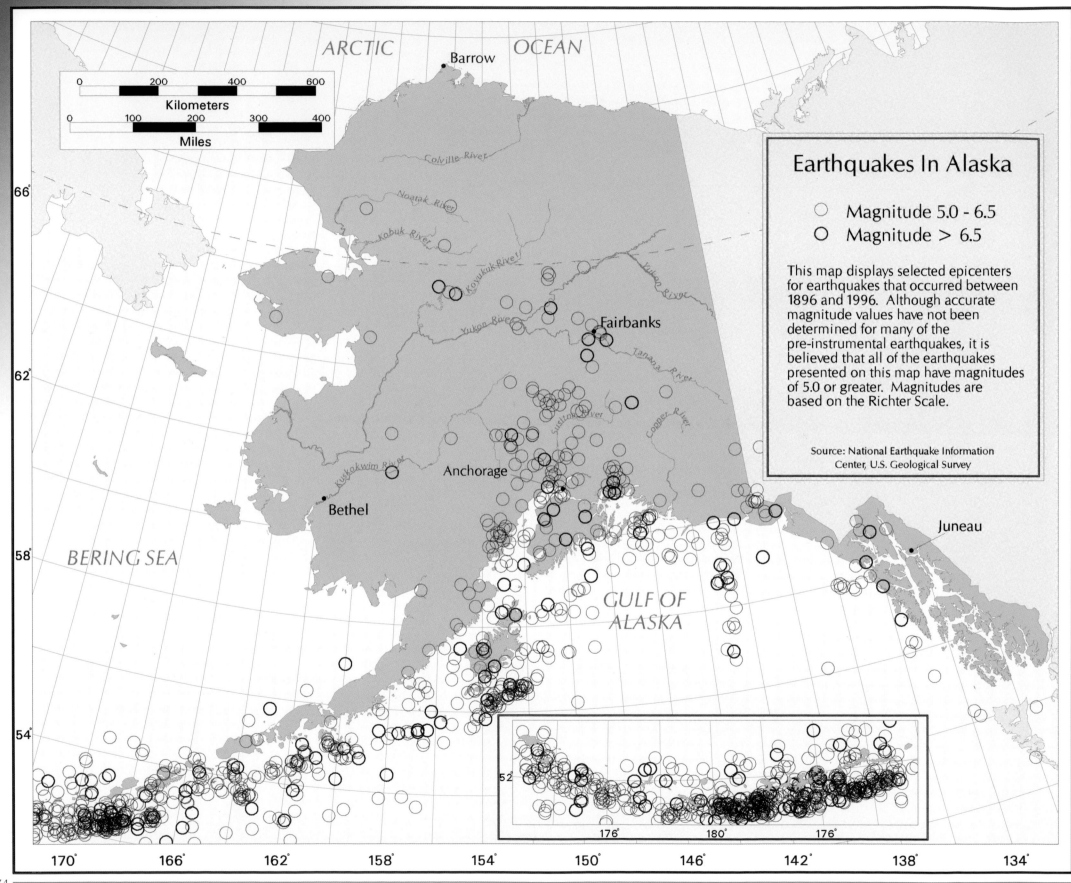

ARCTIC OCEAN

Barrow

Colville River

Noatak River

Kobuk River

Koyukuk River

Yukon River

Fairbanks

Tanana River

Susitna River

Copper River

Anchorage

Kuskokwim River

Bethel

BERING SEA

Juneau

GULF OF
ALASKA

Earthquakes In Alaska

○ Magnitude 5.0 - 6.5
◯ Magnitude > 6.5

This map displays selected epicenters
for earthquakes that occurred between
1896 and 1996. Although accurate
magnitude values have not been
determined for many of the
pre-instrumental earthquakes, it is
believed that all of the earthquakes
presented on this map have magnitudes
of 5.0 or greater. Magnitudes are
based on the Richter Scale.

Source: National Earthquake Information
Center, U.S. Geological Survey

0   200   400   600
Kilometers
0   100   200   300   400
Miles

66°
62°
58°
54°

52°

176°   180°   176°

170°   166°   162°   158°   154°   150°   146°   142°   138°   134°

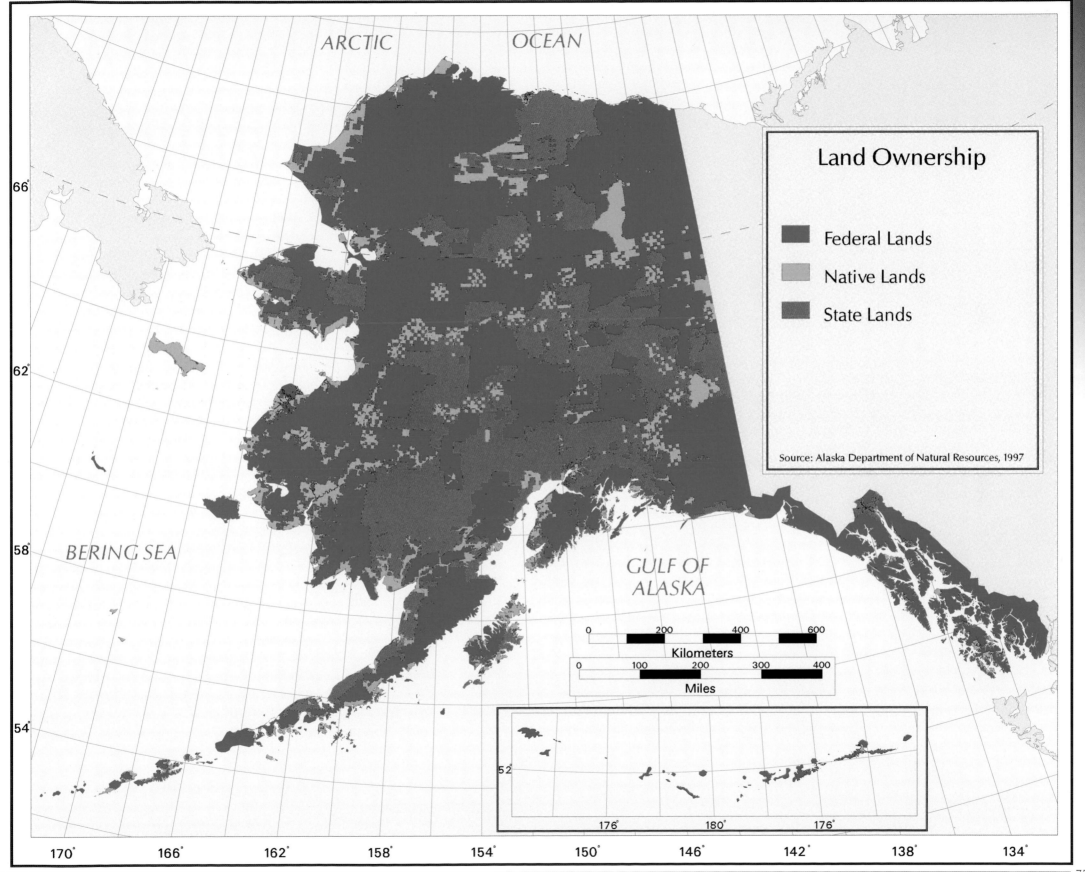

ARCTIC OCEAN

Land Ownership

- Federal Lands
- Native Lands
- State Lands

Source: Alaska Department of Natural Resources, 1997

BERING SEA

GULF OF ALASKA

0 200 400 600
Kilometers

0 100 200 300 400
Miles

Map 39–Selected State and National Parks

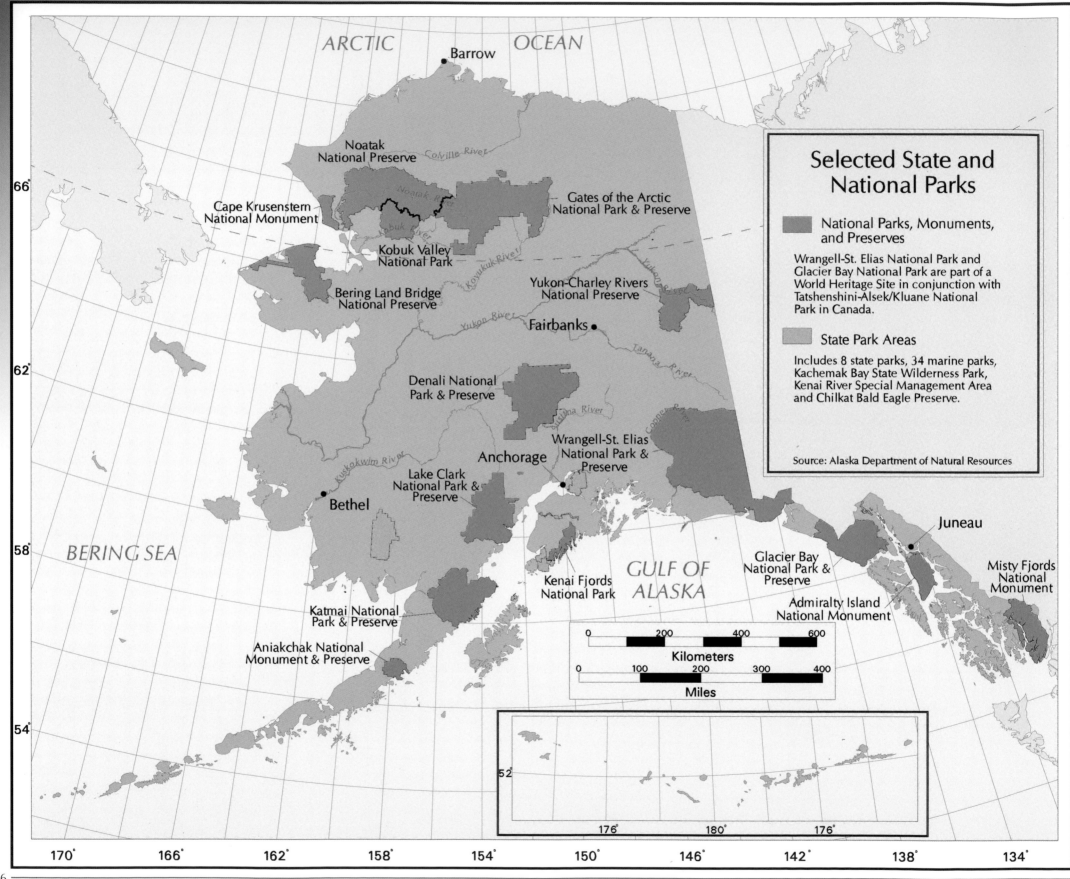

ARCTIC OCEAN

Barrow

Noatak National Preserve

Colville River

Gates of the Arctic National Park & Preserve

Cape Krusenstern National Monument

Kobuk Valley National Park

Noatak River

Kobuk River

Koyukuk River

Yukon River

Bering Land Bridge National Preserve

Yukon-Charley Rivers National Preserve

Yukon River

Fairbanks

Tanana River

Denali National Park & Preserve

Susitna River

Wrangell-St. Elias National Park & Preserve

Copper River

Kuskokwim River

Anchorage

Lake Clark National Park & Preserve

Bethel

BERING SEA

Juneau

Kenai Fjords National Park

GULF OF ALASKA

Glacier Bay National Park & Preserve

Misty Fjords National Monument

Katmai National Park & Preserve

Admiralty Island National Monument

Aniakchak National Monument & Preserve

Selected State and National Parks

National Parks, Monuments, and Preserves

Wrangell-St. Elias National Park and Glacier Bay National Park are part of a World Heritage Site in conjunction with Tatshenshini-Alsek/Kluane National Park in Canada.

State Park Areas

Includes 8 state parks, 34 marine parks, Kachemak Bay State Wilderness Park, Kenai River Special Management Area and Chilkat Bald Eagle Preserve.

Source: Alaska Department of Natural Resources

Kilometers
0   200   400   600

Miles
0 100 200 300 400

66°
62°
58°
54°

52°

176°   180°   176°

170°   166°   162°   158°   154°   150°   146°   142°   138°   134°

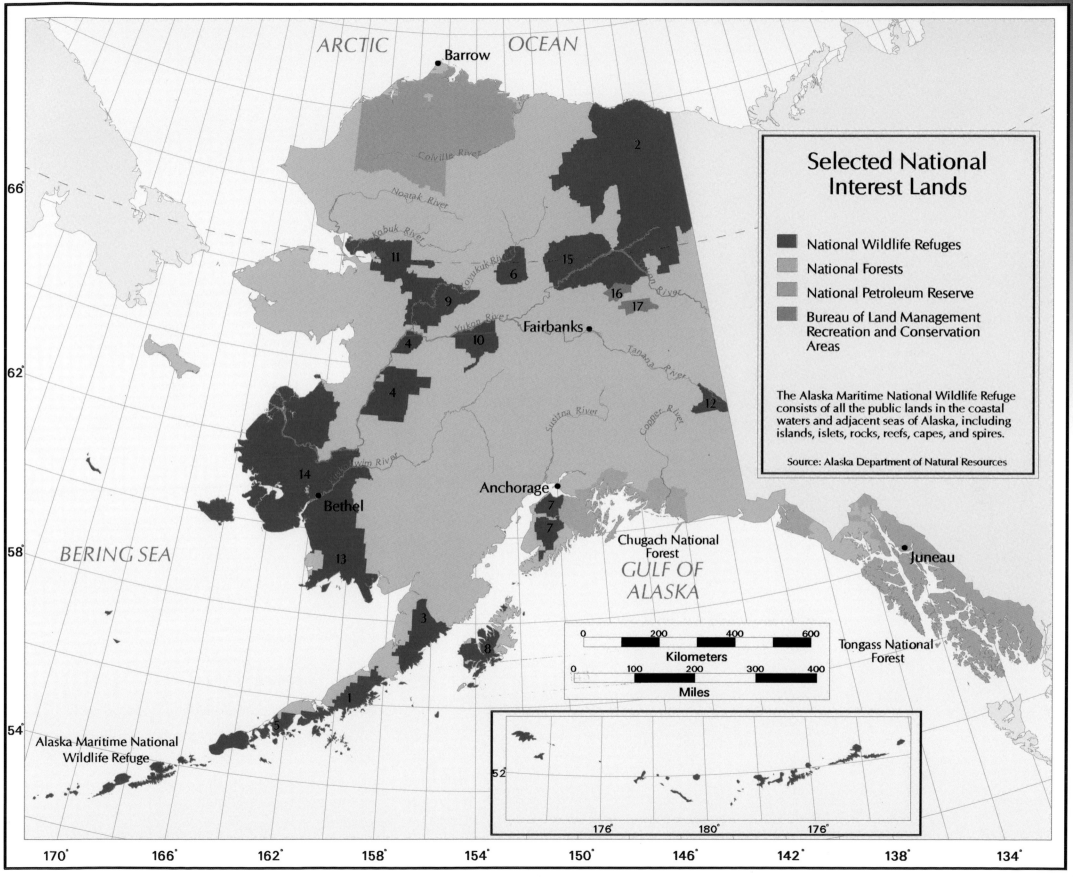

ARCTIC OCEAN

Barrow

Colville River

Noatak River

Kobuk River

Koyukuk River

Yukon River

Fairbanks

Tanana River

Susitna River

Copper River

Kuskokwim River

Bethel

Anchorage

Chugach National Forest

GULF OF ALASKA

Juneau

Tongass National Forest

BERING SEA

Alaska Maritime National Wildlife Refuge

Selected National Interest Lands

- National Wildlife Refuges
- National Forests
- National Petroleum Reserve
- Bureau of Land Management Recreation and Conservation Areas

The Alaska Maritime National Wildlife Refuge consists of all the public lands in the coastal waters and adjacent seas of Alaska, including islands, islets, rocks, reefs, capes, and spires.

Source: Alaska Department of Natural Resources

| 0 | 200 | 400 | 600 |
Kilometers

| 0 | 100 | 200 | 300 | 400 |
Miles

Map 41–Historic and Archaeological Landmarks

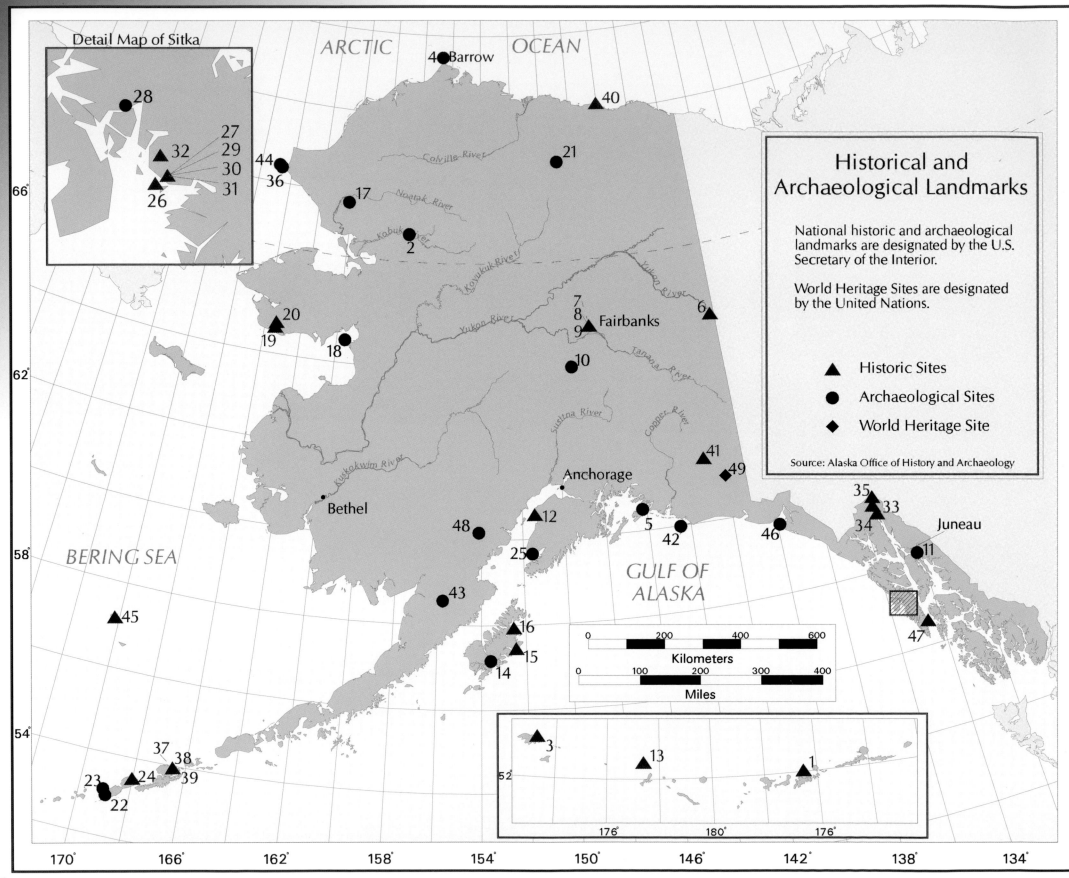

Detail Map of Sitka

ARCTIC OCEAN

4 Barrow

40

Colville River

21

44
36

Noatak River

17

2

Kobuk River

66°

Kovukuk River

Yukon River

7
8
9 Fairbanks

6

20

19

Yukon River

18

Tanana River

62°

10

Historical and Archaeological Landmarks

National historic and archaeological landmarks are designated by the U.S. Secretary of the Interior.

World Heritage Sites are designated by the United Nations.

▲ Historic Sites

● Archaeological Sites

◆ World Heritage Site

Source: Alaska Office of History and Archaeology

Susitna River

Copper River

41

49

35
33

34

Juneau

Anchorage

58°

BERING SEA

Bethel

12

48

5

42

46

11

25

GULF OF
ALASKA

43

45

16

15

14

0   200   400   600
Kilometers

0 100 200 300 400
Miles

47

54°

37
38
23 24
39

22

3

13

52°

1

176°   180°   176°

170°   166°   162°   158°   154°   150°   146°   142°   138°   134°

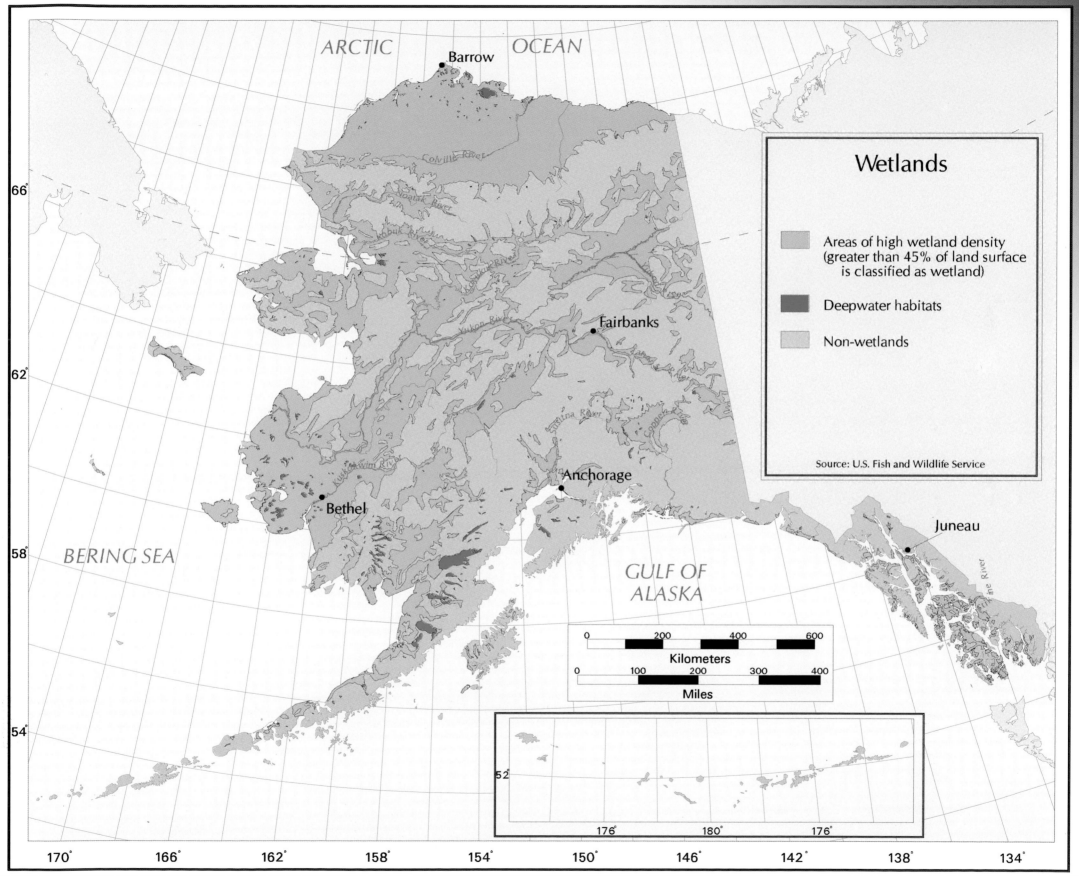

ARCTIC OCEAN

Barrow

Colville River

66°

Noatak River

Kobuk River

Fairbanks

62°

BERING SEA

Bethel

58°

Anchorage

Juneau

GULF OF
ALASKA

Wetlands

Areas of high wetland density
(greater than 45% of land surface
is classified as wetland)

Deepwater habitats

Non-wetlands

Source: U.S. Fish and Wildlife Service

Kuskokwim River

Yukon River

Susitna River

Copper River

Stikine River

0   200   400   600
Kilometers

0   100   200   300   400
Miles

54°

52°

176°   180°   176°

170°   166°   162°   158°   154°   150°   146°   142°   138°   134°

Map 43–Subsistence Harvests in Seven Villages

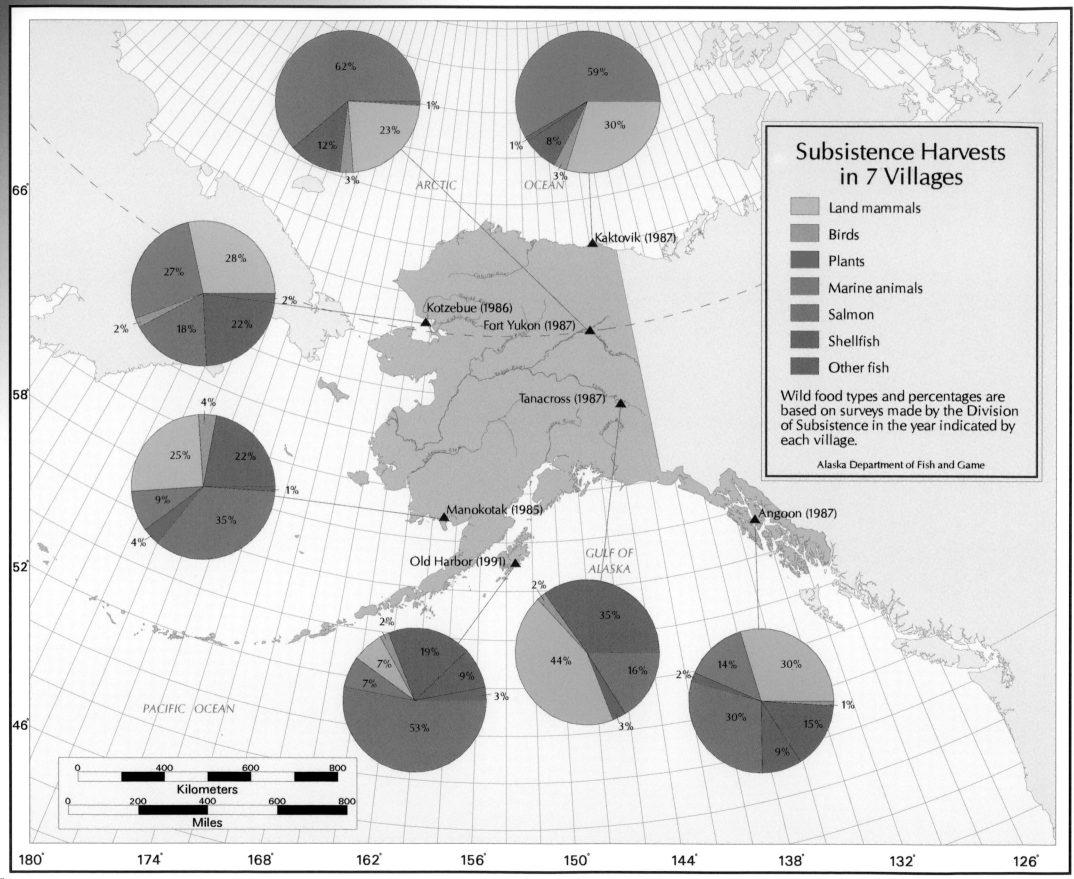

Subsistence Harvests in Seven Villages

Kaktovik (1987)

Kotzebue (1986)

Fort Yukon (1987)

Tanacross (1987)

Manokotak (1985)

Old Harbor (1991)

Angoon (1987)

ARCTIC   OCEAN

GULF OF ALASKA

PACIFIC OCEAN

Subsistence Harvests in 7 Villages

- Land mammals
- Birds
- Plants
- Marine animals
- Salmon
- Shellfish
- Other fish

Wild food types and percentages are based on surveys made by the Division of Subsistence in the year indicated by each village.

Alaska Department of Fish and Game

Kilometers
0   400   600   800

Miles
0   200   400   600   800

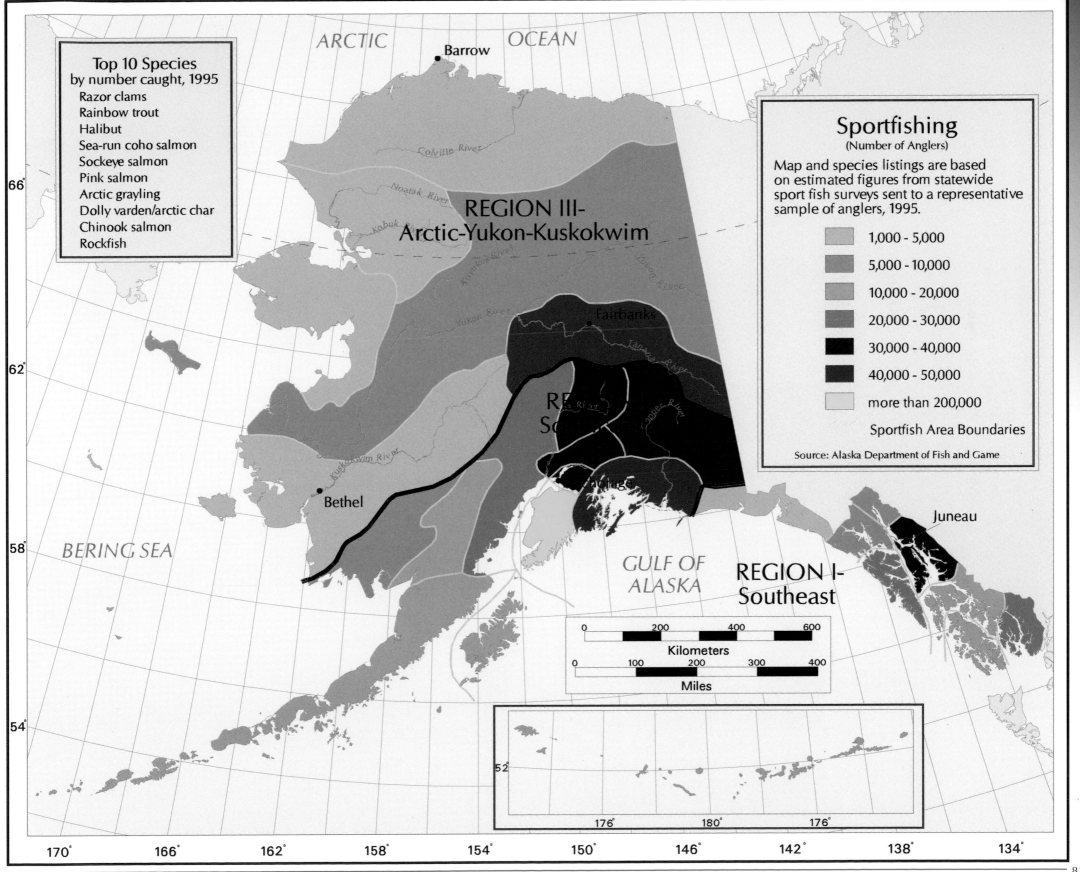

Top 10 Species
by number caught, 1995
Razor clams
Rainbow trout
Halibut
Sea-run coho salmon
Sockeye salmon
Pink salmon
Arctic grayling
Dolly varden/arctic char
Chinook salmon
Rockfish

ARCTIC OCEAN
Barrow

Colville River
Noatak River
Kobuk River

REGION III-
Arctic-Yukon-Kuskokwim

Koyukuk River
Yukon River
Fairbanks
Tanana River
Copper River

Kuskokwim River

Bethel

Anchorage

BERING SEA

GULF OF
ALASKA

REGION I-
Southeast

Juneau

Sportfishing
(Number of Anglers)

Map and species listings are based
on estimated figures from statewide
sport fish surveys sent to a representative
sample of anglers, 1995.

1,000 - 5,000
5,000 - 10,000
10,000 - 20,000
20,000 - 30,000
30,000 - 40,000
40,000 - 50,000
more than 200,000

Sportfish Area Boundaries

Source: Alaska Department of Fish and Game

| 0 | 200 | 400 | 600 |
Kilometers
| 0 | 100 | 200 | 300 | 400 |
Miles

52°

176°   180°   176°

170°   166°   162°   158°   154°   150°   146°   142°   138°   134°

66°
62°
58°
54°

Map 45–Hunting and Trapping

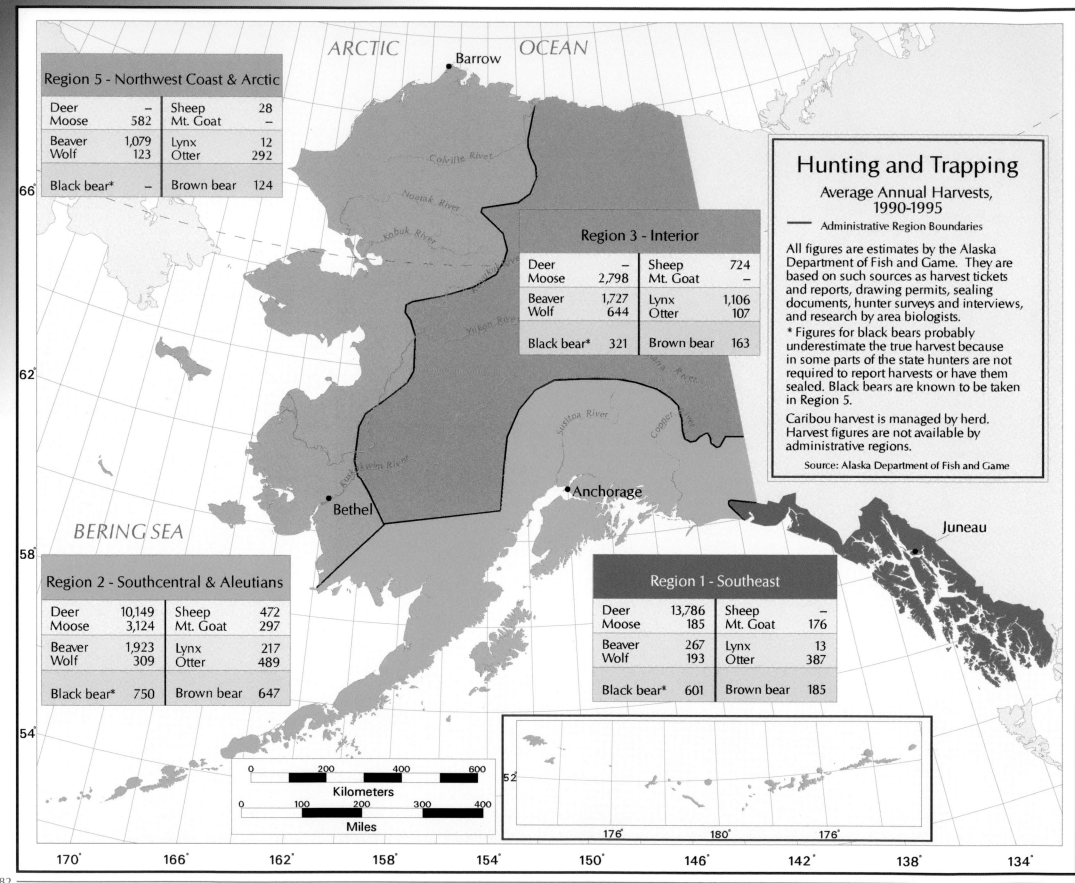

Region 5 - Northwest Coast & Arctic

Deer	–	Sheep	28
Moose	582	Mt. Goat	–
Beaver	1,079	Lynx	12
Wolf	123	Otter	292
Black bear*	–	Brown bear	124

Region 3 - Interior

Deer	–	Sheep	724
Moose	2,798	Mt. Goat	–
Beaver	1,727	Lynx	1,106
Wolf	644	Otter	107
Black bear*	321	Brown bear	163

Hunting and Trapping

Average Annual Harvests, 1990-1995

—— Administrative Region Boundaries

All figures are estimates by the Alaska Department of Fish and Game. They are based on such sources as harvest tickets and reports, drawing permits, sealing documents, hunter surveys and interviews, and research by area biologists.

* Figures for black bears probably underestimate the true harvest because in some parts of the state hunters are not required to report harvests or have them sealed. Black bears are known to be taken in Region 5.

Caribou harvest is managed by herd. Harvest figures are not available by administrative regions.

Source: Alaska Department of Fish and Game

Region 2 - Southcentral & Aleutians

Deer	10,149	Sheep	472
Moose	3,124	Mt. Goat	297
Beaver	1,923	Lynx	217
Wolf	309	Otter	489
Black bear*	750	Brown bear	647

Region 1 - Southeast

Deer	13,786	Sheep	–
Moose	185	Mt. Goat	176
Beaver	267	Lynx	13
Wolf	193	Otter	387
Black bear*	601	Brown bear	185

ARCTIC OCEAN

Barrow

Colville River

Noatak River

Kobuk River

Yukon River

Susitna River

Copper River

Kuskokwim River

Bethel

BERING SEA

Anchorage

Juneau

Kilometers			
0	200	400	600

Miles			
0	100	200	300	400

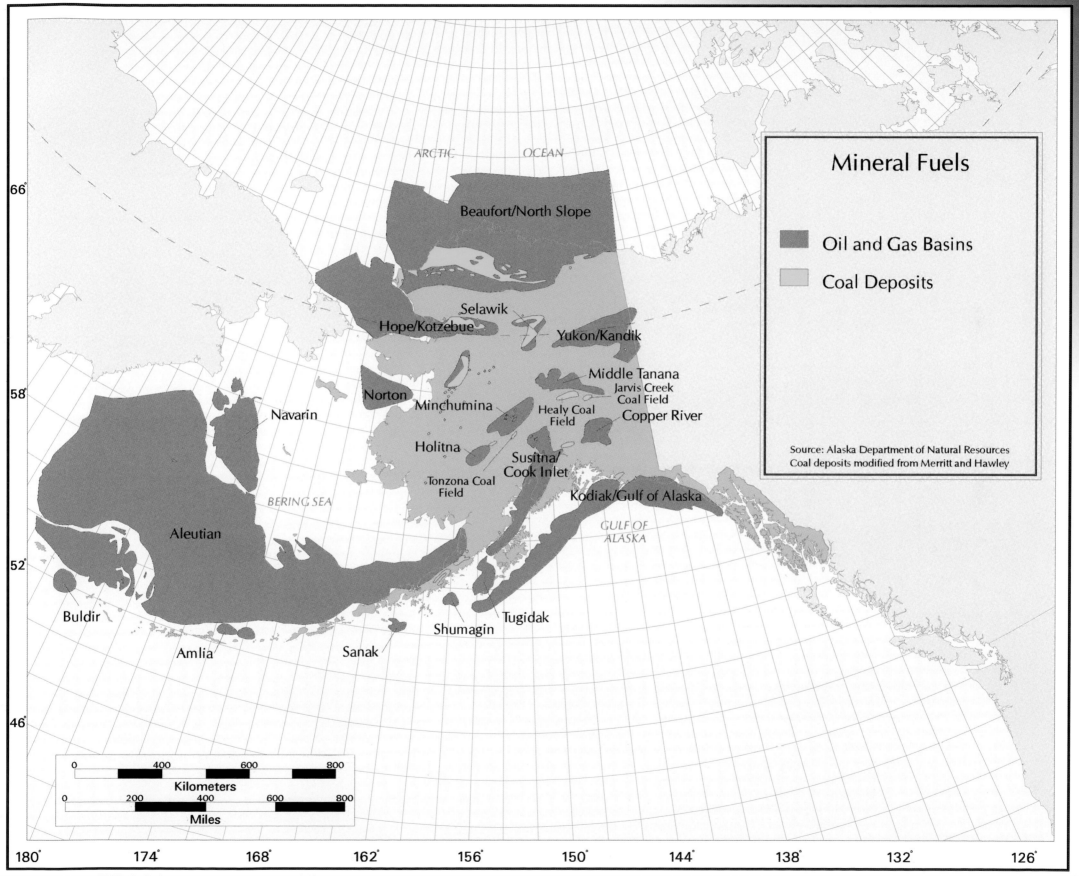

Mineral Fuels

- ▉ Oil and Gas Basins
- ▢ Coal Deposits

Source: Alaska Department of Natural Resources
Coal deposits modified from Merritt and Hawley

ARCTIC OCEAN

Beaufort/North Slope

Selawik

Hope/Kotzebue

Yukon/Kandik

Middle Tanana

Jarvis Creek
Coal Field

Norton

Minchumina

Healy Coal
Field

Copper River

Navarin

Holitna

Susitna/
Cook Inlet

Tonzona Coal
Field

BERING SEA

Kodiak/Gulf of Alaska

GULF OF
ALASKA

Aleutian

Buldir

Tugidak

Shumagin

Amlia

Sanak

Kilometers

Miles

Map 47–Commercial Fisheries

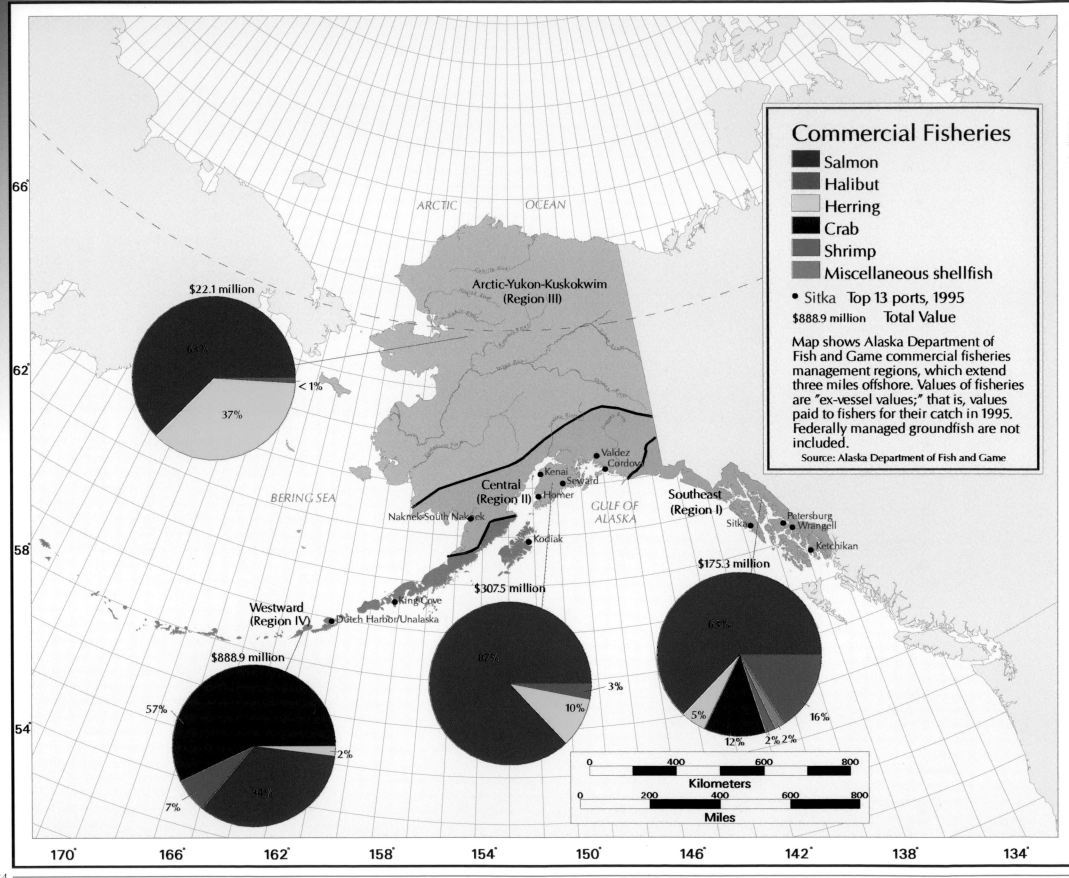

ARCTIC OCEAN

Arctic-Yukon-Kuskokwim
(Region III)

Commercial Fisheries

- Salmon
- Halibut
- Herring
- Crab
- Shrimp
- Miscellaneous shellfish

● Sitka Top 13 ports, 1995

$888.9 million Total Value

Map shows Alaska Department of
Fish and Game commercial fisheries
management regions, which extend
three miles offshore. Values of fisheries
are "ex-vessel values;" that is, values
paid to fishers for their catch in 1995.
Federally managed groundfish are not
included.

Source: Alaska Department of Fish and Game

$22.1 million

63%

< 1%

37%

BERING SEA

Central
(Region II)

●Kenai
●Seward
●Valdez
Cordova
●Homer

Naknek South Naknek

Southeast
(Region I)

GULF OF
ALASKA

●Sitka
Petersburg
Wrangell
Ketchikan

●Kodiak

$175.3 million

63%

Westward
(Region IV)

●King Cove

●Dutch Harbor/Unalaska

$307.5 million

87%

3%

10%

5%

12%

2% 2%

16%

$888.9 million

57%

2%

7%

34%

0   400   600   800
Kilometers

0   200   400   600   800
Miles

170°   166°   162°   158°   154°   150°   146°   142°   138°   134°

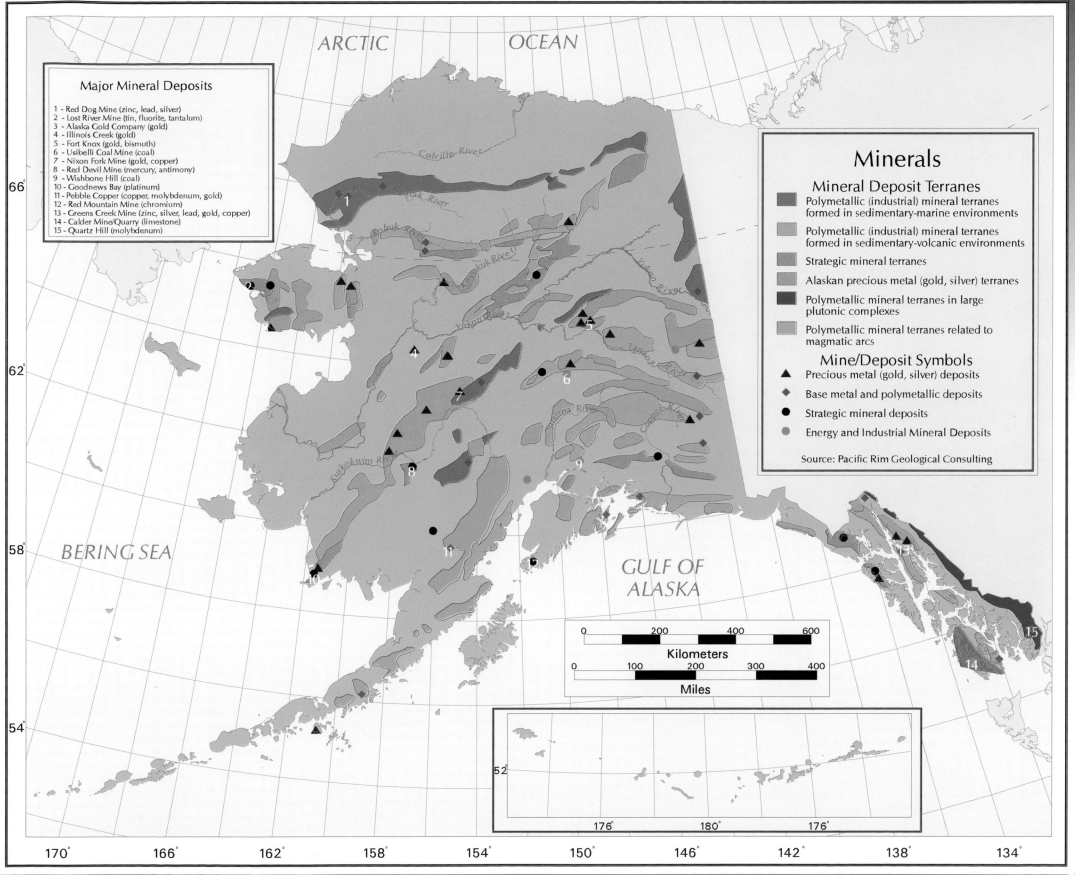

Major Mineral Deposits

1 - Red Dog Mine (zinc, lead, silver)
2 - Lost River Mine (tin, fluorite, tantalum)
3 - Alaska Gold Company (gold)
4 - Illinois Creek (gold)
5 - Fort Knox (gold, bismuth)
6 - Usibelli Coal Mine (coal)
7 - Nixon Fork Mine (gold, copper)
8 - Red Devil Mine (mercury, antimony)
9 - Wishbone Hill (coal)
10 - Goodnews Bay (platinum)
11 - Pebble Copper (copper, molybdenum, gold)
12 - Red Mountain Mine (chromium)
13 - Greens Creek Mine (zinc, silver, lead, gold, copper)
14 - Calder Mine/Quarry (limestone)
15 - Quartz Hill (molybdenum)

Minerals

Mineral Deposit Terranes

Polymetallic (industrial) mineral terranes formed in sedimentary-marine environments

Polymetallic (industrial) mineral terranes formed in sedimentary-volcanic environments

Strategic mineral terranes

Alaskan precious metal (gold, silver) terranes

Polymetallic mineral terranes in large plutonic complexes

Polymetallic mineral terranes related to magmatic arcs

Mine/Deposit Symbols

▲ Precious metal (gold, silver) deposits

◆ Base metal and polymetallic deposits

● Strategic mineral deposits

● Energy and Industrial Mineral Deposits

Source: Pacific Rim Geological Consulting

ARCTIC OCEAN

Colville River

Noatak River

Kobuk River

Koyukuk River

Yukon River

Tanana River

Kuskokwim River

Susitna River

Copper River

BERING SEA

GULF OF ALASKA

Kilometers

0   200   400   600

Miles

0   100   200   300   400

Map 49–Potential Agricultural Lands

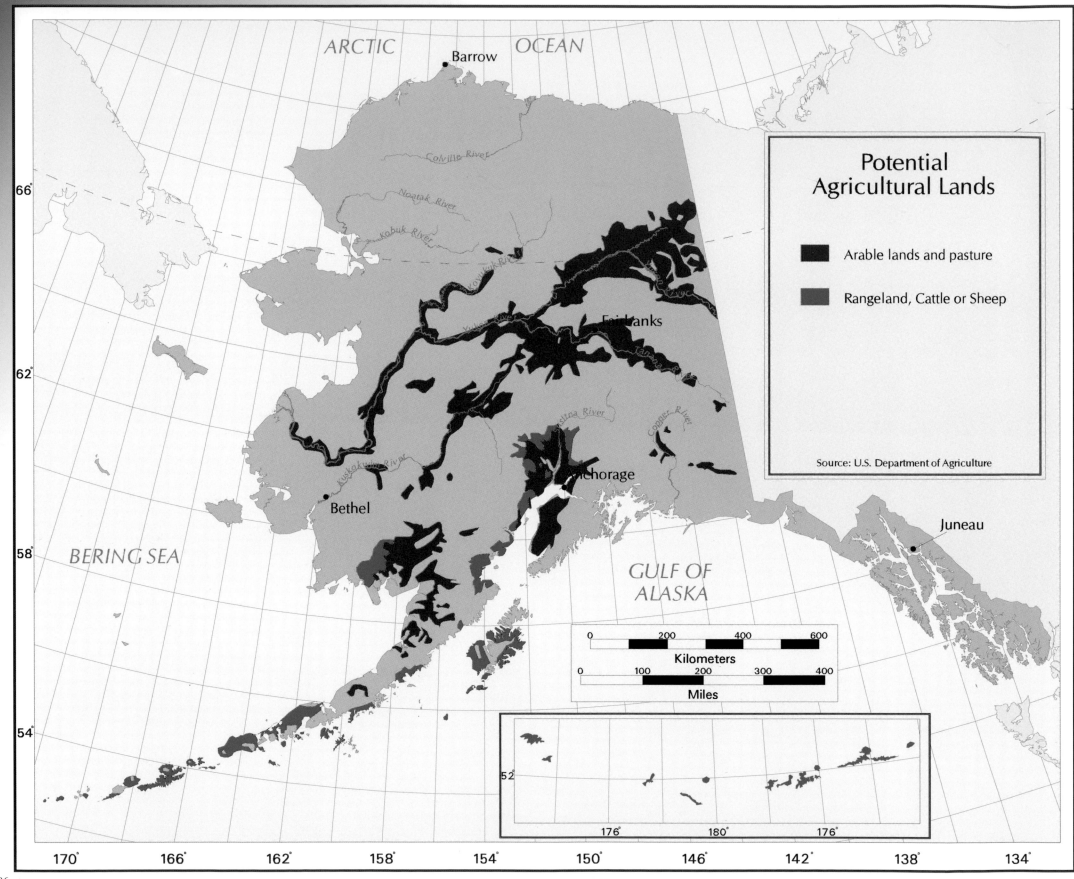

ARCTIC OCEAN

Barrow

Colville River

Noatak River

Kobuk River

66°

62°

Yukon River

Fairbanks

Tanana River

Susitna River

Copper River

Anchorage

Kuskokwim River

58°

BERING SEA

Bethel

GULF OF ALASKA

Juneau

Potential Agricultural Lands

■ Arable lands and pasture

■ Rangeland, Cattle or Sheep

Source: U.S. Department of Agriculture

54°

0   200   400   600
Kilometers
0   100   200   300   400
Miles

52°

176°   180°   176°

170°   166°   162°   158°   154°   150°   146°   142°   138°   134°

Uses of Geography

Section 5 brings together many of the themes and concepts incorporated in the preceding four sections of the atlas. In all seven articles in this section, people use geography to interpret the past, to understand the present, and to plan for the future.

Uses of Geography shows just seven of the many ways modern Alaskans are observing and describing their homeland: in hand-drawn maps sketched during on-the-ground field studies, in colorful thematic maps that illuminate connections between physical features and oral tradition, in complex maps on Geographic Information Systems, and in interactive maps available to the public through the Internet. These articles show just a few examples of how professional geographers, city planners, archaeologists, authors and publishers, toponymists, Native elders, GIS technicians, and Alaska students are contributing to a growing understanding of Alaska's physical and human geography.

People in these articles see Alaska from many perspectives. Some make large-scale maps of stream beds or a single beach, some compare aerial photos to track land use changes over time, some document land uses centuries old, some compile data on resources and how they have been or might be affected by human activities. No less important is the role many people featured here play in making geographic information available to large numbers of citizens and decisionmakers. In a society as populous and technologically advanced as modern Alaska, people want and need accurate information about Alaska's physical geography and the opportunities and considerations related to life in this particular place on earth.

Perhaps the clearest message of all these articles, and of the atlas as a whole, is the interconnectedness of people and the physical environment in Alaska. People are inevitably influenced by characteristics of climate, terrain, natural resources, and Alaska's spatial characteristics, including its location in the Northern world. The physical environment is to some degree inevitably impacted by all human activities and by population, transportation, communication, economics, and trade. Within this web of space and time, the past influences and informs the present.

From Barrow on the Arctic Coastal Plain to Juneau in the Southeast Panhandle, these articles show modern Alaskans—government employees, scholars, Native elders, naturalists, professional geographers, GIS technicians, townspeople, and students using geography to improve their lives and surroundings. By applying geography to the past, they help us understand how physical and human factors intersected to make the world as it was and as it is today. By applying geography to the present, they help us understand how our daily lives affect and are influenced by the world around us. Looking to the future, they show us how we can use what we have learned to influence what our lives and the world that surrounds us will be like in generations to come.

Richard Carstensen

Stream mapping. *Students Hannah Lager and Monika Bethers from Dzantik'i Heeni School sketch onto a map form such features as stream edge, tree trunks, overhead canopy gaps, trails, brush, and fallen logs. Students create maps by stretching a 200-foot tape down the stream. They lay a second 100-foot tape perpendicular to it, extending 50 feet to both sides. Then they gradually move the 100-foot tape downstream in 25-foot steps and complete the rough field draft.*

(See story on following pages)

Exploring Your School

Forest, stream, and wetland studies at Dzantik'i Heeni Middle School

By Richard Carstensen,
Naturalist,
Discovery Foundation

In the Tlingit language, *Dzantik'i Heeni* means "creek of the baby flounders." The beautiful school now known by that name was built in 1992 on ground that biologists described as *forested wetland*, a fragile habitat. The City of Juneau's building permit requires that students of the school learn about the surrounding wetlands, streams, and forests. The city has contracted with Discovery Foundation, a natural history education group, to work with the school's teachers and students. Gradually students, government researchers, and consultants are creating a detailed description of what we call today the Switzer Creek Watershed.

Dzantik'i Heeni offers extraordinary opportunities in nature study. Ancient old-growth forest is literally only seconds from the school doors. Students can study *succession*, the change in natural communities over time, by visiting nearby clearcuts of different ages. A large, undeveloped wet meadow to the southeast can be reached quickly by boardwalk, and the salt marshes of the Mendenhall Wetlands Refuge are only 15 minutes away. Black bear, deer,

Art by student Dävin Savikko

goshawk, and marbled murrelets inhabit the rarely visited forest immediately above the school. Mountain goats gaze down from their cliffs in Switzer's headwaters.

How do we study all this? We take the first step in most environmental research projects, whether they are aimed at fish habitat, glacial landforms, or effects of human development: **We make maps!**

As part of Water Watch, a nationwide stream study organized and partly funded by the Environmental Protection Agency, we study Switzer Creek, mapping stream sections and taking monthly water quality measurements. The most pristine part of Switzer Creek we named Robin Trib. (See D-12 on the habitat map on the next page.) With our data this tributary can be compared to more heavily impacted sections of Switzer Creek, such as Marriott Pond (shown in the large scale inset map from the habitat map) and the extremely damaged Duck Creek in nearby Mendenhall Valley, which we study with students from Floyd Dryden Middle School.

We hope the examples of our work on these pages give other students some ideas about ways to study natural and human surroundings around their schools.

Aerial photographs are extremely useful to habitat mappers. The Forest Service, city planning departments, and other government agencies are good sources of aerial photos. Agencies may allow schools to make copies from their 9"x9" prints. We like to photograph them as 35mm slides because they can then be projected onto paper and traced at any scale and orientation. To see even more in these photos, we look at pairs of them in 3D using viewers called stereoscopes.

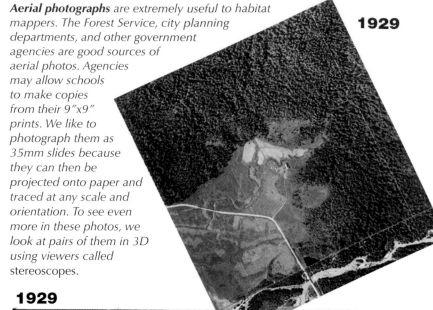

1929

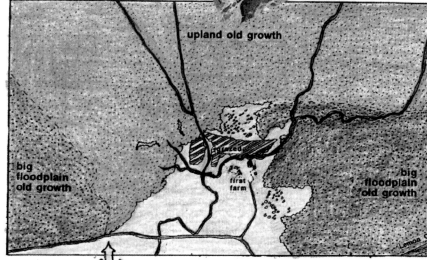

1929

upland old growth

big floodplain old growth

cut'd

first farm

big floodplain old growth

Lemon Cr

1992

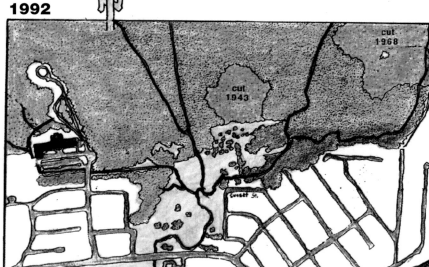

cut 1968

cut 1943

1992

Historical series by Inua Blevins, student

These two maps show the area around Dzantik'i Heeni Middle School in Juneau. They were traced from projected aerial photographs taken in 1929 and 1992. There are many differences between them. The 1968 and 1943 clearcuts don't appear in the earlier map. In 1929, only one dirt road passed through the Lemon Creek Valley.

The major difference between the maps is the disappearance of the floodplain old-growth forests. They are shown only in the 1929 photo because they were sold away after that for lumber. Later the land was used for mobile homes (southwest corner) and housing tracts (southeast corner). Long ago Switzer and Lemon Creeks left deposits of coarse sand and gravel that make well-drained sites for housing.

Inua Blevins and Richard Carstensen

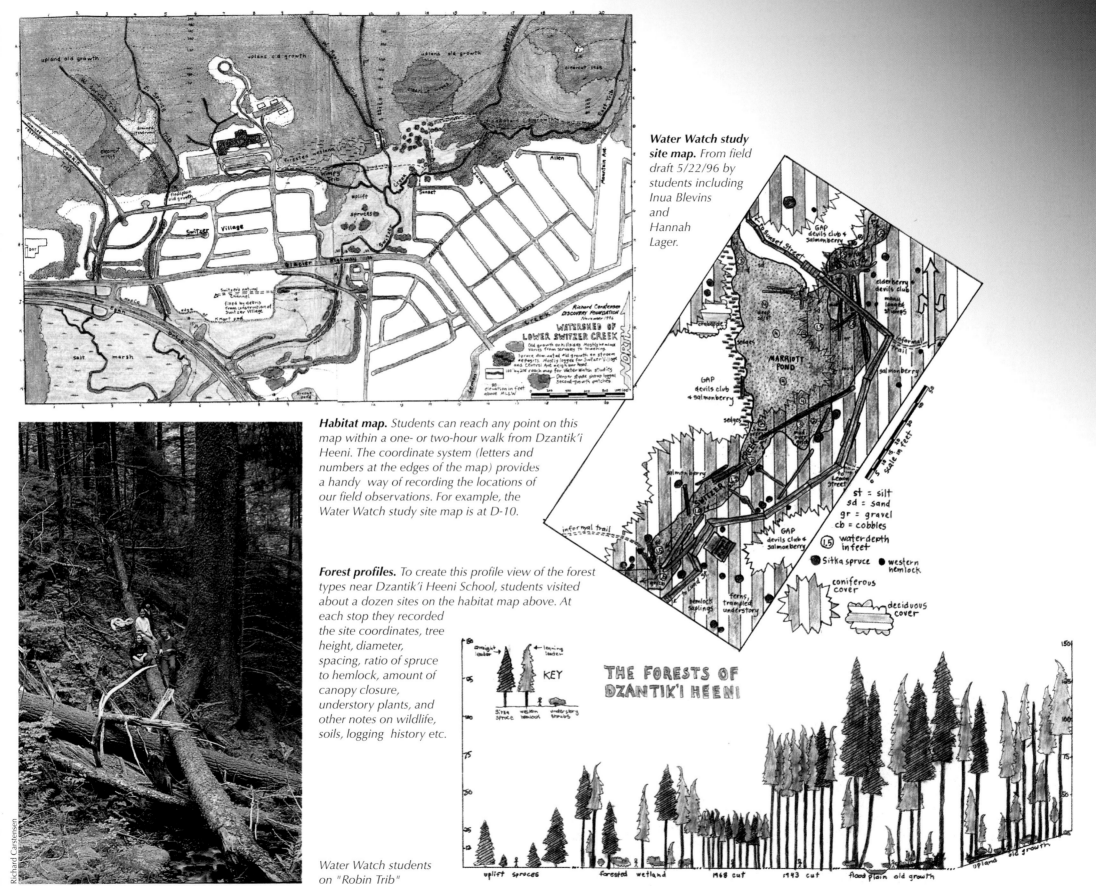

Water Watch study site map. From field draft 5/22/96 by students including Inua Blevins and Hannah Lager.

Habitat map. Students can reach any point on this map within a one- or two-hour walk from Dzantik'i Heeni. The coordinate system (letters and numbers at the edges of the map) provides a handy way of recording the locations of our field observations. For example, the Water Watch study site map is at D-10.

Forest profiles. To create this profile view of the forest types near Dzantik'i Heeni School, students visited about a dozen sites on the habitat map above. At each stop they recorded the site coordinates, tree height, diameter, spacing, ratio of spruce to hemlock, amount of canopy closure, understory plants, and other notes on wildlife, soils, logging history etc.

Water Watch students on "Robin Trib"

Richard Carstensen

st = silt
sd = sand
gr = gravel
cb = cobbles

THE FORESTS OF DZANTIK'I HEENI

uplift spruces   forested wetland   1968 cut   1943 cut   flood plain old growth   upland old growth

Oil Spill Mapping Along Alaska's Southcentral Coast

By Greg Chaney,
Geomorphologist and
City Planner

I said, "Never underestimate the power of maps" to a co-worker who commented on how the result of six months of shoreline surveys, involving hundreds of people, was displayed on a single sheet of paper. It was September of 1989, and I had spent the past six months working as a member of the *Exxon Valdez* Oil Spill response team. We had attempted to recover more than 11 million gallons of Alaska North Slope crude oil spilled into Prince William Sound.

I first learned about the spill from a newspaper article that showed a map of Prince William Sound with an arrow pointing to the leaking tanker *Exxon Valdez* grounded on Bligh Reef. My concern grew as each subsequent newspaper displayed an updated oil spill map showing an expanding ink blot tracing the oil's expansion westward. Soon news reports accompanying these maps were accompanied by photographs of dead and dying wildlife that had been overwhelmed by black crude. Oil spread more than 500 miles across Alaska's southcentral coast, reaching Kodiak Island and the Alaska Peninsula.

At first, efforts to clean up oil from beaches were inefficient, partly because crews did not have accurate maps to guide them to the beaches where the most oil remained. Reality was far more complex than the expanding ink blot of oil reported in the media. Oil floated on the sea in large swirling patterns resembling great octopuses with trailing tentacles.

To make things more complicated, the shoreline consisted of steep glacially carved bays and headlands with pocket beaches strung like beads between them. When random ribbons of oil touched the irregular coast, a wild variety of oil concentrations resulted. In places oil distribution appeared to be the work of a crazed giant who had run along beaches with a broad paintbrush dipped in crude oil. It looked as if he had splattered droplets here, painted a broad band there, and farther down the beach dumped the rest of the bucket in a gooey continuous sheet.

Accurate maps showing where the oil was were needed to direct cleanup crews. First, helicopters flew along shorelines in the spill zone to videotape stranded oil. These video tapes were brought back to an emergency cartography lab in Valdez and combined with eyewitness reports.

The information was then transferred to preliminary computer maps. Unfortunately, maps made from aerial videos were not always accurate because regions of black wet rocks might appear to be covered with oil or oil could be missed if it was buried. Buried oil was impossible to find without digging, so these maps were then forwarded to Shoreline Cleanup Advisory Teams (SCAT) who surveyed oiled beaches on foot. This is where my job started.

SCAT teams were composed of a geomorphologist to map oil distribution, a biologist who primarily documented intertidal organisms so cleanup workers would not harm them, and an archaeologist to ensure archaeological sites were not accidentally damaged. As the team's "oil geomorphologist" I used the aerial video maps as a general guide and drew sketch maps of specific sites. The hand drawn sketch maps showed reference landmarks to guide cleanup crews to the oil we found. In addition, oil concentration was classified into categories and entered into computerized shoreline maps. These reports, based on maps, were then used to establish cleanup priorities and recommend appropriate treatment methods. Ultimately the massive response effort was prioritized, directed, and carried out using maps as its primary guidance tools. Without the rapid deployment of multiple mapping teams, the army of cleanup workers and equipment that descended on Alaska's southcentral coast during 1989 would have been blind and directionless.

Crew cleaning an oiled beach

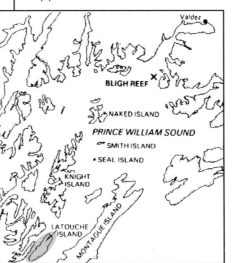

Field map made by Greg Chaney during the Exxon Valdez *oil spill cleanup.*

Debbie Corbett, center, and other archaeologists measure a site in the Aleutians.

Debbie Corbett, an archaeologist with the U.S. Fish and Wildlife Service, works on Alaska's farthest west Aleutian Islands.

Since 1983, when she worked for the Bureau of Indian Affairs, Corbett has been using geography by mapping pre-European village and house sites in the Aleutians. Corbett says archaeologists look for tools, artifacts, houses, and other remains of early people, but their goal is really to understand the people who left those things behind.

Corbett studies archaeological sites on the Near Islands, islands originally named because they were "near" to Russia. The Near Islands include Attu, Agattu, and the three Semichi Islands of Shemya, Nizki, and Alaid.

Corbett says evidence shows the Eastern Aleutians were occupied as far back as 8,000 to 9,000 B.C., but the oldest evidence of early people in the Near Islands dates back 3,500 years ago, to about 1,500 B.C. Archaeologists believe people from the eastern Aleutians gradually worked their way west. They developed settlement patterns different from those of the eastern Aleuts.

"We know people in this area made a living off the ocean," Corbett said, "so we focus our search along the coastline. We also know everyone needs fresh water and a place to physically build a home, so we look for places low and flat with a stream nearby."

Corbett has located 107 sites, and she measured the size of more than 90 of them to create the map shown on this page. By correlating the locations and sizes of the sites with the surrounding landscape, she learned a great deal about the western Aleuts.

Corbett found the largest and most complex settlements were near the greatest variety of resources. They were near reefs, where there were shellfish and inshore fishes. They were near shallow offshore waters, where there were halibut, cod, and rockfish and where harbor seals hauled out on the rocks. They were near but not too close to sea lion rookeries. They were also on the eastern ends of the islands, where people could watch for enemy raiders from islands to the east.

Each island had one or two very large sites. Corbett believes these large settlements were winter villages and that at other seasons of the year people spread out to smaller "home" sites to hunt, fish, and pick berries. The presence of many small "single family" houses in the Near Islands suggests a different social grouping than among the Aleuts on the eastern Aleutians. In the East a single structure might house an entire village of 50 to 100 people.

Corbett is finding other clues about the western Aleuts in the remains at various sites. For example, Near Islands people made tools such as arrow and spear tips and knives from stone. Certain types of stone, however, are found on only one or two islands. Agattu, for example, has a fine-grained sedimentary rock like argillite that makes beautiful tools. Yet tools made from this rock are found on all the Near Islands. That suggests that people visited and traded among the islands.

Other remains tell a great deal about life among Near Islands Aleuts. There are tools made from sea mammal bone: needles, wedges for working wood, harpoon points, handles, and digging sticks. There are remains of grass baskets, matting, and ropes.

Aleuts no longer live on the Near Islands, but Corbett still hopes to learn more about the islands' early inhabitants. "We're trying to understand how people lived in a place that seems tremendously difficult and forbidding to us," she said. "We know they survived and had real comforts. They were happy and healthy. But we still have a lot to learn about their way of life. The whole thing is a mystery, and we're just starting to follow the clues."

Aleut Settlements in the Western Aleutians

"Every time you dig a hole in the ground you're learning something more about the past."

–Debbie Corbett

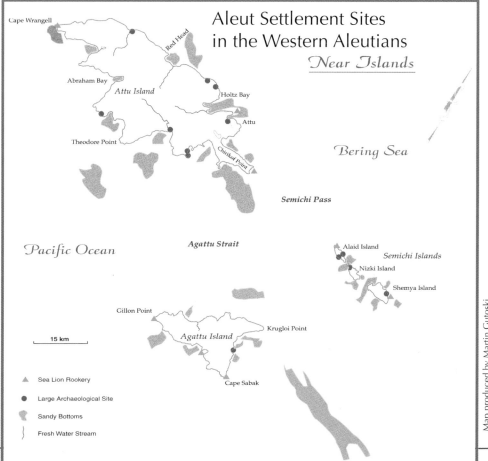

Aleut Settlement Sites in the Western Aleutians

Near Islands

Cape Wrangell

Red Head

Abraham Bay

Attu Island

Holtz Bay

Attu

Theodore Point

Chirikof Point

Bering Sea

Semichi Pass

Alaid Island

Semichi Islands

Nizki Island

Shemya Island

Gillon Point

Pacific Ocean

Agattu Strait

Krugloi Point

15 km

Agattu Island

Cape Sabak

▲ Sea Lion Rookery

● Large Archaeological Site

Sandy Bottoms

Fresh Water Stream

Map produced by Martin Gutoski

D. Corbett

Sharing the excitement of discovery

30 years of *Alaska Geographic*®

One of the best-known and respected sources of information about Alaska geography is housed in a modest, one-story building in Anchorage. Located appropriately on International Airport Road, The Alaska Geographic Society is a crossroads for information about Alaska, much as the nearby airport is the nerve center for people visiting or traveling throughout the state.

The non-profit Alaska Geographic Society was formed in 1968 by Bob Henning, a long-time supporter of geography education in Alaska who was then publisher of *Alaska*® magazine, *The Milepost*®, and a series of books on the North. The Society's stated goal has changed little in the 30 years since then. It is "exploring new frontiers of knowledge across the lands of the Polar Rim" and "sharing in the excitement" of what its writers and photographers discover.

In Alaska and elsewhere, the Society is best known for its quarterly publication *Alaska Geographic*®. Each issue is like a combination diary, photo album, and field notebook about some aspect of life in Alaska. Together, the 99 issues published since 1972 create one of the most complete portraits available of Alaska's landscapes, people, natural features, and industries.

Penny Rennick is editor of Alaska Geographic Society publications, and Kathy Doogan is production director. The two women have worked together at the Society for some 20 years. With a total staff of five and occasional student interns to help them, they coordinate the writing, editing, production, and marketing of four issues of *Alaska Geographic*® each year.

"Once we choose a topic for a monograph," Rennick said, "we have to decide what aspects we want to cover, who knows about those subjects, whether we can reach them, and where we can get photos." For the next six to nine months, Rennick works with writers and photographers, researches and writes certain sections, and provides Doogan with information for creating maps. Doogan designs the book, creates maps on the computer, and lays out the pages in a desktop publishing program. Photos and page layouts are sent to Seattle for conversion into film, which goes to Minnesota, where books are printed, bound, and packaged for delivery.

Over the years, *Alaska Geographic*® has shared the changing story of Alaska with people around the state and throughout the world. Some issues contain stories, maps, and photos of Alaska mammals, glaciers, volcanoes, and weather. Some cover industries such as salmon fishing, forestry, oil, gas, and minerals. Some depict places and regions: Kodiak Island, Sitka, the Pribilof Islands, the Brooks Range, and Lake Clark/Lake Iliamna.

"If you cover a very large area, you have to leave things out," Rennick said. "If you use a smaller area, you can cover more detail." Over the years various issues have focused on Alaska's Great Interior, Cook Inlet Country, Prince William Sound, the Yukon-Kuskokwim Delta, the Kotzebue Basin, Southeast Alaska, and the Tanana Basin.

Alaska Geographic® also deals with current events. In 1972, as preparations for oil drilling began near Prudhoe Bay, the first issue of *Alaska Geographic*® focused on the North Slope. In 1978, when people throughout the world became concerned about whaling, an issue on Alaska whales and whaling was published. Some issues have carried short articles on current topics such as Alaska's wolves, research at archaeological sites, and work by Northern artists.

Rennick came to the Society in 1976 as assistant to the managing editor. "I've always liked geography," she said, "ever since the fourth grade. Since then I've continued to acquire geographic knowledge on my own by taking college classes, traveling, and just looking at the world around me. I like the physical environment. I like geology. I like visualizing mountains, trees, rivers, and seeing what people do with their environment in different places." It is also important that she knows writing and proper use of the English language.

Doogan got her training on the job. "I learned to make maps because I had to," she said. "I had a little training in design, but I've learned a lot by studying other people's publications. Computers have made my work so much easier. Using them is a really important part of my job."

Translated literally, geography means *earth* (geo) *description* (graphy). Through *Alaska Geographic*® Kathy Doogan and Penny Rennick share accurate descriptions of Alaska—and "the excitement of their discoveries"—with thousands of readers both inside and outside the state.

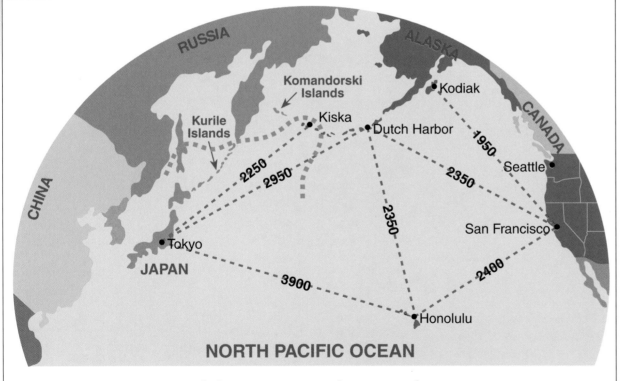

World War II on the Pacific Rim

```
······  Extent of Japanese expansion in Alaska
------  Distances between points, in statute miles
```

(**Source:** *Distances Between Ports*, U.S. Govt. Pub. 151, Defense Mapping Agency, 1995)

Source: © Alaska Geographic Society, map by Kathy Doogan

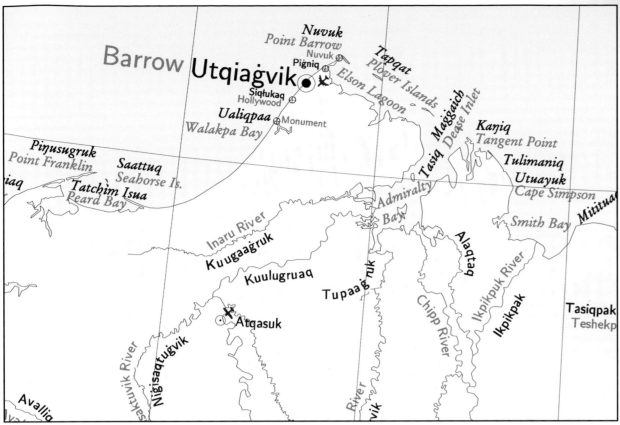

Detail from the Iñupiat-English map of the North Slope Borough

Map excerpt courtesy of North Slope Borough

Technology and Tradition in the North Slope Borough

The North Slope Borough's official map is bilingual. The map is printed with place names in both English and Iñupiaq. The city named Barrow in English is *Utqiaġvik* in Iñupiaq. What is labeled Nigisaktuvik River in gray type (English) has two labels in dark blue type (Iñupiaq). It is *Niġisaqtuġvik* in its southern reaches and *Kuulugruaq* in its northeastern part.

The use of both Iñupiaq and English names on the map reflects strong ideas about how the land should be understood and cared for. The map also reflects the North Slope Borough's decision to use the latest in GIS technology to preserve the past as well as prepare for the future.

Most of the Borough's 6,800 residents are Iñupiaq Eskimo. Their families have lived in the region for generations. In the mid-1970s Borough leaders started a project to record all that could be learned from the region's elders about the history and traditional uses of the land. What the elders said has been compiled into the Traditional Land Use Data Base (TLUD), which describes thousands of sites in the borough. The Data Base also cross-references two computerized archaeological inventories: the state-sponsored Alaska Heritage Resource Survey and archaeologist Ed Hall's descriptions of some 2,800 sites. The TLUD, written in both English and Iñupiaq, allows people to create maps and extract information from all three data bases. The site descriptions tell where people traditionally hunt or camp, where graves or ruins are found, where birds nest or caribou feed. They identify fishing areas, traditional whaling sites, or places where people trap foxes or dig roots.

Gordon Brower of Barrow works in the Permitting Office of the Borough Planning Department, and he is also a member of a respected whaling crew. "It would be a big mistake for anybody to try to decide how land should be used without traditional knowledge," Brower said. He explained that when someone requests a permit to construct a building or drill for oil, the Borough officials who must decide whether to grant the permit need to know if the site is important for other reasons. A place may be an ancient burial site, a source of good drinking water, or a place where people have traditionally found shelter from storms.

Information about such traditional uses of the land has been gathered from elders in all parts of the Borough, Brower explained. Once it has been approved by all eight village councils, it is recorded in the Traditional Land Use Inventory in both English and Iñupiaq. The inventory also describes how people use the land today.

Brower began his work at the Borough in early 1995 after he broke his back while working as a mechanic at Prudhoe Bay. Brower said he had had no experience with computers at the time, but on the job he learned ArcView and ArcInfo, the GIS programs the Borough uses. "I also spoke my language and was able to speak to the elders," he said, so he was able to combine working on GIS mapping and traveling to villages to interview elders.

"It's very critical that someone be able to handle this information," Brower said. "Once the elders are gone, we're not going to see it anymore. Tradition can be lost really easily."

Coordinating data about traditional uses with precise GIS mapping is important for other reasons. According to Brower, the Borough's GIS and Traditional Land Use Data Base are used for search and rescue efforts, to help borough residents locate shelter cabins and trails, and even to study caribou migrations.

Detail from the North Slope Borough Traditional Land Use Data Base

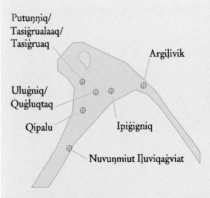

Traditional land Use Inventory Legend

1. Cabins/shelter cabins today
2. Graves/cemetery
3. Ruins/ sod houses/bone
4. Fishing area
5. Trapping area
6. Hunting/camping area
7. Cellars
8. Other (nesting, seals, roots)
9. Whaling settlement
10. Important event/old site
11. Reindeer herding area

Adapted from data courtesy of North Slope Borough

Arġiḷivik - 4, 5, 6, 8.
Igaruni siḷakun. Tatchim iḷuliaŋa tatkimnatchiq, kanagnam nalaani. Aaqhaalliqivik. Ukiumi tiġiganniaġvik, upinġaami iqaluaqpagvik. Kuvraqtuġvik natchiġnun. Upinġirriġviat mitqutaiḷat.

This site is the northern bight of Elson Lagoon, a traditional hunting area for old-squaw ducks. Winter fox trapping area and summer salmon fishing area. Seal hunting is done with gillnets. Summer home to Arctic terns.

Qipalu - 1,5,6,8,9.
Umiaqaġvik atuqtaat ukialliqsiuġmata. Tatkivani iglu suli naparuq ukialliqsiuqtuat atuġuuraat. Ukiumi naniġiaqtuġvik suli upinġaami aivvaksiuġvik, natchiqsiuġvik, suli ugruksiuġvik.

Harbor area used during fall whaling. A shelter cabin used by whalers is still standing. Winter trapping area for fox and summer hunting area for walrus, seal and bearded seal.

New Tools for Land Management

Welcome to the NPR-A Web Site

In 1969 the U.S. Environmental Policy Act took effect. Among other things, it required the writing and distribution of Environmental Impact Statements on proposed development of any federal lands. Environmental Impact Statements (EISs) are intended for the general public as well as for scientists and others with specialized knowledge, but they are usually long and complex. Readers often find it difficult to move from the mass of information presented in writing to a clear understanding of how specific proposals might affect future landscapes.

In 1997-98 the Bureau of Land Management took advantage of new geographic tools and innovative technology to make an EIS more accessible. They worked with John Stroud in the Anchorage office of Environmental Systems Research Institute Inc. (ESRI), a computer mapping company. The result: an Internet web site for what is technically called the Northeast National Petroleum Reserve-Alaska Draft Integrated Activity Plan/Environmental Impact Statement, or the NPR-A IAP/EIS.

The 23.4-million-acre National Petroleum Reserve-Alaska was created in 1923 by President Warren G. Harding to provide for the possibility that the nation might one day need oil. The Reserve is located in arctic Alaska (See Map 40 **Selected National Interest Lands** in Section 4 of this atlas.) The NPR-A Draft IAP/EIS focuses specifically on 4.6 million acres in the northeast corner of the Reserve, where drilling for oil has been proposed. It addresses the question of whether drilling for oil and gas should be allowed in that 4.6-million-acre portion of NPR-A (also called the "planning area"), and if so, what should be done to protect other extensive natural and human resources in the area. It provides vast amounts of information about the environment and offers five "alternatives" for managing the area, whether oil drilling is allowed or not.

The printed Draft IAP/EIS takes up 800 pages and is 2.5 inches (6.25 centimeters) thick. It can be ordered by mail. But the NPR-A web site (*http://aurora.ak.blm.gov/npra/*) makes that entire document available instantly to anyone with access to the Internet, and it offers other features as well.

Stroud created 56 interactive maps showing biological, physical, and social resources and how they relate to areas of low, medium, and high potential for oil. Web site users can zoom in, zoom out, or pan maps showing everything from caribou calving areas, moose density, and major coal bearing rocks, to historical subsistence use, the existing pipeline network, and densities of bird populations, including shorebirds, geese, swans, loons, and pintails.

Comparing the maps with each other and with levels of oil potential reveals the full range of resources in the proposed drilling area and shows how various resources overlap. It is only one step further for web site users to begin evaluating how particular resources could be affected by drilling for oil and building the necessary infrastructure under the various alternatives offered in the IAP/EIS.

"Visitors to the web site are viewing the very same mapping information that the scientists on this project use firsthand," Stroud said. "Then they are invited to send in their comments on the IAP/EIS and the proposed management alternatives.

"It's very exciting that people can see the document, view these maps, search out specific information, and submit their comments in a matter of minutes," Stroud said. "That's quite an improvement over the time it would take through conventional mail."

Over a period of several months, nearly 1,000 visitors used the NPR-A site, averaging 12 minutes per visit. A number of people used the site to file their comments about the draft plan.

In creating the NPR-A site, Stroud integrated a number of new and different technologies, including HTML, component architecture, Internet scripting languages, and client/server programs, all while taking into account current limitations and requirements of web browsers and the Worldwide Web.

And there's more to come. He says, "The next wave of technology will be distributed databases found on both the Internet and CD-ROM. Those will contain documents such as the NPR-A IAP/EIS that work in concert with GIS maps. People will be able to draw polygons around areas of interest and call up information about them almost instantaneously. Very exciting!"

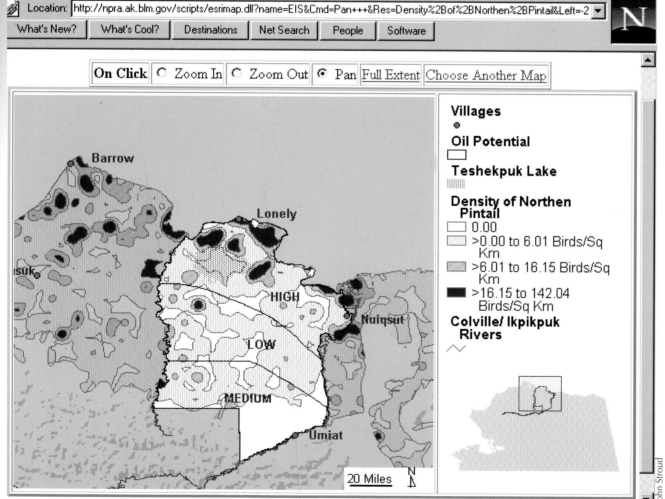

An interactive map from the NPR-A web site

John Stroud

Map produced by Martin Gutoski

Athabaskan River Names in Alaska

Official name	Language	Native name	Meaning
Western southcentral Alaska			
1 - Holitna River	Dena'ina	Haghelitnu	grease-current river
2 - Talkeetna River	Dena'ina	K'dalkitnu	food-is-stored river
3 - Nowitna River	Koyukon	Nogheet No'	frog river
4 - Kanuti River	Koyukon	Kk'oonootno'	? -island river
5 - Nenana River	Tanana	Neenayh No'	camping-place river
6 - South Fork Koyukuk River	Koyukon	Neek'eeleh No'	fish-run-ends river
7 - Chena River	Tanana	Ch'eno'	river of something (game)
8 - Hoziana River	Koyukon	Oodzaa No'	? river (uncertain meaning)
Eastern Alaska at boundary on Yukon River			
9 - Beaver Creek	Gwich'in	Tsenjik	beaver (fur) creek
	Koyukon	Tsogho Neekk'e, Tsonjek	
10 - Porcupine River	Gwich'in	Ch'ôonjik	quill river
11 - Black River	Gwich'in	Draanjik	cache river
at boundary on Tanana River (both stems are used)			
12 - Goodpaster River	Tanana	Jiize Na'	camp robber (gray jay) river
	Tanacross	Jiiz Ndíig	(same)
13 - Fortymile River	Tanacross	Ch'edzagh' Ndíig	ear river
14 - Nabesna River	Upper Tanana	Naabiah Niign	? stone river

Athabaskan Place Names for Rivers in Alaska

People like to name things—other people, objects, ideas, and geographic features such as Mt. Redoubt or the Tanana River. Names help identify features when we are describing them to others. Names may express a group's sense of ownership of a place. Names can show that people attach special value to a place. They might describe distinctive features that help travelers find their way.

The most extensive study of place names in Alaska was conducted by Donald J. Orth in 1967. Orth's *Dictionary of Alaska Place Names* includes more than 27,000 names for rivers, lakes, settlements, and other geographic features.

Orth's study focused on "official" names—those accepted by the U.S. Board of Geographic names at the time he compiled the *Dictionary*. Orth recognized, however, that these were not all the names of places in Alaska.

The official place names of Alaska are enriched by the many thousands of oral place names in the various Alaska Native languages. For example, names long used by the Athabaskan Indians, one group of Alaska Natives, extend in a vast,

This map shows Athabaskan place names for some important rivers and streams in western and southcentral Alaska. Most Athabaskan stream names there end in **-na', -no',** *or* **-nu.** *They are shown as green lines. Streams in eastern Alaska, where most Athabaskan stream names end in* **neekk'e, njik, ndíig,** *or* **niign,** *are shown as red lines. A blue line shows the boundary between areas where the two different stems for stream are used. The boundary reflects the meeting point of areas historically occupied by different language groups of Athabaskan people.*

continuous network from Alaska through northern Canada to Hudson Bay. Only a fraction of these oral place names, such as *Tanana, Talkeetna, Chena,* and *Nenana* appear on modern maps. Native people, however, memorized the oral place names as they traveled the country in their language areas (See **Map 27 Alaska Native Languages**).

Athabaskan names have very interesting meanings. They often refer to food resources, land features, vegetation, or human activities. Sometimes they express direction, or indicate the condition of water flow in a major river system. Unlike people in the European tradition, Athabaskans almost never use personal names for places.

Jim Kari, a toponymist at the Alaska Native Language Center in Fairbanks, has studied Athabaskan place names for more than 20 years. He is currently working to unravel the story behind Athabaskan names for rivers in Alaska.

Kari has found that there is a division in Alaska Athabaskan names for rivers and streams. In the Athabaskan languages of western and southcentral Alaska the stem for *stream* is usually **-na'** (with several other spellings such as **-no'** or **-nu**). In eastern Alaska the stem for *stream* is usually **-niq'e** (with several spellings such as **neekk'e, nik'a, njik, ndíig, niign**).

The shift in stems for *stream* in the place names seems to signal an ancient boundary marker between different groups of Athabaskan people. The boundary cuts across the Yukon River around the village of Beaver at the Koyukon-Gwich'in language boundary, and across the Tanana River around Big Delta at the Tanana-Tanacross language boundary.

As Kari and other toponymists study such features as these about Alaska Native place names, the map of Alaska becomes much richer. Layer upon layer is added to our basic understanding, and we develop increased appreciation for the significance of places and the people who live near them.

Traveling on the Yukon River in Interior Alaska

Tom Eley

Sources for GIS Maps

INTRODUCTION
1. **Alaska** (basic topography). Modified from U.S. Geological Survey

1 PERSPECTIVES ON ALASKA
2. **Alaska** (composite satellite image). National Mapping Division Office, Alaska Branch, U.S. Geological Survey.
3. **Alaska as Part of the North.** National Mapping Division Office, Alaska Branch, U.S. Geological Survey.
4. **Alaska and the North Pacific.** Modified from Defense Mapping Agency.
5. **Alaska as Part of North America.** U.S. Geological Survey, Reston, VA
6. **Distances Within Alaska.** Modified from Charles W. Hartman and Philip R. Johnson. *Environmental Atlas of Alaska.* Second edition. Fairbanks: University of Alaska, 1978.
7. **Alaska as Five Regions.** Map, "Five Regions of Alaska" in Nancy Warren Ferrell. *Alaska, A Land in Motion.* Fairbanks: University of Alaska Fairbanks, Alaska Department of Education, and Alaska Geographic Alliance, 1994.
8. **Alaska as Six Regions.** Map, "The Six Alaskas" in *A Photographic Geography of Alaska.* **Alaska Geographic.** Vol. 7, no. 2. Anchorage: Alaska Geographic Society, 1980.
9. **Election Districts, 1960.** State of Alaska
10. **Election Districts, 1994.** Modified from Alaska Department of Natural Resources GIS Database.

2 PHYSICAL GEOGRAPHY
11. **Topography.** Modified from U.S. Geological Survey
12. **Terranes of the Bering Region.** Modified from W.J. Nokleberg, L.M. Parfenov, J.W.H. Monger, B.V. Baranov, S.G. Byalovzhesky, T.K. Bundtzen, T.D. Feeney, K. Fujita, S.P. Gordey, A. Grantz, A.I. Khanchuk, B.A. Natal'in, L.M. Natapov, L.M., Norton, W.W. Patton, G. Plafker, D.W. Scholl, S.D. Sokolov, G.M. Sosunov, D.B. Stone, R.W. Tabor, N.V. Tsukanov, T.L. Vallier. "Summary Circum-North Pacific Tectono-Stratigraphic Terrane Map." Geological Survey of Canada Open-file report 3428 and U.S. Geological Survey Open File Report, No. 96-727, scale 1:10,000,000, 1996; and David Stone, personal communication, spring-summer 1998.
13. **Glaciation.** Modified from H. W. Coulter, D. M. Hopkins, T. M. V. Karlstrom, T. L. Péwé, C. Wahrhaftig, and J.R. Williams. "Map showing extent of glaciations in Alaska." Compiled by the Alaska Glacial Map Committee of the U.S. Geological Survey. U.S. Geological Survey Miscellaneous Geologic Investigations Map I-415, 1965; Tom Bundtzen, personal communication, December 1997; and Alaska Department of Natural Resources GIS Database.
14. **Permafrost.** Modified from O. J. Ferrians, Jr. "Permafrost Map of Alaska." U.S. Geological Survey Miscellaneous Geologic Investigations Map I-445. Washington, D.C: U.S. Government Printing Office, 1965; and J. Brown, O.J. Ferrians, Jr., J.A. Heginbottom, and E.S. Melnikov. "Circum-Arctic Map of Permafrost and Ground-Ice Conditions." U.S. Geological Survey, Map CP-45, 1997.
15. **Climatic Regions.** Modified from map by Mark Evangelista and the Alaska Geographic Society. *Alaska's Weather.* **Alaska Geographic.** Vol. 18, no. 1. Anchorage: Alaska Geographic Society, 1991.
16. **Major Rivers and Lakes.** Modified from Alaska Department of Natural Resources GIS Database.

17. **Drainage Regions and River Discharge.** Based on David W. Moody, Edith B. Chase, and David A. Aronson, compilers. *National Water Summary 1985 - Hydrologic Events and Surface-Water Resources.* U.S. Geological Survey Water-Supply Paper 2300.
18. **Ocean Currents in Waters Around Alaska.** Modified from *Atlas of Pilot Charts: North Pacific Ocean.* Third Edition. NV PUB108. Washington, DC: Defense Mapping Agency, 1994.
19. **Ocean Basin Topography Around Alaska.** Modified from Helen Beikman. "Geologic Map of Alaska." U.S. Geological Survey, 1980;
20. **Extent of Sea Ice (Alaska Coastal Region).** Joint Federal State Land Use Planning Commission For Alaska. Map, "Major Ecosystems of Alaska." Anchorage. July 1973.
21. **Coastline of Alaska.** Alaska Department of Natural Resources GIS Data Base.
22. **Forests.** Adapted from Joint Federal State Land Use Planning Commission For Alaska. Map, "Major Ecosystems of Alaska." Anchorage, July 1973.
23. **Brown Bear Density.** Alaska Department of Fish and Game; Sterling Miller *et al.* "Brown and Black Bear Density Estimation in Alaska Using Radiotelemetry and Replicated Mark-Resight Techniques." *Wildlife Monographs* Vol. 133; and Harry Reynolds, personal communication, November 1997 and March 1998.
24. **Ecoregions of Alaska.** Alisa L. Gallant, Emily F. Binnian, James M. Omernik, and Mark B. Shasby. *Ecoregions of Alaska.* U.S. Geological Survey Professional Paper 1567. Washington: U.S. Government Printing Office, 1995.

3 HUMAN GEOGRAPHY
25. **Alaska Population by Boroughs and Census Areas, 1997** and **26. Ethnic Groups by Region.** Based on data from J. Gregory Williams, *Alaska Population Overview: 1996 Estimates.* Juneau: Alaska Dept. of Labor, Research and Analysis Section. 1997; and J. Gregory Williams, personal communication, March 1998.
27. **Alaska Native Languages.** Adapted from Michael E. Krauss. Map, "Native Peoples and Languages of Alaska." Revised edition. Fairbanks: University of Alaska Fairbanks, Alaska Native Language Center, 1982; and Michael E. Krauss, personal communication, February 1995.
28. **Communities** and **29. Regional Governments.** Modified from Alaska Department of Community and Regional Affairs. "Community and Borough Map." May 1997; Alaska Department of Natural Resources GIS Data Base; and George Plumley, personal communication, March 1998.
30. **Government Employees by Region.** Based on data from *Employment and Earnings Summary Report for Alaska and 27 Census Areas, 1996.* Diana Kelm, Editor. Juneau: Alaska Dept. of Labor, Research and Analysis Section. 1997; and Jo Donner, personal communication, April 1998.
31. **Health Care Facilities.** Based on data from "Listing of Licensed and Certified Health Facilities." State of Alaska Department of Health and Social Services, Division of Medical Assistance, Facilities Licensing and Certification, February 1998; and Ron Cowan, personal communication, March 1998.
32. **Transportation.** Alaska Department of Natural Resources GIS Data Base; Map, "Public Airports in Alaska." Alaska Department of Transportation and Public Facilities (DOT&PF). Information compiled by the DOT&PF Statewide Aviation Section. Map prepared by the DOT&PF Statewide Mapping Section, 1994; Carl Siebe, personal communication, March 1997, February 1998; and David Oliver, personal communication, February and March 1998.
33. **Newspapers, Television Stations, Radio Stations.** Based on information from *The Alaska Almanac.* 20th Anniversary Edition. Anchorage: Alaska Northwest Books, 1996.

34. **Legislative Information Offices.** Based on information from the Alaska Legislative Affairs Agency, 1997 session.

35. **Alaska Native Regional Corporations.** Alaska Department of Natural Resources GIS Data Base.

4 ENVIRONMENT AND SOCIETY

36. **Volcanoes of Alaska.** Alaska Department of Natural Resources. Division of Geological and Geophysical Surveys and associated web site: *http://www.avo.alaska.edu/*.

37. **Earthquakes in Alaska.** National Earthquake Information Center, U.S. Geological Survey. *http://wwwneic.cr.usgs.gov/neis/epic/epic.html*, and the University of Alaska Geophysical Institute Seismology site: *http://www.giseis.alaska.edu/Seis/seis.html*.

38. **Land Ownership.** Alaska Department of Natural Resources GIS Data Base.

39. **Selected State and National Parks.** Alaska Department of Natural Resources GIS Data Base.

40. **Selected National Interest Lands.** Alaska Department of Natural Resources GIS Data Base.

41. **Historic and Archaeological Landmarks.** Based on information from the Office of History and Archaeology, Division of Parks and Outdoor Recreation, Alaska Department of Natural Resources, March 1997; and Joan M. Antonson, personal communication, March 1998.

42. **Wetlands.** Modified from Jonathan V. Hall. "Map of Wetland Resources of Alaska." National Wetlands Inventory. Anchorage: U.S. Fish and Wildlife Service, 1991.

43. **Subsistence Harvests in Seven Villages.** Alaska Department of Fish and Game, Division of Subsistence. Based on information from Robert J. Wolfe, "Subsistence Food Harvests in Rural Alaska, and Food Safety Issues." Paper presented to the Institute of Medicine, National Academy of Sciences Committee on Environmental Justice, Spokane, WA, August 13, 1996; "Subsistence In Alaska: 1998 Update." Division of Subsistence. Juneau: Alaska Department of Fish and Game, 1998; and Robert J. Wolfe, personal communication, February 1997 and April 1998.

44. **Sportfishing.** Alaska Department of Fish and Game, Division of Sport Fish. Based on information from Allen L. Howe, Gary Fidler, Allen E. Bingham, and Michael J. Mills. *Harvest, catch, and participation in Alaska sport fisheries during 1995.* Anchorage: Alaska Department of Fish and Game, Fishery Data Series No. 96-32. 1996; and Mike Mills, personal communication, February 1997 and March 1998.

45. **Hunting and Trapping.** Alaska Department of Fish and Game, Division of Wildlife Conservation. Based on information from Enid Keyes, Rebecca Strauch, and Suzan Bowen. *Alaska Wildlife Harvest Summary, 1994-1995.* Juneau: Alaska Department of Fish and Game Division of Wildlife Conservation, 1996; and Steve Peterson, personal communication, November 1997, April 1998.

46. **Mineral Fuels.** Alaska Department of Natural Resources. Division of Geological and Geophysical Surveys. Coal deposits modified from "Alaska's High-Rank Coals." Alaska Department of Natural Resources. Division of Geological and Geophysical Surveys. Information Circular 33. Fairbanks: August 1990; and R.D. Merritt and C. C. Hawley. Map of Alaska's Coal Resources Alaska Division of Geological and Geophysical Surveys. Special Report 37. 1986; and Pacific Rim Geological Consulting, personal communication, March 1998.

47. **Commercial Fisheries.** Alaska Department of Fish and Game, Commercial Fisheries Management and Development Division; and National Marine Fisheries Service. Based on data from Brian Frenette, Marianne McNair, and Herman Savikko. *1995 Catch and Production of Alaska's Commercial Fisheries.* Juneau: Alaska Department of Fish and Game, Commercial Fisheries Management and Development Division, 1997; National Marine Fisheries Service, Fisheries Statistics Division. *Fisheries of the United States, 1995.* Washington: Superintendent of Documents, 1996; and Herman Savikko, personal communication, February 1997 and April 1998.

48. **Minerals.** Pacific Rim Geological Consulting, March 1998.

49. **Potential Agricultural Lands.** U.S. Department of Agriculture, Soil Conservation Service. Alaska Rural Development Council, "Alaska's Agricultural Potential." Publication No. 1, Cooperative Extension Service, University of Alaska, 1974; and Carol Lewis, personal communication, April 1998.

Sources for Figures and Diagrammatic Maps

1 PERSPECTIVES ON ALASKA

1. **Alaska Time Zones, October 29, 1983 and October 30, 1983.** *The Milepost®.* Edmonds, WA: Alaska Northwest Publishing Company, 1983 and 1984.

2. **Distance and Cost of Air Travel from Anchorage, January 1997.** Concept by Roger W. Pearson. Chart by Elizabeth Knecht. Costs based on information from *Anchorage Daily News*.

2 PHYSICAL GEOGRAPHY

3. **Physiographic Regions of Western North America.** Modified from N.M. Fenneman, *Physiography of Western United States.* New York: McGraw Hill, 1938.

4. **North-South Transect of Alaska.** Adapted from "Alaska Natural Landscapes." Joint Federal State Land Use Planning Commission For Alaska. Commission Study 33. Anchorage, May 1978.

5. **Permafrost in the Soil.** Adapted from Lidia L. Selkregg, editor. *Alaska Regional Profiles: Arctic Region.* Anchorage: University of Alaska Arctic Environmental Information and Data Center, 1975.

6. **Climographs for Six Alaska Locations.** Based on information from Western Regional Climate Center Web site: *http://www.wrcc.dri.edu/summary/climsmak.html*

7. **Ten Longest Rivers** and **8. Areas of Selected Lakes.** Based on information from *The Alaska Almanac.* 20th Anniversary Edition. Anchorage: Alaska Northwest Books, 1996.

9. **Drifting Objects on the Ocean.** Map by Elizabeth Knecht. Based on information from Curtis C. Ebbesmeyer and W. James Ingraham, Jr. "Drifting Objects on the Ocean." In *Atlas of Pilot Charts: North Pacific Ocean.* Third Edition. NV PUB108. Washington, D.C.: Defense Mapping Agency, 1994; "Lost logs menace mariners, but help track rich fisheries," *Anchorage Daily News,* November 17, 1996; and Jim Ingraham, personal communication, April 1998.

10. **Barrow Canyon.** Adapted from K. Perry and H.S. Fleming, "Bathymetry of the Arctic Ocean." Naval Research Laboratory. Boulder, CO: The Geological Society of America, 1986; and Ned Rozell. "Barrow Canyon: Where Atlantic meets Pacific." *Fairbanks Daily News Miner*, Heartland, August 25, 1996.

11. **Four Ecoregions of Alaska.** Modified from Alisa L. Gallant, Emily F. Binnian, James M. Omernik, and Mark B. Shasby. *Ecoregions of Alaska.* U.S. Geological Survey Professional Paper 1567. Washington: U.S. Government Printing Office, 1995.

3 HUMAN GEOGRAPHY

12. **Population by Age and Gender, 1996.** Adapted from "Alaska and U.S. Population—Percent Distribution by Age and Male/Female, 1996" in J. Gregory Williams, *Alaska Population Overview: 1996 Estimates.* Juneau: Alaska Dept. of Labor, Research and Analysis Section, 1997; and J. Gregory Williams, personal communication, March 1998.

13. **Population of Alaska, 1880-2000.** U.S. Census and Alaska Department of Labor; and J. Gregory Williams, personal communication, March 1998.

14. **Urban Population of Alaska, Percent of Total, 1910-1997** and **15. Urban and Rural Places of Alaska, 1996; Percent of Population in Places of Various Sizes, 1996.** Based on data from J. Gregory Williams, *Alaska Population Overview: 1996 Estimates.* Juneau: Alaska Dept. of Labor, Research and Analysis Section. 1997; and J. Gregory Williams, personal communication, March 1998.

16. **Air Routes in the Nome and Kotzebue Area.** Map by Elizabeth Knecht. Based on a sketch map by Carl Siebe, Alaska Department of Transportation and Public Facilities, Statewide Aviation Section. February 1997.

17. **Export Partners, 1996** and **18. Value of Alaska Resource Exports, 1996.** Based on information from the Alaska Center for International Business. University of Alaska Anchorage. *http://www.acib.uaa.alaska.edu*

4 ENVIRONMENT AND SOCIETY

19. **Hours of Daylight.** Based on Sue Ann Bowling, personal communication; and data from the Geophysical Institute, University of Alaska Fairbanks. *http://climate.gi.alaska.edu/weather/tourist/information.html/DAY.*

20. **Seasonal Changes in the Lower Kuskokwim Region.** Based on "Work Feasibility in Southwest Alaska" in Lidia L. Selkregg, editor. *Alaska Regional Profiles: Southwest Region.* Anchorage: University of Alaska Arctic Environmental Information and Data Center, 1975.

21. **Subsistence Harvest Cycle in Tununak, 1985.** Adapted from research by Mary Pete. In Robert F. Schroeder, David B. Andersen, Rob Bosworth, Judith M. Morris, and John M. Wright, "Subsistence in Alaska: Arctic, Interior, Southcentral, Southwest, and Western Regional Summaries." Technical Paper No. 150. Juneau: Alaska Department of Fish and Game, Division of Subsistence, 1987.

22. **Top Ten Earthquakes in the World, 1904-1997.** Map by Elizabeth Knecht. Based on data from the Geophysical Institute, University of Alaska Fairbanks. *www.giseis.alaska.edu*

23. **State Parks** and **24. National Interest Lands.** Based on data from the Alaska Department of Natural Resources and *The Alaska Almanac.* 20th Anniversary Edition. Anchorage: Alaska Northwest Books, 1996.

25. **Historic and Archaeological Landmarks.** Based on data from the Office of History and Archaeology, Division of Parks and Outdoor Recreation, Alaska Department of Natural Resources, March 1997; and Joan M. Antonson, personal communication, March 1998.

26. **Oil Production and Value, 1978-1997.** Based on data from the Alaska Department of Revenue; and Chuck Logsdon, personal communication, September 1997.

27. **Fishery Landings of the Top Five U.S. States**. Based on data from *Fisheries of the United States, 1995.* Silver Spring, MD: National Marine Fisheries Service, Fisheries Statistics Division, 1996.

28. **Seafood Harvests and Value, 1995 and 1996.** Adapted from "Seafood Harvests 1990-1996" and "Ex-Vessel Value 1990-1996" in *Alaska Seafood Industry.* Juneau: Alaska Department of Commerce and Economic Development, Division of Trade and Development, 1997.

29. **Summer Visitor Arrivals in Alaska, 1985-1996** and **30. Visitors by Mode of Arrival.** Based on statistics from Alaska Department of Commerce and Economic Development, Division of Tourism; and John Byler, personal communication, January 1998.

31. **Wood Exports in Alaska, 1985-1996.** Adapted from "Average Value and Volume of Alaska Wood Exports, 1985-1996" in Alexandra Hill and Teresa Hull, *Timber Harvest and Wood Products Manufacture in Alaska: 1996 Update.* Anchorage: University of Alaska Anchorage, Institute of Social and Economic Research, 1997; and Alexandra Hill, personal communication, October 1997 and February 1998.

32. **Gold Production and Value in Alaska, 1880-1996.** Adapted from "Amount and Value of Gold Production in Alaska 1880-1996 in *Alaska's Mineral Industry, 1996.* Special Report 51. Fairbanks: Alaska Department of Natural Resources, Division of Geological and Geophysical Surveys, 1997; and Joanie Robinson, personal communication, October 1997 and March 1998.

5 USES OF GEOGRAPHY

Aleut Settlement Sites in the Western Aleutians. Map by Martin Gutoski. Based on data from Debbie Corbett.

World War II on the Pacific Rim. *Alaska Geographic*© map by Kathy Doogan. Based on *Distances Between Ports*, U.S. Govt. Pub. 151, Defense Mapping Agency, 1995. In **World War II in Alaska.** *Alaska Geographic.* Volume 22, no. 4. Anchorage: Alaska Geographic Society, 1995.

Detail from Iñupiatullu Taniktullu Nunauraq. Iñupiat-English Map. Compiled by the North Slope Borough Geographic Information System using data from the U.S. Geological Survey, North Slope Borough, state and other federal sources. Iñupiat place names were provided by the borough village Tribal and City councils. Revised May 1997. Reproduced with permission.

Excerpt from North Slope Borough Traditional Land Use Data Base. Reproduced with permission.

Athabaskan River Names in Alaska. Map by Martin Gutoski. Based on data from Jim Kari, Alaska Native Language Center, University of Alaska Fairbanks.

Sources for Narratives

Most of the sources listed in the two preceding sections provided information, statistics, and background for the narratives. In addition, the following references were particularly useful:

Alaska Economy Performance Report, 1996. Juneau: Alaska Department of Commerce and Economic Development, Division of Trade and Development, 1996.

Geography for Life: National Geography Standards, 1994. Developed on behalf of American Geographical Society, Association of American Geographers, National Council for Geographic Education, and National Geographic Society. Washington: Geography Education Standards Project, 1994.

Hardwick, Susan Wiley and Donald G. Holtgrieve. *Geography for Educators: Standards, Themes, and Concepts.* Upper Saddle River, New Jersey: Prentice Hall, 1996.

Selkregg, Lidia, editor. *Alaska Regional Profiles.* Six volumes: Vol. I: Southcentral Region. Vol. II: Arctic Region. Vol. III: Southwest Region. Vol. IV: Southeast Region. Vol. V: Northwest Region. Vol. VI: Yukon Region. Anchorage: University of Alaska Arctic Environmental Information and Data Center.